Diana
Secrets
& Lies

BY NICHOLAS DAVIES

American Media, Inc.

DIANA
Secrets & Lies

Copyright © 2003 AMI Books, Inc.

Cover design: Carlos Plaza
Interior design: Debbie Browning

ISBN: 1-932270-21-3

First printing: August 2003

Printed in the United States of America

10 9 8 7 6 5 4 3 2 1

About the Author

Nicholas Davies lives in England not far from Windsor Castle. He is accepted in Britain as an authority on the royal family, having written 10 royal biographies including New York Times best sellers on Princess Diana and Queen Elizabeth II. Davies, a former British Army officer, war correspondent, newspaper editor and polo player, was the only writer to know both Prince Charles and Princess Diana before they dated.

Table of Contents

$\mathcal{I}$ first met the teenage Lady Diana Spencer at the Guards Polo Club in Windsor Great Park during the early summer of 1979, shortly before she began dating Prince Charles. I found her to be a quiet, shy girl, young for her age with no hint of the sophistication and elegance that would one day mark her out as one of the 20th century's most beautiful and striking young women.

The 1979 Diana wore no hint of makeup and her hair was tousled and slightly unkempt. That day she wore a white, short-sleeved cotton blouse and a calf-length, flowered cotton skirt and carried a navy blue sweater. As she walked alone across the polo ground treading in the divots thrown up by the galloping ponies, she seemed lost in a world of her own, unsure whether she was placing the divots correctly. She seemed both lonely and nervous, so I walked over to her.

I had no idea of her identity but everyone chats to everyone else on the polo field in the knowledge that players and their friends are all of the same set. Her face lit up when I spoke to her as though she was relieved to find someone to talk to and she gave me her natural, dazzling smile that was to capture the hearts of millions and grace the covers of magazines across the world.

I remarked on the light pumps she was wearing,

which were totally unsuitable for treading in divots, and she gave me that innocent look and laughed. "I'll know better next time," she said.

We talked for a couple of minutes about polo and she told me that she loved the game but hated riding horses because of a childhood riding accident that had unnerved her. I reassured her, saying, "You'll get over it; you'll probably be playing polo here one day."

"I doubt that very much," she said, with a laugh, "I doubt if I will ever get on a horse again, let alone play this game."

We wandered back to the pavilion when the bell rang and went our separate ways. It was the first but not the last time I would see and chat to Diana on the polo field, but by the time of our next encounter some weeks later, her photograph had been on the front page of most newspapers and magazines as the latest girlfriend of the Prince of Wales.

Our next meeting at Windsor was at Diana's instigation. I was walking across the polo field when she came up to me. "Hello, again," she said, "See, I did what you suggested," looking down at her shoes, "are these better for the job?"

"Much better," I replied, "but next time you could try hob-nailed boots," and she pursed her lips and gave me a doubtful look before smiling broadly. "How's it going?" I asked her, wondering what her reply would be. "I've seen your picture everywhere."

"Oh, don't," Diana replied, "it's all so dreadfully embarrassing. I just want to curl up and hibernate."

"I would just enjoy it," I commented, "and see what happens."

"I know," she said, "but it's all so embarrassing. I don't like the limelight."

"I can tell," I said jokingly.

"Oh don't," Diana replied. "It's not me; honestly."

"Well, good luck," I told her, "you might need it."

"Might?" she replied with an ironic smile, and the bell rang for the start of play. We parted company and she walked back, this time not to the pony lines, but to the royal enclosure.

I met Diana on other occasions, including bumping into her at Harrods and also at her favorite London store, Harvey Nichols. Surprisingly, she remembered me and on both occasions we stopped and chatted for a few moments. Teasingly I said, "Not shopping again?" and she gave me a knowing look, followed by her broad, friendly smile.

"A girl has to look her best," she said and I replied, "Well, you had better continue shopping 'cos you're looking great."

"Thanks," she said, and added with a laugh,

"Don't worry, I will." With a wave she was off and then turned and said, "I'll probably see you at polo."

"Yes, fine," I said — and she was gone.

We did occasionally meet at Windsor with Charles during those first few years during the polo season until the paparazzi became too much. Later still, she would sometimes bring along young Wills and Harry and they would play around together in the royal pavilion.

And then in 1988, nearly 10 years later, when the tabloids were full of rumor and speculation about Diana's loneliness and unhappiness, I was approached by a senior royal aide, someone who had been close to both Diana and Prince Charles. At that time, many of the rumors were half-truths and many of the stories were fabricated by a press that was keen to feed the nation's insatiable appetite for any tidbit about Charles or Diana.

I agreed to write a comprehensive, objective account of their marriage and when the warts-and-all manuscript was completed I sent it off to a number of British publishers. They were outraged, accusing me of writing untruthful rubbish, of bringing the royal family into disrepute and of having the audacity to ask them to publish a book in which I had written that both Charles and Diana had lovers whom I had named. They sent me away.

So I turned to the United States where the manuscript was welcomed as manna from heaven and the book *Diana: A Princess and Her Troubled Marriage*' became a *New York Times* best seller and sold in 50 countries.

In the 1990s, two polo-playing friends of mine became lovers of Diana and they asked my advice as to how deeply they should become involved with the estranged wife of the Prince of Wales. They told me everything about Diana, discussing her character, her personality, her mood swings, her demands and her fantasies, but until now I decided not to write of such failings.

And throughout the last 12 years I have been kept informed by two or three people who have worked in the royal palaces about what has been going on within the royal family with particular reference to Charles and Diana. Now I believe the time has come to tell all.

To all these people who have provided me with on-going information, I owe a debt of gratitude. Without their help this book could not have been written.

On Aug. 31, 1997, I was awakened shortly after 1 a.m. and informed that Princess Diana had been involved in a fatal car crash in Paris while traveling to the home of her Egyptian lover, Dodi Fayed. I was told that she was injured but fine and that she had suffered no life-threatening injuries. Two hours later, I was phoned again and told that both Diana and Dodi were dead, along with their chauffeur. Her royal bodyguard, Trevor Rees-Jones, had been seriously injured but was expected to survive.

Since that time, I have been involved in putting together a dossier and trying to ascertain the facts of what really happened that night. I have spoken to countless people and tried to speak to others who refused to cooperate. However, in 2001, a retired member of Britain's security services, whom I had known for some 10 years, agreed to provide me with the facts of Diana's death.

I have waited until now before publishing this book for two reasons. One, to wait until Prince William and Prince Harry reached maturity and were therefore, better able to cope with the revelations I have included about their mother. And secondly, that the two young men will hopefully be able to accept the dramatic revelation that the tragic death of their beloved mother was no accident.

Chapter 1

Lamb to the Slaughter

*P*rince Charles, the world's most eligible bachelor, and his beautiful, shy young bride Lady Diana Spencer had captured the imagination of people across the globe and never before had so many people paid such close attention to a royal wedding. This would be the first royal wedding ceremony in history to be covered by satellite television and people everywhere watched it live either at home or in their offices. Scores of television cameras were poised along the route from Buckingham Palace to St. Paul's Cathedral to transmit the royal nuptial ceremony to the millions around the world who wanted to witness this fairy-tale romance with the prince and his bride making their solemn vows.

Everyone who watched that wedding ceremony wished the couple well and silently hoped that their marriage would be long, happy and fruitful.

Champagne toasts to the royal couple were made not only in Buckingham Palace but in homes, pubs, bars and cafes in many towns and cities in many countries. A few emotional tears were shed that day by women everywhere for the innocent, natural, unaffected and lovable Diana. But few had any idea of what was really going on in her heart and mind. Many viewers commented that Diana looked nervous and uncertain, but most dismissed her troubled demeanor as a natural phenomenon in the extraordinary circumstances that had catapulted an unknown, bashful young woman into the glaring limelight of the royal House of Windsor and the ever-present photographers.

In fact, the young Diana was indeed a worried and anxious woman that day in July 1981. She was in turmoil. Diana's natural instincts were telling her that she should not go through with the wedding ceremony while her head was telling her that she must. She believed she had no alternative. In those few days before the wedding, Diana found herself in an impossible situation, when the world was ready and waiting to see the royal marriage – her marriage – and she simply couldn't let everyone down. That morning her stomach sank and she felt physically sick because she knew it was simply too late; there was no escape.

These doubts had been gathering in her mind

for weeks before the wedding and, as the big day approached, the more nervous and unsure Diana became. She kept telling herself, over and over, that she was only suffering the normal prewedding nerves that many brides experience, but her nerves were in shreds because this was no ordinary wedding. She was the reluctant star of the show. Major problems had surfaced in the weeks and months before the wedding that worried Diana greatly.

On the one hand, she had been thrilled and flattered to be on the arm of Prince Charles, invited to quiet, intimate dinners in his apartment at Buckingham Palace, where they would drink champagne before dinner and share jokes. She had laughed at his wit, adored his attention, felt overcome by his words of love and the intimacy they shared. Rapidly, Diana had fallen in love.

Never before had Diana been in love; never before had she enjoyed a relationship with a steady boyfriend. She was 18 and still a virgin at a time when most of her girlfriends were dating, falling in love and enjoying love affairs. Diana's experience with men was so limited that even a passionate kiss from a man was rare and she yearned to be like the other girls with whom she shared an apartment in London – dating, dining out and enjoying the companionship, love and passion of being with a man.

All this had been denied to Diana before Prince Charles, out of the blue, invited her to accompany him to polo on the odd weekend and then asked her to join him for dinner in his private apartment at Buckingham Palace.

As she arrived on that first date, Diana suspected that Charles only wanted to chat with her about her elder sister Sarah, with whom Charles had been enjoying a year-long, on-and-off intimate relationship. Diana knew the couple was happy most of the time, but she also knew that Sarah was an emotional and often challenging character. Diana would say later that after Charles called to invite her to the palace, she dared to wonder whether there was a chance that Charles might actually fancy her. It would transpire that during her teenage years Diana had dreamed of dating the Prince of Wales, whom she had known slightly since childhood.

Her feelings of joy in those early days turned into tears on the morning of her wedding, but it wasn't simply prewedding nerves. The reasons for her apprehension were far more fundamental. She was awake at the crack of dawn after a sleepless night tossing and turning and she peeped through the curtains to see the crowds gathering in the Mall. It was at that moment that the tears fell. But they weren't tears of simple emotion or apprehension of what lay ahead that day. They were tears for the decision that she could no longer escape — to go ahead with the wedding and marry Prince Charles.

Weeks before the wedding, Diana had come to the realization that she could never find true happiness with Charles. Later, Diana would tell her close friends the reasons why the marriage had gone so wrong, but to only a few very close friends would she discuss the *principal* reason why she knew before the wedding that she could never be truly happy.

There were, in fact, three main reasons; the first was the dreadful realization that she could never enjoy any freedom, privacy or obscurity for the rest of her life; the second, that Prince Charles had so many duties and responsibilities that they had little or no quality time together, and the third, equally important, was sexual.

During the previous decade, Prince Charles had enjoyed the companionship of many young women, including a couple of friendly lunches with Camilla Parker Bowles, which over the years would develop into a lasting friendship. Charles had also enjoyed perhaps some 20 or more romantic affairs with young women and most were close, intimate relationships. Many of those relationships Charles had been able to hide from the prying eyes of the press as well as the public. The press understood that Charles should be permitted to conduct his love life in privacy — he was simply enjoying the life of a bachelor, sowing his wild oats — and should be permitted to do so, more or less in private, until he found the woman he wanted to marry. From the moment there was a real likelihood that Prince Charles was viewing Lady Diana Spencer as a potential wife, the press were let off the leash and from then on they were never to leave her alone.

For her part, Diana was totally unprepared for the reality of becoming the world's No. 1 attraction for the newspaper and magazine editors who quickly realized that here was a delightful young woman who sold their papers and their magazines like no one before her. Many editors could see from their sales charts that a cover picture of Diana sold far more copies than when she was not on the cover. They demanded more and, as a result, a new industry took off as photographers discovered that pictures of Diana sold for high financial rewards. Life as Diana had known it completely disappeared and she hated it. Embarrassed, fearful, bashful and nervous in front of any camera, Diana simply wasn't equipped to cope with such extraordinary attention.

Her life had been spent in the country on the large private family estate of Althorp with only her two older sisters, Sarah and Jane, for company and they mostly ignored her. The arrival of younger brother Charles, three years her junior, gave her life some form and she lavished her love and attention on him. But at the tender age of 5 Diana discovered, to her horror, that her mother was leaving the family home, their father and the children to live in London.

It is difficult to exaggerate the effect that single event had on Diana, deserted by the one person who had shown her love and affection and protected her from her two older, bossy sisters. For the rest of her life, Diana could never forget and never forgave her mother for deserting her in her hour of need. That horrendous shock was followed by life at boarding schools, where most of the time she lived a quiet, unadventurous life. Later, Diana would confess, "I never could forget that my mother had walked out on me. I don't think I ever got over it."

From the moment of the announcement of her official engagement in February 1981, there was no hiding place for Diana. She was thrilled when Charles asked her to marry him and she felt she was in seventh heaven, the bride-to-be of the man she had dreamed might one day ask her to marry him. It was the stuff of fairy tales that had become reality.

The reality, however, would be far different from

the dream. From the moment she accepted his offer of marriage, Diana found herself physically confined to palaces and royal households, cut off from the outside world, unable to participate freely in her favorite pastime — shopping — and not permitted to walk or drive anywhere without an armed police bodyguard. She hated losing her freedom and she hated being unable to hide, unrecognized, in a crowd, a shop, a street or a restaurant. Diana had always lived a very private life and she cherished her privacy, wearing ordinary, comfortable, unfashionable clothes so that she would never stand out in a crowd or draw attention to herself. It was for that reason that Diana hated being a tall girl and, at 5-foot-10, she had always been one of the tallest young women in her school class.

It was unfortunate for Diana that her notoriety and fame had arrived in the early 1980s, a time when there was real concern that IRA terrorists were targeting the royal family. It was in August 1979 that Earl Mountbatten, Charles' great uncle, whom he loved and adored, had been assassinated by the IRA while vacationing in Ireland and there was real fear that the IRA killer squads might target another member of the royal family. Those senior MI5 officers responsible for royal security fully realized that if the IRA gunmen managed to kill the young Diana, her murder would be hailed as a magnificent success by the IRA leadership. Those responsible for Diana's safety knew the very real danger and they could take no chances with her safety. They escorted her everywhere and they were always armed. There was no escape, though. Diana constantly begged to be allowed to go shopping on her own.

The realization that her life was no longer hers was disturbing enough for the young Diana. But there were other matters, equally important, that would have a profound affect on her personal life. She had never fully realized just how many royal duties Charles was called upon to perform each and every week, from early morning to late at night, leaving him very little time to spend with her. His was no 9-to-5 job. His day would usually start at 6 a.m. because he would need to travel some distance to his first appointment. More often than not he was out most of the day, welcoming visiting dignitaries, chairing meetings, attending official lunches, opening factories, schools or hospitals, running the Prince's Trust, writing official letters and reading the government papers that arrived every day. And once a week or so he would have to attend some official dinner or some other function. On those occasions he would be fortunate to be home by 10 o'clock.

Charles' life was so hectic that he might need to return to the palace to change his clothes perhaps four times a day, dashing in, changing and then away again to the next call of duty. For that was the word : duty — the moral obligation that bound him to serve his country because he was the queen's son and heir. Diana came to realize during those few months of sublime happiness of her engagement, when she all but lived with him in his apartment at Buckingham Palace, that she saw very little of the man she was about to marry. Duty always came first with Charles and she realized she was a very distant second.

In those few months from the February engagement to the July wedding Diana hardly had a moment to herself. Her life was one hectic round of appointments, meetings and conferences. However, the task of buying an extensive new wardrobe of clothes was the bit that Diana loved more than anything else. It suddenly dawned on her, some weeks after the engagement was announced, that she could now have whatever clothes she wanted — for the rest of her life. And the realization changed Diana overnight from a girl who hardly spent any money on her wardrobe to a fashion conscious icon the world admired for her style, elegance and choice of outfits.

In those early months of 1981, from the

moment Diana awoke until she happily climbed into bed beside Charles for some love, affection and gentle sex, Diana had not a spare moment to herself. "I hardly have time to grab a bite," she would happily tell her roommates, "life's absolutely wonderful."

One of the reasons Diana so enjoyed her life at that time was the fact that she was never on her own. Diana had a fear of being left on her own. Whenever she was left alone she would feel as though she had been deserted and she couldn't cope with that haunting feeling. The phobia originated after her mother had left her and the family. It was one of the reasons she had been so shy about becoming involved with a young man for fear that one day he might dump her. Diana knew that she couldn't face being deserted. She came to understand that she needed a man who would love and cherish her totally.

In retrospect, Diana came to understand that there were some problems with her sex life with Charles. Following the engagement it was announced that Diana, in an effort to escape the media circus that followed her every move, would leave her London apartment and, until her wedding day, would live at Clarence House in the Mall, the Queen Mother's London home, a hundred yards from the palace. Unknown to the world, however, within days Diana had moved from Clarence House to an apartment next to Charles' rooms in Buckingham Palace and the two young lovers spent the next five months living together. Diana was blissfully happy, dining by candlelight most nights in private with Charles, falling in love and making love, and sleepily kissing him goodbye in the morning when he would set off on his royal duties and Diana would rise and shower and ready herself for another hectic day preparing for the great event.

Those were Diana's happiest times. She was unashamedly in love and she adored Charles, believing that he was the most wonderful man in the world. Whenever he was making a speech, Diana would look at Charles with adulation, admiring everything about him and brimming with love for the man she was to marry. She would tell her friends, "I am the luckiest girl in the world and Charles is just wonderful." During these months, Diana idolized Charles, unable to find fault with the man she was to marry.

Such adoration would not last. The more Diana saw of Charles the more she realized that he was fallible. All too quickly his halo slipped and, only weeks before the wedding, Diana was faced with the stark reality.

Subsequently, Diana confessed to Howard, a

City banker who for some months became her lover in the 1980s, "Charles and I had problems with our sex life and that didn't help at all. At first, everything seemed wonderful because, I suppose, I was so in love with the man and I adored him. I thought sex with him was wonderful, but then he was my first lover. I was totally inexperienced. In time I came to realize that the earth wasn't moving for me and had never done so. It had all been in my mind."

Diana read books about sex and lovemaking with the hope that she could find the missing ingredient which would produce the orgasms and the fulfillment that were missing. But the books and magazines didn't seem to help. She also found it incredibly difficult to raise the subject with Charles and she confessed to faking orgasms so that he believed that she was in seventh heaven whenever they made love. But that proved to be a short-term solution and she found herself becoming more agitated, frustrated and nervous. Their lovemaking rapidly deteriorated as Diana found herself making excuses. Where once she had been willing to make love "at the drop of a hat," she suddenly found herself wanting to do anything but have sex. Diana blamed it on prewedding nerves, which her mother, her sister and her girlfriends readily discussed with her. Diana never, however, mentioned to them the problems she was experiencing with her sex life.

Diana would also confess to her lover, "To be fair to Charles, he showed me kindness and understanding and he tried everything. But I was certain that I was at fault. Perhaps it was my inexperience, my naivete, but nothing seemed to work for me and I worried. The more I worried, the worse things became. I felt so guilty that everything was my fault. When Charles left in the mornings, I would sometimes break down in tears feeling so frustrated and angry with myself. It was awful for both of us and it caused a rift from which I don't think we ever really recovered. It was no one's fault as such and we tried to sort it out but no luck. It just wasn't right."

Some years later, Diana would confess that she came to blame Charles for their sex problems simply because he was the man and she believed that he should have taken responsibility to ensure that she was enjoying her sex life as much as he seemed to be. Almost overnight, the respect and adoration that Diana felt toward Charles evaporated and the two found themselves in a loveless marriage with little physical contact between them after their honeymoon cruising the sunny Mediterranean. Within weeks of returning home, Diana discovered she was pregnant. This made her feel more confident and the problems with their sex life were put aside. While Diana was focused on her pregnancy, Charles threw himself once again into his never-ending round of royal duties and the couple found themselves drifting apart.

Charles appeared to be more capable of putting up with this unfortunate but disastrous state of affairs, but poor Diana found it almost impossible to be living such a lie. Cut off from her friends and the outside world, trapped in the palace, she yearned for love and affection, yet she had received precious little from the two most important people in her life – her mother and her husband.

At times, Diana believed she was going mad for she had nowhere to turn and no one to turn to. She felt she couldn't talk to her mother about the situation because they had never really gotten along and she didn't want to talk to her sisters or her brother Charles. Nor did she want to confess her personal problems with roommates and friends. She felt there was no one to turn to for help or advice.

In desperation, Diana made friends with the servants and the cooks in the same friendly way she had always done back home at Althorp. The staff were taken aback by her appearances because it simply was not appropriate for any member of the royal family to chat with maids and cooks as though they were her friends. To Diana's astonishment, they didn't want her there. After a dozen or more visits to the kitchens, senior staff objected to her frequent appearances and demanded an end to them. One day, as she popped into the kitchens, the yeoman approached, pointed to the door and told her, "Through there, Ma'am, is your side of the house; through here is our side of the house."

Diana was shocked, unsure how to respond to this blunt piece of advice. The yeoman stood his ground, in effect barring Diana from moving further into the kitchen. Diana looked around for a friendly face but there were none. She blushed madly, turned and fled through the door, never to return. It seemed the one set of people with whom she could enjoy a friendly chat had put an abrupt end to any chance of any friendliness. She felt even more alone.

Every morning it was necessary for Charles' private secretary, Sir Edward Adeane, to discuss official matters with Charles, check his diary arrangements, go over the plans and times for that day, that evening and for the days and weeks ahead. Most mornings, Sir Edward would need to spend at least 30 minutes to an hour with Charles on his own with no distractions. Diana hated this. She barely coped with the intrusion in the early months of their marriage, but after she became pregnant and, even more so after the birth of William in June 1982, she did her utmost to put an end to these early morning talks. She would plead with Charles to change the time of the meeting and stay with her. Her pleading became desperate and she would quite often scream and cry, sometimes physically restraining Charles from leaving the room, tugging at his clothes.

In a raised voice, Diana could be heard saying, and sometimes screaming through her tears, "I need you here; William needs you here. For God's sake, can't you tell them to go away and leave us alone? You're the bloody Prince of Wales, one of the most important people in the whole country and you can't do anything you want. They always tell you what to do and you go along with that. Can't you just tell them to go away just for an hour or so?"

Charles would try to calm her, explain to her that his life was not his own; that he had duties to perform, royal obligations which he could never defer — whatever domestic crisis might be going on at home. Time and again Charles would tell Diana, "There is no alternative. There are no 'ifs' and 'buts' in my life. I have duties which I must perform that take precedence over everything."

Later, during some ferocious spats, Diana would accuse Charles of not loving her or loving

William, shouting, "If you loved us, you would stay here with us. Even when I beg you to stay, you don't. What kind of man are you!"

For the majority of the time, Charles would try to calm the situation. He would explain that he had to adhere to a strict timetable and that he could never be seen to keep people waiting. He explained that he had to go; he had no choice in the matter. That was his job, his duty. When Diana realized that Charles was not going to alter his routine to please her, she turned on his senior advisers and particularly the bachelor private secretary, Sir Edward Adeane, whom she came to treat with venom, sarcasm and obvious loathing. She blamed him for ruining their life together, spoiling their relationship, destroying their marriage. It wasn't surprising that Sir Edward eventually quit the job.

As the world now knows, the effect of these traumas culminated in Diana becoming ill and refusing to eat properly, which led to her suffering from bulimia and anorexia. Diana became a classic case of *bulimia nervosa*, eating mountains of a single food at one time — for example, scoffing an entire carton of ice cream — and then making herself sick by putting her finger down her throat. Diana would say that making herself ill would make her feel in control of her eating habits and, she claimed, relieve the inner tension she felt. At the height of her anorexia, which lasted on and off for some four years, Diana's weight plummeted from around 125 pounds to under 100 pounds. At these times Diana would describe herself as "a bag of bones."

To make matters worse, Diana suffered from postnatal depression only weeks after William was born. This psychological reaction to the birth triggered more black moods for Diana. In effect, she was unable to cope with the depression and her bulimic eating habits. Her mood swings, which had started during the latter months of her pregnancy, returned with a vengeance and her personal staff never knew from hour to hour how they would find Diana. At times, of course, Diana was wonderfully happy, the life and soul of the party, joyful and smiling and great company. At other times, her euphoric mood would change in an instant, for no apparent reason, and the black mood, irritability and self-loathing would reappear, frequently accompanied by floods of tears. Charles became seriously worried and so did the queen and Diana's close relatives.

It was time for action. Doctors, psychiatrists, counselors and psychologists were called in to advise in a bid to help Diana rid herself of these inner conflicts and encourage her to eat normally and somehow come to terms with her life as the wife of the Prince of Wales and the mother of the future king. But Diana didn't really want to know. Sometimes she would be happy to see these people for she rather enjoyed being the center of attention, but on other occasions she hated the idea of being like a goldfish in a bowl with hordes of different people with different medical expertise coming to see her, gaze at her and question her.

When Diana felt that way, she simply refused to see them or talk to them. She would retire to her bedroom and refuse to come out while eminent doctors, physicians and psychiatrists would wait patiently outside in the hope that she might change her mind. But Diana hardly ever did change her mind on those occasions and they would have to leave without having been able to see or talk to her. From time to time, various prescription drugs were advised and proffered and, on occasion, Diana would take them as prescribed. But then she might simply refuse to take anymore drugs, complaining they were either "useless" or doing her more harm than good. Consequently, the doctors who prescribed them would tell her, patiently but succinctly, that if she wanted to get well she had better take their advice and the drugs, otherwise, their effect would be less and, at worst, totally useless. Such advice, however, had no effect on Diana. She simply did what she wanted when she wanted.

In the autumn of 1983, however, a year after the birth of William, Diana seemed to be making a recovery. Her moods became less black, her eating habits less bizarre. The change came about some months after she met a dashing young Guards officer by the name of James Hewitt.

Chapter 2

The Open Prison

*T*he gilded cage never suited Diana's temperament or character. The girl who used to roam with total freedom around her father's Althorp country estate in Northamptonshire found great problems coming to terms with having to reside in an open prison — able to move around the palace and the grounds where she lived but forbidden to leave the sanctuary of the place.

On one famous occasion, shortly after moving to Kensington Palace, Diana decided to go for a walk, simply to escape the confines of the place and to get a breath of fresh air. She would later tell what happened: "I simply walked out of the house and down the little road to where the police were on guard and I said a polite 'hi' to the two officers at the barrier that crossed the road and I just kept on walking. They looked at each other, unsure how to react, and I suddenly felt this mad desire to keep walking. I knew I would come out in Kensington High Street and I thought it would be fun to wander around a couple of shops. I was wearing a coat and scarf and I didn't think anyone would recognize me. I must have walked some 200 yards beyond the barrier when I heard the sound of running feet some distance behind me. I looked quickly over my shoulder and saw two officers running toward me, so I quickened my pace and believed I could make it into Ken High Street and into a shop before they reached me. The street was quite crowded but just as I was about to dive into the first shop they caught up with me. 'Excuse me, Ma'am', said the first breathless officer, 'but I've been instructed to escort you back to the palace.'

" 'Please,' I said, 'I'm only going to take a quick peek at some clothes and then I'll come straight back; promise.'

" 'Ma'am,' said the other officer politely, 'we can't permit that. It would be worth more than our job to let you go shopping on your own and we can't accompany you dressed in uniform. We'll have to ask you to accompany us. I'm sorry.' "

Diana said that she pleaded with the officers to let her go but they were adamant and she was forced to return. "I walked back toward the palace sandwiched between the two officers and I felt as though I was under arrest, being escorted back to prison."

Before William was born, Diana had come to the conclusion that Kensington Palace had indeed become her prison from which there was no escape. She tried to persuade her personal police bodyguard, senior courtiers, Sir Edward Adeane and she had constantly begged Charles to order the police to permit her to go shopping occasionally — entirely on her own or, perhaps, with a girlfriend.

It was an argument that kept erupting, for Diana hated the idea that she was being confined to live in a palace with no escape. This led to frequent rows between Diana and Charles. Some of which were heated, their voices raised, swear words exchanged. What really annoyed Diana was that Charles kept telling her that he could not give her permission to go out alone because her safety was not his responsibility but the responsibility of the police officers whose duty it was to protect and guard her at all times.

"But you're the Prince of Wales," Diana would shout at him. "They must obey you, they have to obey your f***ing orders."

"But the police are not under my authority," Charles would argue in his rather desperate way. "I cannot tell them what to do and what not to do.

They have to obey the orders that they take from their senior officers and I cannot countermand them. It is their job, their duty."

Understandably, these arguments between Diana and Charles contributed to the rapid erosion of their relationship. From Diana's standpoint it simply showed that Charles had no power and no authority. She began to see Charles less as a leader of men, a man of authority, but as a man with little power. Indeed, in time Diana came to understand that Charles, too, was a prisoner of the system. And yet, despite these thoughts, Diana was still convinced that if Charles *really* wanted to be his own man, there was no way that anyone could stop him. She knew that Charles could, if he wished, simply tell them to "f*** off" and leave him alone — and she was convinced that they would obey such an order because they were trained to obey orders.

But in her heart, Diana realized that Charles would never order an adviser, a bodyguard, a police officer or any member of his staff to carry out an order he knew went against their duty. Whereas Diana knew that she would have happily issued such orders to staff and police officers, she knew that Charles didn't have the courage to do so because he was hidebound by his upbringing and his respect for the system. Frequently, in those first few months at Kensington Palace, Diana pleaded with Charles to break the rules, demand his freedom and go shopping or for a walk without his bodyguard. But what infuriated Diana was that Charles would simply refuse to do so or even contemplate the idea because he said it would be "grossly unfair" to those responsible for his safety. And he would never put them in that impossible position. Diana would disagree, sometimes shouting and pleading with him, but Charles would never be moved.

Occasionally, Diana would try to make a break for freedom, leaving the palace in disguise, pretending she was one of the office workers employed at Kensington Palace. She would wear a long coat and a scarf over her head in an effort to hide her face. She would walk with her hands in her coat pockets and her head down in the hope that she could escape their notice as she slipped past the police barrier. But she failed every time. Diana became convinced that the police manning the barrier were tipped off by other staff members inside the palace. She was right and that annoyed her greatly, because she hated the ignominy of being stopped and instructed to return to the house like some schoolgirl playing truant.

It is difficult to emphasize how important this

issue of personal freedom was to Diana and to her relationship with Charles. She felt she was living in a prison without bars. "There are armed guards who would physically stop me from walking out of the palace and they would then insist on escorting me back to the palace just like any prison officer would if a prisoner tried to escape from jail. There really is no difference, no difference at all."

Diana believed her enforced confinement was responsible, in large measure, for her bulimia because there was nothing for her to do all day but sit around Kensington Palace, watch television, listen to music, phone friends, read magazines or eat. She never really enjoyed reading books because she had never been taught to do so. Back home at Althorp, she had spent her childhood roaming around the extensive grounds, playing with her sisters or younger brother, chatting to the staff or watching television.

As a result, at Kensington Palace, Diana would find herself constantly raiding the refrigerator, picking at things, having a snack or eating chocolate simply because she was so damned bored. "I'm bored, I'm bored to death; don't you understand that," she would yell at Charles. "There's nothing for me to do, nothing except watch bloody TV and eat. Don't you understand that I want my freedom? I want my freedom desperately, otherwise I'll go stark raving mad stuck here all day in this Godforsaken place." And, as a result of her boredom, Diana would raid the pantry and munch away until the feeling of guilt struck her and she would throw away whatever food she was eating and make herself sick. For a while that would re-establish her equilibrium, her peace of mind, but the gorging quickly became a vicious cycle. The downward spiral had begun but, at that time, Diana didn't recognize the symptoms.

She became convinced that if she had been allowed to go shopping on her own, to spend a couple of hours buying clothes, wandering around her favorite stores, having lunch with a friend, she would then have felt fulfilled because she was enjoying herself in the way she liked. There would have been no need, no compulsion for her to stuff herself full of food she didn't want in a bid to bring some pleasure into her boring life.

Of course, Diana was permitted to leave the confines of the palace at any time, to come and go as she pleased — but only if accompanied by her personal armed bodyguard. But doing so irked her. She knew there was the possibility that the IRA might try to kidnap or kill her, but she considered that idea so unlikely she thought it a preposterous excuse for insisting that she had to be accompanied whenever she left the palace grounds.

She didn't want some policeman going into shops with her, sitting at another table whenever she lunched with a girlfriend, watching everything she did. As Diana put it to some of her girlfriends, "Does a girl really want some policeman standing by watching her while she buys her bra and knickers?!"

Her friends would laugh, but to Diana it was all too serious. To most of them, of course, Diana was the luckiest woman in the world, the envy of everyone — married to the Prince of Wales, with servants, cooks and maids, magnificent homes to live in, wardrobes full of designer clothes, never wanting for any material goods and all the money she could spend.

But not to Diana.

Diana wasn't the only non-royal married to a member of "The Firm," as the royals refer to their own family. There were others who shared her anxieties, who yearned for freedom, who found life almost impossible with the tiresome restrictions on a royal life. The present royal family of the House of Windsor is littered with broken marriages and one of the primary reasons for those casualties was not the problem of personal relationships but the never-ending life of duty, obedience, confinement and of living their lives in a goldfish bowl with the world examining — and frequently criticizing — their every movement, remark, every dress and outfit, their hairstyle.

From the day she became queen in February 1952, Elizabeth wanted her family to be the epitome of a loving, caring nuclear family, a beacon of moral example to the British people. Born in 1926, Elizabeth grew up in the knowledge that divorce was an abomination to the royal family and to those courtiers whose duty it was to uphold the good name of the monarchy. Divorcées were treated like lepers, ostracized by the court and no divorced person was ever permitted to be in the presence of the monarch. Elizabeth understood that two world wars had weakened the nation's moral fiber as well as their sense of duty and obligation and she determined to do all in her power to persuade the British people to return to the golden age when no divorces were even contemplated let alone condoned.

Even in 1967, Elizabeth's attitude to divorce was unforgiving and, in a remarkable demonstration of her principles and belief in the old moral code, Elizabeth acted in a draconian fashion toward the divorce of her own cousin, George Lord Harewood, with whom, until that moment, she had been on close family terms. His wife, the beautiful and talented concert pianist Marion Stein, wanted to divorce Lord Harewood after he met a beautiful Australian model, Patricia Tuckwell, who, in 1965, bore him a son. Harewood went to see Elizabeth to seek permission for a divorce but she refused, calling in the Prime Minister Harold Wilson and the Archbishop of Canterbury in an effort to gain their support. She was adamant that, as a matter of principle, no close member of the royal family should be allowed to divorce. In the end, Elizabeth did agree to a divorce but only because the young woman had born Harewood a child. However, the consequences were severe.

Elizabeth ordered that Harewood be banished from court and Harewood's total ostracism ended much of his public life. On Elizabeth's explicit instructions, Harewood was forced to resign his position as Chancellor of York University and also as artistic director of the famous Edinburgh Festival. And yet, two years after the Harewood divorce, Elizabeth had to sign her government's 1969 Divorce Reform Act, permitting easier and quicker divorce with no blame attached to either party. She had no choice because the British Constitution gave Parliament the right to pass laws as they saw fit. The monarch has no power to refuse to bring any new act of Parliament into law.

In 1980, only two years after her sister

Margaret's official divorce, Elizabeth was shocked to be confronted with the same problem, but this time it was closer to home and much more embarrassing. Her only daughter, Princess Anne, then sixth in line to the throne, was involved in a liaison with her personal police bodyguard, Sergeant Peter Cross. Unnerved at the revelation, the queen ordered a close watch be kept on the couple and she demanded weekly reports of the lovers' meetings. On hearing that the couple were having a full-blown affair, Elizabeth ordered the immediate removal of Peter Cross from royal protection duties.

The gutsy Anne was furious, turned on her rather meek husband, Captain Mark Phillips, whose nickname was "Fog," and accused him of telling tales behind her back. Eventually, Mark confessed that he had told the queen's personal bodyguard about Anne's adultery, which infuriated Anne further. But Mark Phillips had never enjoyed his high-profile position married to the queen's only daughter. Indeed, for most of the marriage he was deeply embarrassed at the idea of being a member of the royal family and refused to become involved in any royal matters at any time during his marriage. He felt he could never be himself or relax — except in the confines of his own home.

However, neither the queen nor Mark Phillips knew at the time that Anne was pregnant and that the father of the unborn child was Peter Cross. After being withdrawn from royal duties, Cross resigned from the police protection squad and was then free to see Anne at any time. Anne's daughter, blue-eyed, blonde Zara, was born in 1981. When the queen finally learned that Peter Cross was Zara's father, she permitted Anne and Mark Phillips to divorce. She had no real option but to grant the divorce, but she was totally embarrassed that her daughter would let her down by committing adultery and having a baby out of wedlock.

The queen refused to permit Anne to live openly with Peter Cross until some time had elapsed after the divorce and the public had no idea that Zara was not Mark Phillips' daughter. After Zara's birth, Anne and Cross continued to see each other and Anne would phone him at his office using the name Mrs. Wallis. (It was Anne's mischievous idea to use the name of the most famous adulteress known to the House of Windsor, the American divorcée Wallis Simpson, who married King Edward VIII after he abdicated the throne in 1937). However, Cross did not want to spend the rest of his life in the shadows and became convinced that the queen would never permit her only daughter to marry a cop, so he began looking for another woman. Eventually, he met and fell in love with a dental nurse and devastated Anne had to accept that she had lost the man she loved. Understandably, she blamed her mother.

To the queen, who had fought all her life to restore faithfulness in marriage among the British people, the fact that divorce had entered her own family was difficult to accept. And, as the world now knows, Anne's divorce was only the start of a catastrophic period in the queen's family as the marriages of two of her sons fell apart amidst dreadful scandals and bitterness, which gripped the attention of the world.

These unions, in which royals married out-siders, had all come to embarrassing ends before Diana arrived on the scene — but she would be a witness to other royal marriages ending in acrimony and embarrassment for the monarchy before she, too, found it impossible to continue as a member of "The Firm."

The celebrated, flame-haired Sarah Ferguson, daughter of the late Major Ronald Ferguson, who played polo with both the Duke of Edinburgh and later Prince Charles, arrived on the royal scene with big smiles and great enthusiasm — but little decorum. Overnight, Fergie, as the world called her, caught the eye of Prince Andrew and within weeks the two were inseparable, apparently spending the majority of their time in bed together. Andrew was bowled over by the audacious, bubbly, boisterous Fergie, who enjoyed the reputation of being a very sexy lady.

A matter of months after their first date, Andrew married Fergie in the summer of 1986. Two years later, daughter Beatrice arrived and, in 1990 Eugenie. But royal life never suited extrovert Fergie, for she was too outgoing, too enthusiastic and there seemed no possibility that she would ever calm down and lead a quiet existence in the background, dutifully carrying out royal duties by the side of Prince Andrew. Fergie also discovered that Andrew was not the man whom she had hoped would be able to quench her sexual appetite and she had begun to look around for other likely prospects. It didn't help that Andrew had spent most of their married life away at sea with the Royal Navy, providing Fergie with free rein to indulge herself.

In November 1989, when three months pregnant with Eugenie, Fergie went on an official royal visit to Houston, Texas, to represent the queen at the British Festival at the Houston Grand Opera. There she met Steve Wyatt, 35, a serious, athletic, handsome man with a mahogany suntan who did not smoke, drink or take any form of drugs. Fergie became smitten by his seductive talk of karma, astrology, divinity and other New Age subjects, interests which were dear to her heart and a million miles from the conversation she usually had with Prince Andrew. She spent much of the evening dancing with Steve. It was a real-life fatal attraction.

Fergie invited Steve to London, escorted him on a personal tour of Buckingham Palace and arranged invitations for him to lunch at the palace and take dinner at Windsor Castle. She even introduced her new "friend" to Prince Andrew when he was home on leave and, apparently, they all got on famously — having supper and barbecues together. Months after their first meeting, Fergie took Bea and Eugenie on holiday to Morocco and Wyatt went along, too. Unknown to Andrew, the couple were having a passionate fling, which continued back in London.

Fergie's illicit sex exploits had now reached the ears of senior courtiers at the palace and by the autumn of 1990 the queen was informed that Fergie was involved with the young American. Fergie was called in by the queen's private secretary, Sir Robert Fellowes — Diana's brother-in-law — and informed that the queen knew of her affair with Wyatt. Fergie was told to end the affair immediately but she took no notice, oblivious that this potential scandal could be ruinous for her reputation and her marriage as well as proving deeply embarrassing for the queen.

The influential powers of Buckingham Palace had more of an effect on Wyatt. He was quietly and discreetly taken to one side and advised to end his adulterous relationship with Fergie and to leave Britain. He took the advice and fled. Unhappy and upset that "the love of her life" was deserting her for no apparent reason, Fergie was, as it turned out, rightly convinced that the Establishment had been quietly at work in the background and she was furious that they had had the audacity to interfere in her private life. The departure of Wyatt, however, brought Fergie to the edge of a nervous breakdown, for without Wyatt she felt vulnerable and defenseless. She believed that her phones were being tapped, her mail checked, her meetings with everyone spied on. Even the ebullient, cheery Fergie couldn't take the pressure and toward the end of 1991 she began to go to pieces.

In a remarkable interview for the society magazine *The Tatler*, Fergie confessed, "I just have to get away from the system and people saying to me all the time 'no you can't, no you can't.' That's what the system is like. I can't stick to all these guidelines, to all the rules because they're not real. It's not a real life living in a palace. And so I feel inhibited.

"I don't even feel happy at our home at Sunninghill. Some nights I ask every member of staff to leave so that we can be a family, on our own, like any normal family."

The interview continued:

"I like to get away but I feel I can't. If I lived in Europe no one would be any the wiser if, for example, I went to the mountains. I could go skiing for the weekend and no one would bat an eyelid. But here, everyone thinks skiing is an elitist sport. The mountains are my security. I love them. The mountains talk to me and they give me strength. And I'm not allowed to go because of being seen, because of what people might say or write, and all because I'm now owned by the system. Therefore, I don't go and I feel trapped. And it is the system that is trapping me."

All nonroyals, but particularly Diana, sympathized with Fergie's frustration and her description of life inside "The Firm." When Diana read the article she phoned Fergie to congratulate her. "I wish I had the courage to write something like that," she said. "Everything you said was honest, and I feel exactly the same as you do … I could have written that because, like you, I know it's the truth ... People always say that one day the truth 'will out' and you've now told the world what life is really like inside the royal family ... Everyone thinks we have the most wonderful life, but now perhaps they will understand what a bloody awful life we have."

It would be some 10 months later that Andrew Morton's *Diana: Her True Story* was published and some members of the royal family believe that the interview by Fergie in *The Tatler* magazine persuaded Diana to become involved in writing the book that would expose her life to the world and rock the inner sanctums of both the royal family and the palace courtiers, the men responsible for laying down the rules that all royals are expected to follow to the letter. The courtiers are also responsible for ensuring that all members of the extended royal family obey those rules.

There was another royal marriage hiccup that would cause the queen sleepless nights. This new scandal would reach into her marriage to Prince Philip and would be deeply embarrassing if the real story ever emerged. Everything was done at every level inside the palace in a desperate bid to keep the lid on the impending scandal.

In 1987, the queen's first cousin, Princess Alexandra, discovered her strong-willed daughter, Marina, then a talented concert pianist of 21, had fallen in love with Paul Mowatt, a young photographer some three years older. For the first three months of the relationship, Mowatt had no idea that his new girlfriend had any royal connections.

Marina had always been something of a teenage rebel, headstrong and independent. Calling herself "Mo" Marina Ogilvy (her father's surname) she lived the life of a tomboy. She attended Outward Bound adventure schools, dressed in nothing but jeans and sweaters and shunned all connections to the royal family. She also had a strong social conscience and became dedicated to helping youngsters in trouble with drugs and crime. At the age of 17, she worked incognito as a shorthand typist to raise $3,000 for a trip to the West Indies, where she helped to build a new school. She refused to ask her parents for the money.

In December 1988, Paul and Marina began living together in part of Paul's mother's small, suburban, three bedroom, semi-detached house in Kingston-upon-Thames, only five miles from her parents luxurious, large country home, Thatched House Lodge in Richmond Park, 20 miles south-west of London. Princess Alexandra's husband, Sir Angus Ogilvy, worked in the city and, wanting to show they were modern, understanding parents, turned a blind eye to their daughter's new arrangement. Secretly, neither of her parents approved.

Once she began living with her boyfriend, Marina turned her back on her career, left the university and her education at the prestigious London Guildhall of Music, to spend more time with her live-in lover and dedicate her life to rock music.

The drama that would very nearly envelop Elizabeth and Prince Philip in an amazing scandal came in October 1989, when Marina told her parents she was pregnant and that she was determined to have her lover's baby. She also announced that she had no intention of getting married. Marina, then 24th in line of succession to the throne, was to give birth to the first royal baby born out of wedlock for 150 years. (Through the centuries, scores of royal children have, of course, been illegitimate. Very few, however, were officially recognized. Usually, the scandal was hushed up and the mother paid a handsome maintenance allowance).

Princess Alexandra had no choice but to inform the queen of Marina's pregnancy and the very difficult telephone conversation ended with the queen telling Alexandra to "get a grip" on her wayward daughter and sort out the matter. "She is your daughter and, therefore, your responsibility. You must find a way out of this fine predicament and quickly."

Alexandra and her husband explained to their daughter the potential embarrassment of someone in line to the throne giving birth to an illegitimate child, but she refused to follow their orders. In a newspaper article before the baby was born, Marina claimed that her mother had given her two alternatives: either have the baby aborted immediately or get married by special license. Marina retorted that she had no intention of doing either. She then claimed, "My mother gestured with her fingers in front of my face and told me, 'It will only be about this big. You are a healthy young girl and you will conceive easily again.'

"I couldn't believe she could talk to me like that, so coldly about my baby and her grandchild. She said the same thing again the following night when Paul was with me. Paul and I were horrified. My father was furious that we were refusing to have the baby aborted and my mother's mouth turned into a snarl. I asked my parents, 'What comes first, your daughter or queen and country?' My father replied, 'Queen and country.' "

Marina wrote to Elizabeth, imploring her help in sorting out what was happening, telling her of the awful choices her mother had given her, saying that one day she did indeed intend to marry her boyfriend Paul. Elizabeth was now in an extraordinary quandary — she was aware of the terrible secret that the two families had kept closely guarded: that Prince Philip had been Princess Alexandra's secret lover for some 20 years from 1955 to the mid-1970s. The queen had been forced to live with that secret. Though she had been informed about the affair by her private secretary in the late 1950s, Philip refused to end the relationship.

The last thing Elizabeth needed at this time, the late 1980s, was for the world to hear of the relationship – especially since it had continued with her knowledge for so many years. She knew that such a revelation would harm her personally and would do irreparable damage to the royal family and the prestige of the monarchy. The queen, convinced that Marina already knew, had to find a way to make sure she stayed quiet.

Elizabeth called for Alexandra and Angus and told them that, whatever she decided, they both had to comply with her demands. They accepted her intervention and agreed to do whatever she wanted.

Angry beyond words with the recalcitrant Marina, the fearful Elizabeth knew that the only chance of sorting out the problem was to have a woman-to-woman chat at Buckingham Palace with her. Over tea and biscuits, Elizabeth persuaded Marina that it would be best for her and her unborn baby, as well as the royal family, if she would agree to marry Paul before the baby was due. At the end of one of Elizabeth's most difficult private conversations, Marina agreed and the couple were married in a quiet church wedding in February 1990.

Sir Angus did agree to give his daughter away that day, but both Alexandra and Angus refused to attend the wedding breakfast afterward and refused to invite any of the 150 relatives who would normally have been expected to attend the wedding of the 24th in line to the throne. The queen and the entire royal family also shunned the wedding. Baby Zenouska was born four months later, but during the first two years of her life Alexandra only visited her once — for 20 minutes. For Elizabeth, the crisis had been averted — but for how long?

Diana would have to endure years of personal drama before some of these later events came to pass, but she intended to try and dictate the play to her advantage. Diana knew full well the lengths to which The Firm and their courtiers would go to protect the image of the monarchy and the good name of Elizabeth and she was determined that they would not easily get the better of her.

She recognized that she had a powerful hand to

play — she was the mother of William and Harry, heirs to the throne, who, after Charles, were the two most important people in Britain. Diana intended to build on her own image with the ordinary people of Britain, to win their support, their friendship, their love, their belief in fair play and their natural support for the underdog. She would show the women of Britain, whom she believed were her natural allies, that she had become a victim of the royal family, who was treating her as an inferior person who had to yield to their orders and be subjected to their demands.

Diana first conceived this plan shortly after the birth of Harry in September 1984. She put it into operation almost immediately, testing the ground to see how popular she had become with the ordinary British men and women. She found that they had taken her to their collective bosom without knowing anything about her. To most women Diana had become "that darling girl." Although born an aristocrat and with family trees even more royal than the House of Windsor, the British people considered Diana one of them because she had worked as a charwoman, a nanny and a kindergarten teacher.

Her shy smile and bashful appearance won the hearts of most people and even Diana was astonished by the adoration the people showed whenever she made a public appearance. As a result, Diana actually enjoyed many of the royal visits and official engagements she was obliged to attend with Prince Charles because those who turned out to see her, to wave their flags and cheer, were growing in numbers. Their welcomes were becoming increasingly vociferous, chanting in unison: "Di-an-a, Di-an-a," as the royal car drew near. Sometimes, that chant would continue unabated until after she had been driven away — sometimes 30 minutes later. She took great comfort in their enthusiasm and support. That was why, on many of those obligatory occasions that she usually despised so much, Diana was seen happy, smiling and genuinely enjoying herself.

She continued her public appearances while pregnant with William, and even though she was suffering from terrible bouts of morning sickness, she portrayed the image of a happy, smiling princess simply because she came to love those moments of adoration and support. Her public appearances while pregnant also won her praise from every mother in the land. Before Diana, most royal women never appeared in public when pregnant, preferring to hide their bulging waistlines. But Diana was different and British womanhood took her to be one of them — who, by chance, happened to marry a prince.

The arrival of baby William in June 1982 helped concentrate Diana's energies and for the first few months Diana really enjoyed her darling little boy, especially those special moments of cuddling, bathing and breast-feeding her wonderful "little miracle." Diana did have nurses and nannies and maids to care not only for baby William, but also for all the diapers and bottles, the nursery and the washing and ironing. Diana recognized that she was indeed fortunate that she had all the enjoyment and fulfillment of motherhood but with none of the accompanying drudgery.

However, Diana did have problems to confront — problems that seemed, to her, insurmountable.

Chapter 3

Diana Takes a Lover

*I*n late 1983 Prince Charles was informed by his private secretary, Sir Edward Adeane, that he had been led to understand that the Princess of Wales had become involved with a young cavalry officer. At that meeting Adeane did not reveal the officer's name or rank, nor did Charles ask, but Adeane revealed to Charles that he not only knew the officer's name, he confirmed that he was still a serving officer with the Life Guards in the Household Cavalry.

Charles was totally taken aback and unnerved by the news. He knew that the faithful Sir Edward Adeane would not have given him such a delicate and shattering piece of information unless he was absolutely certain that Diana and the unnamed cavalry officer were romantically involved. Charles guessed that the information had probably been passed to Sir William by one of Diana's police bodyguards, as it was their duty to inform Sir Edward as to what was going on.

The bodyguard's duty was to protect the Princess of Wales, but it is never the duty of a police protection officer to judge anyone's morals or faithfulness to their spouse. Diana's guards had been drilled into understanding that the private lives of the royals must remain just that. If any of the royals they were guarding had affairs, committed adultery or attended any wild parties, it was none of their business. The royals had to be permitted to have private lives and feel comfortable that they could indulge themselves in whatever sexual pleasures or dalliances they wished, with the confidence that such behavior was to remain a secret. Police officers were ordered not even to reveal such extramarital matters to their superior officers unless there was a very good reason for doing so.

In the 1980s, however, a new problem had entered the equation which tended to blur the matter of strict confidentiality. The IRA had already assassinated one senior member of the royal family — killing Earl Mountbatten and other members of his family while on vacation in Ireland in August 1979. As a result, police protection officers were ordered to take extra care when guarding their principals and to always think of what the consequences might be as a result of any untoward behavior on behalf of those they were protecting. As a result, of course, Diana's romantic relationship with a cavalry officer was judged as a possible threat to her safety; that her secret movements hidden from Charles and others might, in consequence, expose her to possible danger. Diana's protection officer decided that he had no option but to pass on his knowledge of Diana's clandestine movements outside the palace gates to his superior officer. In turn, he handed the information to Sir Edward Adeane — Prince Charles' principal adviser.

Perhaps it was hearing this news that caused Charles to realize that his marriage to Diana had begun to go downhill shortly after she had become pregnant with Prince William, back in the winter of 1981, only a few months after their wedding.

To give Charles some credit, he had tried everything to please his young bride and he hoped and prayed that her pregnancy would not only rekindle her love for him, but that having a baby to care for and nurture would bring her real happiness. Before their wedding, Diana talked frequently of the thrill of caring and loving a little child of her own. She knew that it was expected that she and Charles would have a family and she felt very happy about it. Diana had always loved babies. Didn't she look after her baby brother Charles when she was only 5 years old? The reason she worked for so little money as a London kindergarten teacher was because it involved caring for very young children, most of them toddlers.

Diana had eagerly looked forward to the prospect of motherhood, perhaps bearing three or four royal children. And she understood that one of the reasons Charles wanted to get married was so that he could, God willing, produce not only an heir for the House of Windsor but also a vibrant young family. They had talked about all of this well before their engagement was announced — Charles knew it was imperative that he should marry someone who was happy to have a large family and a house full of children. After the bitter experience of his own childhood, Charles wanted his children to lead a happy, free life without the dreadful restrictions that had been imposed on him since the age of 4.

As he began dating, Charles discovered that because of his position as heir to the throne, some of his relationships with young women ended disastrously. They soon discovered that dating the Prince of Wales was both awkward and restrictive. He was a straightforward, regular, heterosexual man with what he gauged was a healthy sexual appetite — as probably a dozen or more women can testify.

And yet, despite his interest in the opposite sex, Charles openly recognized that he wasn't in any way a "ladies' man." He always felt somewhat awkward, even gauche, in the presence of a young woman, particularly one to whom he felt a strong sexual attraction.

One of his first girlfriends, Caroline Wisley, whom he dated in the 1970s, confessed, "We had some fun together and he was wonderfully polite and well-mannered, but when it came to going to bed together he seemed unsure of himself, even embarrassed, and yet he had no reason to be. The other problem, which really seemed rather stupid, was that I had been advised that I should call him 'Sir' on all occasions. Every girl can imagine how off-putting it would be to have to call her lover 'Sir' throughout all the passion and lovemaking. It totally put me off."

With some young women, however, he felt no embarrassment whatsoever, particularly with those women who enjoyed his jokes and who were interesting conversationalists with bright, sharp minds and a sense of humor. Indeed, Charles found he actually enjoyed such women far more than those he simply bedded, usually because he discovered that though he had found them sexually attractive, there had been no meeting of minds.

Of course, before Diana came on the scene, Charles had never actually lived with a woman. Indeed, he had hardly ever spent more than a long weekend with a woman at any time of his life. Charles had been the proverbial bachelor and thoroughly enjoyed being a single man. Indeed, if Charles had not been the heir to the throne and if he had not been subjected to constant badgering from his father to get married and produce an heir, it is fair to say that Charles might never have married and settled down.

Since leaving the Royal Navy at age 28, Charles gathered a team of men to organize his life; to manage the multimillion-dollar Duchy of Cornwall, with its large farms and its property empire in London; to run the Prince's Trust for less fortunate young people seeking work and to take care of his homes. Each day, secret government papers were delivered to his home informing him, as heir to the throne, of exactly what the government was doing on a day-to-day basis. Like his mother, who also received these daily reports, he was diligent in reading them, though many of the papers were boring and mundane.

In his spare time, Charles loved to play polo, shoot birds and game, fish for trout in Scottish rivers and, of course, hunt foxes with different packs of hounds throughout Britain. He also found time to attend the theater in London and enjoyed opera and classical music. From time to time he threw parties, usually for his polo friends and others. He also found time to date the occasional young woman but that never seemed to be a priority. He was the young man declared the world's most eligible bachelor who could offer a young woman great wealth, a future kingdom and, one day, the probability of a crown and the title of "Queen of England."

Charles, of course, had never really enjoyed a normal life. He had never enjoyed a mother-son relationship with the queen because she was far too involved and busy with her daunting job as monarch to spend much time with her firstborn. The love and warmth that most children receive from their mothers was missing and though his nannies were kind, loving and gentle, Charles' only true family relationship was with his father, Philip, who proved an absolute disaster in the role. At age 7, Charles was off to boarding school. When he turned 13, he moved on to the tough Scottish school of Gordonstoun, where he was never happy. That experience was followed by university, where he met a few girls but never became really involved. And then he joined the

Royal Navy, which he really enjoyed. He would spend five happy years at sea in the company of men and naval officers whom he respected. (At that time, no women were permitted to serve on Her Majesty's ships). With that start in life, it is not surprising that Charles never really understood girls, never felt at ease with them except on a cerebral level, excepting of course, the occasional lusty romp.

Unfortunately for Diana, Charles' character was not conducive to sitting on a sofa in front of a roaring log fire enjoying long cuddles and chats, engrossed with the young woman at his side; or spending hours over a romantic candlelight dinner with a lover, or lying in bed together making love for hours at a time. To her horror, Diana quickly discovered that such romantic ideas were never a part of Charles' thought processes. Diana quickly became convinced that Charles had never learned how to woo or make love to a girl, never learned to laugh and joke and make a girl feel relaxed, happy and secure in a relationship; never indulged in little intimacies or affectionate kisses. He didn't seem to understand that young women love to be romanced, seduced and made love to, not simply invited to take part and, hopefully, enjoy the act of fornication — but to be fully involved in the passion of making love.

After the marriage had ended in tears, Diana told Sarah, who was married about the same time as Diana but is now divorced, "I found much more romance and affection in a magazine story than I ever found with Charles and that made me really sad. It was all such a terrible waste. Basically, Charles is a nice guy but he simply hasn't any idea, any idea at all how to treat a woman."

At other times, Diana would say, "I accept that it's not his fault; I accept that the whole royal family is lacking in affection, warmth, kindness and understanding; you name it, they lack it. Poor Charles inherited the family traits and he has to live with that ... The trouble was that I fell in love with the whole idea of marrying Prince Charles, perhaps because he was heir to the throne and I didn't see the personal problems and all the royal baggage that came with him ... Stupid me ... I just went into it with my eyes shut, believing the fairy tale would come true ... I really did think that the prince had fallen in love with the girl he had been searching for all his life and that we would live happily ever after."

This was at the heart of what *really* went wrong with the marriage. With her unfortunate upbringing with no mother around to care and love her, and a father who had the will but little or no idea of how to bring up three young daughters in a loving way, Diana was desperate for a close, loving relationship. Charles was the first man who showed her any real commitment and she fell in love with him, hoping that he would give her the confidence she lacked and the love for which she yearned. It is difficult to exaggerate Diana's fundamental need for a caring, loving relationship with someone following her loveless upbringing and what she always considered was her mother's desertion. Unfortunately for Diana, the dutiful, lukewarm and passionless Charles was simply not the man capable of providing those needs. Seemingly, he had little or no idea how he should treat his wife.

Charles did try, but he failed. In the first few months of the marriage, Charles was kind and considerate to Diana, because he desperately wanted the marriage to be "hugely successful." He tried by being generous with money and happily paying all her credit card bills that, with some of her designer clothes, would sometimes amount to hundreds of thousands of dollars a year. He gave her total and complete freedom to do anything she wanted, go anywhere she wanted, buy anything she wanted as long as she agreed to her part of the bargain — to be his consort, attending boring dinners and tedious functions that he knew she hated. And he knew that the great majority of people Diana would meet at such functions were nearly always dull, gray and colorless. Diana always told Charles how much she preferred to be at home, sitting in bed watching TV and sipping a mug of hot cocoa.

Unfortunately for Charles, he had major personality faults that prevented him from having a loving, caring, exciting relationship with any woman — let alone an inexperienced, bashful, shy young woman like Diana. Her interests were clothes, friends and TV soaps. Unfortunately, she was also an immature young woman who had received a poor education and was someone who never read books and had no interest in doing so; who had little or no conversation that could interest or fascinate Charles; whose friends were girls who never extended her intelligence or broadened her horizons. Her music interests extended to 1970s pop songs and she had no interest in Charles' love for opera and classical music. Unfortunately, Diana had no wish to broaden her interests or educate herself in any way or in any discipline. As some critics commented from time to time, "Diana brought very little to the marriage except good breeding, a healthy young body, good legs, lovely face and a radiant smile."

After her death, however, even those who had never warmed to Diana admitted, "She matured with age and during her life she brought compassion and tenderness to a rather cold royal family who have never seemed to learn the meaning of the word compassion."

After his years at Gordonstoun and his stint in the Royal Navy, Charles came to believe, like his father, that order, obedience, duty and firmness were essential in all matters and no deviation from these rules should be considered or condoned. But, unlike his father, Charles did believe in fairness when dealing with people and their problems. Fairness and duty were his criteria for leading his own life. But they were simply useless and probably counterproductive in cultivating a caring, loving, doting relationship with his wife. To that extent, Charles was responsible for the breakdown of the marriage.

From time to time, the queen would try to reach out to Diana and involve her in the family dinner conversations, but Diana's response was usually to blush with embarrassment knowing the queen was only trying to be kind to her, which made her feel worse. After such attempts by the queen, Diana would be so embarrassed that she had nothing of consequence to bring to the conversation that she would sink back into her shell and say nothing as the rest of the family chatted away. And, because Diana paid little attention to what had actually been said, she didn't even catch on to any of the jokes, so that when the rest of the family laughed at some comment, poor Diana would simply blush because she hadn't even heard what was said, let alone understood the joke. Diana put it succinctly to one of her girlfriends, "All they talk about at dinner is f***ing shooting; it makes me sick."

After her first winter at Balmoral, Diana had hoped that now that she was pregnant, all the love that she wanted to share with Charles could now be directed toward the child she was carrying.

Diana would later confess to Howard, one of her lovers, "After the birth of William, it seemed to me that Charles lost interest in me. I knew that he had been forced into getting married because his parents had badgered and cajoled him for years to find a 'suitable' girl, settle down and produce an heir or two for the family. It seemed that after William came along, Charles lost interest in the sex side of our marriage. I felt that he believed he had done his duty by his parents and now he could relax and get on with his own life again — playing polo and all that hunting, fishing and shooting stuff. I think he was quite happy with things, but he must have known that I wasn't."

Diana had tasted the delights of a sexual relationship but had not enjoyed the passion and lust of a full, demanding and satisfying sex life for which she now yearned. In the summer of 1981,

Diana first saw Lt. James Hewitt at a polo match in which he was playing against Prince Charles.

This was first revealed in the book *Princess In Love*, written by Anna Pasternak with much aid, advice and assistance from James Hewitt. In it she revealed that in June 1981, a month before the royal wedding, Hewitt had been playing for the Army in the annual polo match against the Royal Navy team captained by Prince Charles. Watching him that day was Charles' fiancée Diana.

Pasternak wrote, *"The young Diana Spencer had come to watch her fiance, and the world had come to watch her. For the first time in public she buckled under the strain of the engagement — not, as she told James later, so much because of the zeal of the press as because of the nauseous fear continuously washing over her that her relationship with Charles was not as it should be. Try as she might, she could not shake off the ghosts that persecuted her incessantly, telling her to embrace the truth before it was too late."*

Pasternak continues, *"As her thin, weary face crumpled against the car and the tears ran unguarded down her face, it was not her future husband's heart that ached in empathy but James Hewitt's, as he watched from his mount. Disturbed that her sadness was so heavy and so*

*profound, he would gladly have taken her misery
from her and, in any way possible, eased her load.
But, of course, it was impossible."*

According to Hewitt's autobiography, *Love and
War*, they first met by accident in May 1986 at
Buckingham Palace, though he did recall that he
had seen Diana some five years earlier at the
Tidworth Park polo club.

Referring to the 1986 meeting, he recalled, "I
wish I could remember the exact words we spoke
but I do remember exactly what I was feeling:
just completely bowled over by someone so fem-
inine and friendly and captivatingly beautiful."

It seems odd that Hewitt, allegedly, never met
or even saw Diana again until five years later. In
his autobiography, Hewitt boasts in a caption of
a photograph of him challenging Prince Charles
on the polo field, "Polo at Windsor with Prince
Charles. We met frequently on the field, both
being keen players."

Both Prince Charles and James Hewitt were
members of the Guards Polo Club whose headquarters are at Windsor Great Park and they
would have met on many occasions during the
summer season. Being a keen polo player, this
author also frequently attended matches at
Windsor during the 1980s, and on numerous occasions I saw Diana watching Prince Charles

playing polo matches. Sometimes she would take along little William and later, Harry. It seems strange to me that Hewitt, according to his own autobiography, apparently never saw or met Diana during those five years. And if he did, it is even stranger that he should never record or mention such meetings or sightings in his book.

He recalled other meetings with Diana in the middle 1980s — a discussion of horse riding, his offer to teach her to ride and her gushing response of acceptance, riding lessons at Knightsbridge Barracks, walks on horseback in Hyde Park, conversations about Hewitt's girl-friends and then, suddenly, Diana's brutally honest and shocking statement one day when she confessed to Hewitt, "Charles and I are not in love and the marriage is on the rocks."

Hewitt claimed in his autobiography, published in 1999, that Diana had initiated the affair, that she had made the first move by grabbing his hand and with tears in her eyes telling him, "I need you. You give me strength. I can't stand it when I'm away from you. I want to be with you. I've come to love you." And Diana followed that dramatic declaration by leaning forward and sealing her declaration of love with a kiss on his lips.

Hewitt also states that the date of his first meeting and conversation with Diana was in May

1986. But that is not borne out by other facts. Hewitt's name was included in the approved list of people permitted entry to Kensington Palace in 1983 and Prince Charles' former baggage master, the late Sergeant Ronald Lewis, confirmed that Hewitt was a regular visitor to the Princess of Wales' apartment at Kensington Palace in 1983 and 1984. This has since been confirmed by other senior advisers who were working on the staff of the Prince and Princess of Wales at Kensington Palace during the early years of their marriage.

As a result of Earl Mountbatten's assassination, security had been dramatically stepped up at all royal residences. At Kensington Palace, where Charles and Diana as well as four other royal family members had apartments, armed police were on duty 24 hours a day. Everyone was checked on arrival and no one was permitted to pass the vehicle checkpoint some 50 yards from the entrance to Kensington Palace. Of course, the regular, well-known visitors were permitted entry, waved through with a salute.

For a number of years following the birth of Prince Harry in September 1984, no one ever suggested that Prince Charles was not Harry's biological father, but throughout his teenage years Harry has come to look more and more like James Hewitt and less like Prince Charles. Questions were raised, comparisons made. Harry's hair color was one of the principal reasons why people put forward the suggestion that Harry looked like James Hewitt. His hair, his eyes, his mouth and his demeanor seemed to suggest that Harry not only looked increasingly like Hewitt but both his personality and character traits seemed more like those of Hewitt than of Prince Charles.

This allegation of paternity, that Hewitt is Prince Harry's father, has always been strenuously denied by Hewitt whenever the matter has arisen. Of course, there is absolutely no suggestion of such an allegation in either Hewitt's autobiography or, more importantly, the book, *Diana: Her True Story*, which Diana helped to write and edit.

Hewitt's latest denial came in September 2002, when he issued a statement in response to gossip about Harry's paternity, which had reached a crescendo after portraits commemorating the prince's 18th birthday were released by Buckingham Palace. It is customary for photographs to be released of the younger royals when they turn 18 and 21.

Hewitt, comparing Harry's looks with his own said, "There really is no possibility whatsoever that I am Harry's father. I can absolutely assure you that I am not."

Putting on record for the first time his denial of

the persistent rumors, Hewitt went on, "I can understand the interest, but Harry was already walking by the time my relationship with Diana began. Admittedly, the red hair is similar to mine and people say we look alike. I have never encouraged these comparisons, and although I was with Diana for five years, I must state once and for all that I am not Harry's father. When I first met Diana, Harry was already a toddler."

Hewitt, who claims he was drummed out of the British Army because of his adulterous affair with Diana, continued, "Now Harry is a grown man and he has very different features to Prince William. William looks very much like his mother — Harry is rather different. There is still some family resemblance but it is a lot less noticeable. All this talk of Harry is really very unfair. I think he has been through enough without having his parenthood questioned in public. I am hoping to nail this nonsense once and for all."

One of Diana's former police bodyguards, Ken Wharfe, who published a book in 2002 about his six years as Diana's personal bodyguard, wrote: *"The nonsense should be scotched here and now. Harry was born on September 15, 1984. Diana did not meet James until the summer of 1986, and the red hair gossips so love to cite as proof is, of course, a Spencer trait."*

However, Inspector Ken Wharfe only became Diana's personal bodyguard in 1988, when Harry was 4 years of age, though he had previously been employed as one of the four armed police officers in the "backup" car, which escorted the Prince of Wales wherever he traveled.

After selling his memoirs, Ken Wharfe found himself *persona non grata* with the Establishment for "betraying" a member of the royal family, in this case Diana, by writing about his life with the princess and revealing certain intimate details of her love life for a lucrative publishing contract.

Wharfe may not have known the true facts of Hewitt's first meeting with Diana, or he may simply have chosen to be economical with the truth so as not to embarrass Harry, Prince Charles or the queen, which would have brought him even more ignominy.

James Hewitt claimed in his book that Diana initiated the affair between them after giving her riding lessons at the Household Cavalry's indoor riding school at Knightsbridge Barracks and, later, around Hyde Park's Rotten Row. When Hewitt was moved to Windsor, Diana would be driven there two or three times a week by her personal bodyguard so that she could go riding with Hewitt in the privacy of Windsor Great Park.

Hewitt claimed that the affair took off some

months after they first met in 1986 when they were sitting alone together in the officers' mess at Windsor after one of her riding lessons. Allegedly, Diana told him that day that she and Charles were no longer in love and that their marriage was over in all but name.

"Diana said that one of her problems was that there was absolutely no one to help her. The palace was against her and she found it hard to know who would be for her," wrote Hewitt. "I said that she could rely on me. She turned to me and, without warning, grabbed my hand. And suddenly it all came out, all in a rush. Her eyes were tearful and she spoke with a passion far removed from her usual teasing flirtatiousness.

" 'I need you,' she said. 'You give me strength. I can't stand it when I'm away from you. I want to be with you. I've come to love you.'

"Then she leaned forward and kissed me.

"And so we embarked on an affair which was to continue for most of the next five years. It was wonderful — exhilarating, passionate and intensely loving. We were young — in our 20s — and when we were together life was carefree and full of fun."

The meeting and that affair would have untold consequences for Diana and would lead to a string of lies and falsehoods. It would also lead to her extraordinary bid to sideline the House of

Windsor, remove Prince Charles as heir-apparent and put her son William on the throne in place of Prince Charles. To achieve her ambitions, however, Diana needed the British public's full support and she had to find a way to win and retain their confidence and, if possible, their love and affection. Without the support of the great British public, Diana realized that she would stand no chance against the queen, the royal family and the Establishment — not to mention the political elite, the Church of England and the millions who adored the royal family.

It was an extraordinary challenge that Diana set for herself and yet, at the time of her death, she had succeeded to a remarkable degree. The nation loved and worshipped her and they showed in their adoration that they fully supported her in her battle against Charles, the queen and the entire royal House of Windsor. But the adulation Diana had sought and gained so completely would instead bring about her untimely death in a fatal car crash in August 1997.

Chapter 4

Diana's Greatest Secret

$\mathcal{P}$rince Harry was born 4:20 p.m. Saturday, Sept. 15, 1984, in the Lindo wing at St. Mary's Hospital, London.

In *Diana: Her True Story*, her life in the months leading up to Harry's birth included these surprising words, *"Charles and Diana enjoyed the happiest period of their married life. The balmy summer months before Harry's birth was a time of contentment and mutual devotion."*

This sentence was obviously intended to encourage the reader to believe that during those nine months everything in the royal marriage was fine and that they were really happy together. In fact, however, that was far from true. Charles had been made aware that Diana had taken James Hewitt as a lover months before she told him she was pregnant for the second time.

But Diana had no idea that Charles knew that she and Hewitt had become lovers. Throughout the pregnancy, Charles never let on that he knew she had taken a lover. Nor did he let her know that he knew that she continued to see Hewitt during her pregnancy. Nonetheless, it was true that during those months before the birth of Harry, Charles had noted that Diana had become far more attentive, kind and loving toward him.

But, having informed the reader that the marriage was "the happiest" she could remember, Diana then wrote: *"But a storm cloud hovered on the horizon. Diana knew that Charles was desperate for their second child to be a girl. A scan had already shown that her baby was a boy. It was a secret she nursed until the moment he was born ... Charles' reaction finally closed the door on any love Diana may have felt for him. 'Oh, it's a boy' he said, 'and he's even got rusty hair' ... With these dismissive remarks he left to play polo. From that moment, as Diana has told friends: 'Something inside me died.' It was a reaction that marked the beginning of the end of their marriage."*

For some eight months, Charles had hoped that Diana would enjoy a short fling with Hewitt and would return to him after their child was born. Charles had instructed Sir Edward to tell no one of

the affair and also to inform the Royal Protection
Squad officers to carry on with their duty as usual
as though nothing untoward had occurred. The
officers were also instructed to tell no one, not
even their wives.

Prince Charles had hoped and prayed that the
baby would not look anything like James Hewitt
because he knew there was a slight possibility
that the baby could be his. In his heart, however,
Charles felt fairly certain that the baby Diana
was carrying was not his because, for all intents
and purposes, their sexual relationship had never
really recovered following the birth of William in
June 1982.

It was with some trepidation that Charles took
the elevator to the Lindo wing that September day
and went to see the newborn baby, then just a few
hours old. Charles looked at the tiny baby in the
cot next to Diana's bed and his worst fears were
realized — the baby had rust-colored hair. In fact,
Charles had steeled himself to say nothing about it
to Diana immediately following the birth because
he knew that would be the wrong thing to do in
the wrong place at the wrong time. Yet, he simply
couldn't stop himself making the remark about the
"rusty hair" though he metaphorically kicked himself for doing so the moment he had spoken those
words.

Afterward, Charles was angry at himself for blurting out the statement and not having the patience to keep quiet until a much more appropriate time. He would confess later that seeing the baby's rusty hair was a traumatic moment for him, believing that his wife had given birth to another man's baby while pretending the boy was his. Although it was just a gut feeling, it had shaken him to the core.

He stormed off to play polo because that was the best way Charles knew to get rid of anger and frustration. As he drove away from the hospital and the cheering crowds who had gathered, he confessed to feeling physically sick. He hoped that racing around a polo field and swearing at everything that went wrong might provide some perspective to his distressing situation.

The passage in the book relating to Charles' reaction to Harry's birth illustrates the lengths Diana was prepared to go to deceive the world into believing not only that Charles was an impossible and awful husband but that she was determined to attempt to destroy Charles in whatever way was necessary to protect her character. In retrospect, the book became the core of a clever and unscrupulous plot on Diana's behalf to influence the nation into believing that because Charles wanted a baby girl and she had produced a boy, his reaction had such an effect on her that it was enough to kill her love for him. The idea that Charles' disappointment that the baby was not a girl should have had such a dramatic impact on Diana's feelings toward her husband after their nine months of "mutual devotion" seems almost impossible to accept. Yet, Diana was asking the world to believe that Charles' remark at the birth of Harry was the basis of the breakup of their marriage.

The majority of people reading *Diana: Her True Story* had no reason not to believe what they had read. They even appeared to believe her sentiment that this vital passage proved beyond a reasonable doubt that Charles was a heartless, cold-blooded man, for no husband would behave in such a way to the woman he loved just hours after she had given birth to their son. And yet Diana was asking readers to accept her belief that Charles was just such a man. These stories, passed to the author from Diana and subsequently published in newspapers and magazines across the world, had the effect of damning Charles in the opinion of most who read them.

Nowhere in the book, however, did Diana reveal that Hewitt was her lover. She only confessed to the affair years later during her famous and frank *Panorama* television interview on Nov. 14, 1995 –

Prince Charles' 47th birthday. The interview was seen by tens of millions of viewers throughout the world. By then, of course, the world had known for some years that Hewitt had been her lover — but this was confirmation from Diana herself.

The program also won much praise and ever increasing sympathy for Diana as she explained in a quiet, somber voice of the problems she had to face being married to the Prince of Wales. Her composure and fluency were remarkable; her replies to questions polished and articulate; no question took her by surprise and no answers seemed fluffed. Diana's makeup was subdued and she looked pale and wan, some thought gaunt. Her gut-wrenching honesty was compelling when she spoke movingly of her eating disorders, of her postnatal depression and the effect it had on her marriage, her self-mutilation and her love affair with Hewitt. She told the world, "Yes, I did mutilate myself. I didn't like myself, I was ashamed because I couldn't cope with the pressures ...Well, I just hurt my arms and my legs."

Despite her apparent honesty, which everyone praised, Diana did not mention a word about any suicide attempts, leaving many to believe that she had, in fact, never attempted to kill herself. Perhaps Diana, realizing that she had embellished the stories in the book written with

Andrew Morton, decided the best policy was simply not to mention the subject.

Many viewers watching the program felt they were eavesdropping on a confessional burial of a marriage. More ominously, others highlighted Diana's determination not to obey the wishes of the queen and her advisers and disappear quietly into the background but, instead, it seemed she was preparing to put herself forward as a direct alternative to the queen herself.

In the latter part of the interview, Diana laid down her plans for her future saying, "I would like to be an ambassador for Britain, my country. I would like to offer my talents to serve the victims of society across the world. I would like to be the queen of people's hearts. Someone's got to go out there and love people and show it ... The perception that has been given of me for the last three years has been very confusing, turbulent and, in some areas, I'm sure, many, many people doubt me. I want to reassure all those people who have loved me throughout the last 15 years that I'd never let them down. That is a priority to me. The man on the street matters more than anything else to me."

Diana would be true to that promise of using her talents to serve the victims of society. But, in outlining her plans for the future, Diana had not only given a description of her new career but, more importantly, she had unwittingly set in motion the chain of events that would lead to her death, less than two years later.

Princess Diana knew exactly what she was doing when she gave that interview. Diana did not seek permission from the queen to give such an interview. Some thought this courageous, while others considered it foolhardy. Nor did Diana have the courtesy of informing the queen that she had given the interview, which many considered rash and injudicious. Somehow, Diana even managed to keep the interview secret from her private secretary Patrick Jephson. In doing so, she made him appear incompetent to the senior courtiers who were absolutely furious that Diana had given such an interview without permission. The first that the queen, her advisers and Jephson knew of the interview was exactly one week before it was to be broadcast when it was promoted for the following week's *Panorama* program. Diana's choice of programs was brilliant, for *Panorama*, a prestigious weekly current affairs program, concentrated solely on the most important events of the week.

In retrospect, Diana's television interview marked a major turning point in her life and, importantly, in her relationships with the queen, all members of the royal family and particularly the queen's close advisers including her own brother-in-law, Sir Robert Fellowes, the queen's private secretary — her closest and most important courtier. The interview also ended any possibility of support from Charles — Diana could hardly have been more lethal in her efforts to belittle and disparage him, suggesting that he really wasn't capable of being a good monarch even if he actually wanted the job, which she doubted. It was cruel indeed.

The aftermath of the sensational program had the effect of highlighting the problems surrounding the British monarchy. Royal commentators and constitutional lawyers recognized that the monarchy was in serious trouble. Crisis meetings were held at the palace, ideas suggested, new policies put forward, but all seemed little more than window dressing compared to the problem the royals faced. They had hoped Diana would be a fleeting phenomenon — like a butterfly enjoying a few months of summer before falling to earth as the autumn winds turned cold. This was not the case.

Diana arrived on the scene in a blaze of glory only 15 years before, but had little impact on the nation until the public began to read in newspapers in the late 1980s of cracks appearing in her royal marriage. From then on, Diana's hold on the British people, particularly women, increased dramatically as they rushed to support Diana in her one-sided battle against the wayward, adulterous, hardhearted Charles, who they knew would be supported by the queen, Prince Philip and the Establishment.

Indeed, every article about "Princess Di," as the media referred to her, was avidly read and every television program about her was watched by millions. Diana, her problems, her marriage and her children had become the major topic in most tabloid newspapers and the principal talking point wherever people gathered. Discussion over the royal marriage was not only conducted in the pubs and clubs and bingo halls of the nation but also at the dinner tables and cocktail parties of the middle and upper classes.

Whenever there was an opportunity to actually see Diana in the flesh, even if only for a moment, people would flock from miles around to catch a glimpse. Her life may have been a mess, but to her army of loyal women supporters, her failing marriage became an added attraction. Millions of British women recognized Diana as a fellow victim just like millions of them who also had lived, or were still living, with selfish, philandering, adulterous men. By 1995, Diana's magnetism had taken a grip on the nation that some in the royal family and the British Establishment found quite frightening. Many admired her courage in standing up to the royal family. In their eyes, Diana could do no wrong and her vast army of supporters were prepared to back her to the hilt. And Diana loved it.

Behind the scenes, however, plots were afoot. Some courtiers even wondered whether the queen might one day make the same, famous, rash request that King Henry II (1133-1189) made to his knights when he was having problems with Thomas a Becket, his Archbishop of Canterbury — *"Who will free me from this turbulent priest?"* As the world knows, the king's knights responded by murdering Thomas Becket on the altar as he was saying Mass in Canterbury cathedral. The queen's courtiers knew that she would not have wanted Diana dead, but she may have hoped that someone might come up with an idea that would somehow sideline Diana.

During the last few years of Diana's life, it is true to say that Diana succeeded, without exception, in humiliating every member of the royal family. They felt that Diana was rubbing their noses in the dirt; they looked inconsequential and unimportant in the eyes of the nation. She hurt their pride and their dignity with nonchalant ease.

Monarchs and their extended families aren't

used to that type of treatment and they certainly don't like it. All their lives, the royal family was held in the greatest respect by the nation and, in particular, the queen lived a life apart, the head of state, the most important person in the land, the monarch who signed all the parliamentary bills and to whom everyone, including the prime minister, would bow in obedience.

By the end of the 1980s, the queen was showing signs of stress and she blamed her daughter-in-law. It was the queen herself who described her in 1992 as her *"annus horribilis,"* as the damage to her position and her authority came under increasing pressure from Diana, as well as the embarrassment of the failed marriages of Princess Anne and Prince Andrew.

The queen, however, did pay Diana a remarkable, but silent, tribute when she took a leaf out of her daughter-in-law's book, portraying herself for the first time ever as "vulnerable" to the events punctuating her jubilee year, at the celebration of her 40 years on the throne. It was the most remarkable speech the queen had ever made, which amounted, in effect, to an extraordinary public confession.

The queen appeared before dignitaries from the city of London, leading politicians from the House of Lords and Commons, members of the

Establishment, the cream of Britain's high society as well as leading members of the legal profession and pillars of the nation's financial elite. There were aldermen and councillors in their flamboyant robes and finery and all were gathered in the famous Guildhall for the principal celebration marking the queen's glorious jubilee.

Most of what the queen said that day was as a direct result of the criticism heaped on the royal family, which could be traced directly to Princess Diana and the nation's perception that the royal family — Charles in particular — were behaving badly and unfairly to the young Princess Diana.

The queen confessed to the privileged assembled listeners who attended the lunch, "There can be no doubt, of course, that criticism is good for people and institutions that are part of public life. No institution, city, monarchy, whatever, should expect to be free from the scrutiny of those who give it their loyalty and support, not to mention those that don't. But we are all part of the same fabric of our national society and that scrutiny, by one part of another, can be just as effective if it is made with a touch of gentleness, good humor and understanding."

Queen Elizabeth was hoping not only to rein in the more violent attacks on her and her family over the previous two years, but also to win the moral high ground, going over the heads of critics and the press, appealing directly to the people. Elizabeth was following in her daughter-in-law's footsteps — she saw how well it had worked for Diana.

Since the queen believed the bulk of the nation was still behind her and her family, she was prepared to take the risk of appealing to them directly. "I sometimes wonder how future generations will judge the events of this tumultuous year," she mused. "I dare say that history will take a slightly more moderate view than of some contemporary commentators."

Of course, the royal soap opera and the plight of Princess Diana had become the talking point of the nation, but it was not Britain's only problem in 1992. The country was in a severe recession — 3 million people were unemployed, thousands of families unable to pay their mortgages were being thrown out of their homes, a record number of people were being declared bankrupt and thousands of firms and companies were going bust.

Another tragedy befell the queen that November – a fire erupted at Windsor Castle, the queen's principal home outside London where she spends most weekends. It destroyed the famous St. George's Hall, the adjacent Waterloo Chamber — said to be the most beautiful room in the world

— as well as many priceless paintings and other works of art. Many were moved as they saw the diminutive, rather pathetic figure of Queen Elizabeth beside the tall, well-built firemen battling the blaze. The fire lent an air of unease to the nation and the photographs and television shots of the queen amid the scene of destruction seemed to epitomize the mood of desolation and disaster that had befallen her and her family.

But balanced against this feeling of pity for the queen was the anger the nation felt toward the way the royal family had behaved toward their beloved Diana. It was suggested by the government that the taxpayer should pay the full cost of the repairs estimated at $ 100 million. The nation thought otherwise.

A TV poll asked callers to phone in with their answer to the question, "Who should pay for the repairs to Windsor Castle?" An amazing 95 percent out of a quick poll of 30,282 people watching the program said the taxpayer should not pay the bill. The royal family was castigated by the tabloid press. The *Daily Mirror* accused the House of Windsor of sowing the seeds of its own destruction, saying "meanness, greed and blatant disregard for the feelings of the people are the mark of a dying, not lasting, dynasty."

The Windsor fire became one of the most

traumatic events in Elizabeth's long reign — it brought about the realization that the British people's attitude to the monarchy had undergone a dramatic change. With the fire still smoldering, Elizabeth, the Establishment and Parliament were forced to face the unpleasant fact that the myth that the British people were totally supportive of the monarch and the royal family at any cost had, almost overnight, been swept away. And, undeniably, it had been the arrival of Diana on the scene and the perceived way that she had been treated by the family, which was principally responsible.

It wasn't only the royal family that the nation was turning its back on. As monarch, Elizabeth is also head of the Anglican Church and, throughout her reign, the numbers attending church plummeted dramatically. By the mid-1990s, less than 2 percent of the population attended Sunday services.

Opinion polls made gloomy reading for Elizabeth. The nation wanted a dramatic change from the type of distant, aloof, old-fashioned monarchy Elizabeth had epitomized throughout her reign. According to these polls, people wanted a slim-line, Scandanavian-style monarchy with fewer royals involved. They also demanded that all the lesser royals take proper jobs, rather than simply opening the occasional wing of a hospital or throwing local parties. And perhaps most distressing for Elizabeth, they wanted a cut in the cost of the royals and their upkeep.

Figures published by the Heritage Department in 1994 showed that 268 members of the royal family, relatives and staff were living at the taxpayers' expense. It noted that aunts, uncles and cousins of every member of Elizabeth's family lived rent-free in apartments in royal palaces, all attended to by lavish staff. To service the royals, free homes were provided for 13 chauffeurs, 55 private secretaries, 47 domestic servants, 41 stable and farm staff, and six gardeners, along with 42 additional craftsmen, porters and other staff.

In a desperate bid to halt the slide in the popularity of the royal family, the queen finally came to the decision that she had to take some positive action. First, she grudgingly agreed to a suggestion that Prince Charles had been putting forward for some years — that the royal family should pay tax on their income. She hated the idea, but with headlines in the tabloid press screaming "HM: the tax dodger" she felt she had to bow to the demands of her subjects and pay tax — just like they had to.

The *Sunday Times* commented, *"By joining the ranks of sovereigns who pay income tax, the queen has seized the opportunity to sweep away some of the cobwebs that have surrounded the royal finances for centuries. In doing so, she has taken a historic step toward putting the monarchy on a new, more modern footing, which is to be welcomed."*

Second, the queen decided that those members of her extended family whom the public regarded as "hangers-on" should quietly retreat from the limelight and into oblivion. Until the 1990s, the queen had made it imperative that the family show they were a unit on every possible occasion. Now she ordered that the family should adopt a lower profile and fade into the background. At family celebrations, when the entire royal family would stand on the balcony at Buckingham Palace and wave to the crowds, the numbers were severely curtailed and, from then on, only the queen's immediate family gathered to greet the people.

Elizabeth's rather desperate efforts to re-establish herself and the family's position as beloved and respected leaders of the nation didn't bring back the adoring, cheering crowds. The thousands who had turned out in the earlier decades of her reign had now become only scores and they were mostly children given a half-day off school to stand and wave little flags. She did, however, see thousands of people turning out to cheer Diana whenever and wherever she appeared in public. The queen knew that she was being ignored but had no idea how she could reverse this trend, which she understood could one day sound a death knell for the House of Windsor.

The queen knew that the person responsible for that dramatic change in the nation's respect and affection for the royals was, of course, Princess Diana. In the nation's view, however, the blame was laid not at Diana's feet but at the feet of the queen, Prince Philip and Charles for what they believed was disgraceful, abhorrent and cynical treatment of Diana. One year after her divorce from Charles in 1996, Diana had virtually swept away the nation's interest in any other members of the royal family, usurping their place in the affections and respect of the great majority of the British people. To many, Diana had become the angel of hope, visiting the sick in hospitals and retirement homes throughout London and the world.

In 1997 — the year of her death — Diana had all but eclipsed the royal family. On one occasion, Charles was away on a four-day, high-profile official royal visit to Germany and yet only one reporter and photographer from the entire British media went along to record the event. Five days later, Diana flew to Asia and 400 reporters, photographers and television personnel accompanied her. The game was over for the royal family. Single-handedly, Diana had undermined the prestige and primacy of the monarchy and there was seemingly nothing whatsoever they could do to counter the situation.

Six months later, Diana, Princess of Wales, the one person the House of Windsor believed was responsible for the plunge in the royal family's popularity, was dead.

Chapter 5

"They Want to Kill Me"

$\mathcal{W}$ithin 12 months of giving birth to Prince Harry in September 1984, Diana became convinced that some members of the royal family wanted her dead or, at the very least, out of the way. Quite openly, Diana would discuss the matter with close friends who visited her at Kensington Palace, telling them in a sad, melancholy, resigned voice, "The family knows that I've done my duty. I've provided an heir and even a spare for the House of Windsor and some members of the family would happily be rid of me. I've become a nuisance and some believe I would be better out of the way."

She would relate this startling and extraordinary opinion as though it was a simple matter of fact; as though it was perfectly normal for the queen and the rest of the royal family to want to be rid of the wife to the heir to the throne — the mother of the next generation of royals — simply because she had carried out her duty and produced two offspring. She would give no other reason behind her belief that the royal family wanted her out of the way.

Some would laugh at the suggestion, as though Diana was simply making a rather tasteless self-deprecating joke, but one glance at Diana's sad face would reveal to the listener that she believed it to be true. Other friends would try to humor her, suggesting that it was "preposterous" or "nonsense" for her to even think for one moment that the queen and other members of the family wanted her dead. But Diana could not be persuaded otherwise and she would continue to tell friends of her certainty that there were members of the royal family, senior courtiers and members of the Establishment who thought it might be better for them if she were dead.

Sometimes, Diana would suggest that the reason the royal family wanted her removed from the scene was because of her close relationship with "her darlings," Wills and Harry. Diana believed that those opposed to her thought she had an influence on the two young princes that might eventually prove disastrous to the House of Windsor. She believed that "they," the unnamed, royal flunkies whom Diana despised and some-times loathed, feared that her independence, her anti-royal views and her determination to hog the limelight to the exclusion of the queen and Prince Charles might have a serious effect on William and would lead to the demise of the House of Windsor.

On some occasions, Diana seemed to accept that it was possible that the royal family might be happy enough if she simply agreed to divorce Charles and slip away to live quietly in the country, far from the glare of cameras and publicity. "I do believe that they would be far happier if I agreed to remove myself permanently from public life," she said, "resign from all my charities and lead a life of quiet obscurity somewhere in the country. They would let me see Wills and Harry, of course, but only in the privacy of my country home far from the cameras and the public." However, she would usually go on to say, "From their viewpoint, of course, the best of all conclusions would be for me to disappear, have an accident, die."

During a private chat in 1992 with Max Hastings, the former editor of the broadsheet paper *The Daily Telegraph*, Diana said, "I know of a scheme that has been funded by Canadian gold tycoon Peter Munk of Barrack Mining to hire public relations man David Wynne-Morgan to get rid of me at any price." Hastings was taken aback by the suggestion and assured Diana that he had never heard of such a plot. It didn't matter to Diana that he denied such knowledge — nothing would dissuade her.

Indeed, since the birth of Prince Harry in September 1984, Diana believed that there were a number of plots to remove her by various means and strategies and she continued to believe that right up to the time of her death. Sometimes it felt to Diana that some members of the royal family wanted her dead while, at other times, they just wanted her "to go away, get married to someone, anyone, and disappear from the royal scene."

In his biography of the princess, *Diana: Closely Guarded Secret*, Police Inspector Ken Wharfe, who was her personal police bodyguard for six years, told of another occasion in May 1992 when Diana was visiting Egypt. She had taken a swim in the British Ambassador's private pool at his official residence in Cairo. Photographers were perched on the flat roof of a house in the near distance, but the glint of reflected light from their camera lenses betrayed their presence to Diana and she fled the scene.

Wharfe recounted, *"As Diana wrapped a towel around her shoulders she said, 'Ken, if anything happens to me you'll let people know what I was really like, won't you?'"* Later that morning,

Diana, speaking of her feeling of total isolation within the royal family, revealed, "Ken, I want out of this once and for all."

When visiting the United States during the 1990s, Diana chanced upon a book I had written, *Queen Elizabeth II: A Woman Who Is Not Amused.* She bought the book because she found the title so amusing and I understand she found the book fascinating, providing her with knowledge of the royal family that she had never before known. One passage in particular that alarmed her concerned the late Prince John. Although it occurred many years ago, it proved to Diana how harsh the royal family can be when preserving their image.

Born in 1905, the youngest son of King George V and Queen Mary of Teck, Prince John developed epilepsy at the age of 7, possibly as a result of the harsh treatment and beatings meted out to him by his father. Embarrassed that a son of theirs should develop epilepsy, the family removed poor John and locked him away in a small house on the Sandringham Estate, only a few miles from where Diana would be brought up.

One night at dinner, Queen Mary announced to their other five children, "John is unwell and has gone away to be cared for. It is very unlikely that we will ever see him again." John, who was being cared for in his "prison" by a single nurse was, indeed, never seen again by any of his brothers or sisters. And, to their everlasting shame, neither his mother nor his father ever visited him or set eyes on him. John died in 1919 unloved, unnoticed and unmourned. He was 14.

This story shook Diana and it proved to her how heartless and ruthless Britain's royal family can be in their determination to protect their public image. Prince John was ill and they wanted him removed from their presence because he was an inconvenience and a poor advertisement for the family. Diana was convinced that if it were possible, both the queen and Prince Philip would deal with her in exactly the same way.

It was in the 1990s that Diana decided that she had to rewrite her last will and testament, not just because she had recently divorced from Charles, but mainly because she feared something terrible might happen to her. She always believed, as she illustrated when chatting to the *Daily Telegraph* editor Max Hastings, that she had this "gut feeling" that there was a plot against her, to remove her from the royal scene once and for all. Diana would have serious conversations with a number of friends who believed the royal family were "out to get her" as she put it and she would leave no doubt in anyone's mind that she had this "suspicion," this "feeling," this "premonition" that they wanted her dead.

There were a couple of reasons for rewriting her will. Not only did she believe she might be "removed from the scene" in the near future, she wanted to ensure that Prince Harry would have substantial funds available for him to lead an independent life as a wealthy man in his own right without necessarily having to go out to work to support a wife and family, as well as having the means to run a large country house and maintain an apartment in London. Diana feared for Harry in case the royal family turned against him as they did her. She trusted no one in the royal family. She knew that if the queen and Philip decided something should happen, it did not matter a damn whether Charles, the heir to the throne, agreed or not.

Diana's fear that she might meet a sudden end, though she was only in her 30s, was also the reason that she put so much faith in Paul Burrell, her loyal butler, telling him many of her secrets and entrusting him with access to many of her private papers. This was one of the reasons why Burrell, who had been her butler, friend and confidant for 10 years, took 300 items from Kensington Palace to his home following Diana's death. He admitted taking papers, Diana's private correspondence, private tapes of her conversations, knickknacks and other personal items — a total of 310 separate items which he secreted at his home in Cheshire, 120 miles from Kensington Palace. He explained the removal of the items was solely to keep them safe for Prince William and Prince Harry when they were older.

In reality, Paul Burrell took them because he knew that Diana would have wanted him to hide them for fear that, if she did meet her death when still a young woman, many of her private papers, some damaging to the royal family, would conveniently disappear from her Kensington Palace apartment. She knew that MI5, Britain's security service, would have been quite capable of removing such items following her death, without arousing any suspicion.

In October 2002, Paul Burrell stood trial in London on three theft charges relating to the 310 items that had belonged to his former employer, Princess Diana. Sensationally, the trial was stopped after the personal intervention of the queen, who suddenly remembered that during her conversation with Paul Burrell after Diana's death, he had told her that he was removing some of Diana's "things" for safekeeping.

People commented that it was strange that the queen had suddenly remembered the now-famous conversation with Paul Burrell immediately following Diana's death in 1997. Even more extraordinary was that Burrell stated that the interview with the queen had lasted three hours. Those who have any knowledge of the queen know that, first, she has a remarkable memory and, second, she never has private conversations with people for three hours — not even with the prime minister. And she certainly would not have had such a lengthy interview with a lowly, insignificant servant. According to senior courtiers, Burrell's conversation with the queen lasted less than 15 minutes.

Unbelievably, the queen stepped in to stop the trial only days before Paul Burrell was to give evidence for his defense in court. The queen, Prince Philip, Prince Charles and all her courtiers were aware that Paul Burrell knew nearly all of Diana's most intimate secrets. He also knew how the royal family had treated her since the birth of Prince Harry and since they had forced her to divorce Charles. He knew about the incredible legal haggles over the details of the divorce settlement, the pressure put on Diana by the royal family to force her to leave Britain and he knew the contents of the secret letters from Philip to Diana which would have shocked the nation.

Indeed, the revelations Burrell would have been able to describe to the jury would have shown the royal family in such an appalling, vindictive, revengeful and pitiless light that there might have been serious repercussions for the monarchy. The queen simply could not take the chance of Burrell taking the witness stand and giving testimony before the entire nation — she had no idea what royal secrets he might betray.

The arrest and trial of Burrell took place as a result of a request from both Prince Philip and Diana's sister, Lady Sarah McCorquodale — Charles' former mistress. They approached the police and asked them to obtain private letters they had written to Diana in the final years of her life, which they understood were in Paul Burrell's possession. Apparently, they were worried that these letters might fall into the wrong hands and would end up splashed across the front pages of the nation's newspapers.

The letters from Prince Philip were described as "cruel and insulting." It's no wonder Philip was worried that the contents of his letters might reach the press. They contained strong suggestions that Diana should remove herself from the royal family or face the consequences; that Diana's behavior was a disgrace to the royal family; that she should be ashamed of herself for leading an adulterous life, and that her now-famous book was a catalog of lies and deceit which never should have been written. In one devastating letter Philip called Diana "a harlot."

It is widely believed that the letters from her sister Sarah to Diana mainly concerned Prince Harry and Diana's estrangement from her brother Charles and the Spencer family.

With such a lack of trust and deep suspicion between Diana and senior members of the royal family, it was no wonder that Diana felt under constant threat. She became convinced that "they" wanted her exiled from the royal family, living far from London, where she could have little or no influence over the upbringing of Wills and Harry.

From Diana's viewpoint, her nagging fears were exactly why she never wanted a divorce from Charles. She reasoned that, once divorced from Charles, her removal from London — or worse — her sudden, mysterious death might be the next logical step. Because of this deep conviction, Diana refused requests from the queen to even consider the matter of a formal separation or divorce for almost a decade — until the early 1990s, when she was subjected to so much pressure from so many different sources and so-called friends that she felt forced to agree to the separation and later the divorce. In agreeing to a divorce, Diana recognized that she now had the upper hand. And her terms were tough indeed.

The Diana that the royals were dealing with in the 1990s was a far stronger, confident woman than the nervous, docile Lady Di of the late 1970s. She had developed a remarkable steely character and showed that no one, not even the queen, was going to push her around. This tough, more mature Diana proved to be quite a shock, not only to Prince Charles, but also to the queen, Prince Philip and the courtiers who had to deal with her on a day-to-day basis. To a number of senior courtiers who dealt with the princess on a daily basis, the quiet, innocent, vulnerable Diana, who seemed almost angelic to the general public, was in reality, they claimed, a determined, duplicitous, scheming charlatan who loved to flirt with everyone in a bid to gain their support.

Following the queen's demand for an early divorce, Diana had come to some conclusions as to what she would demand in her settlement. She was determined to keep the title "Princess" and though she recognized that she could not continue to be "Her Royal Highness, the Princess of Wales," she still wished to be known officially as "Her Royal Highness, Princess Diana." In the end, she agreed to be known as "Diana, Princess of Wales." She demanded either a substantial London mansion or the massive apartment she was occupying at Kensington Palace, rent-free.

For all concerned, and especially from a security viewpoint, Kensington Palace was a far more preferable home. Diana also demanded a personal annual income of $2 million U.S. dollars, after expenses, on the understanding that the upkeep of her home, staff salaries, cars and all ancillary expenses should be met by the Duchy of Cornwall, Prince Charles' private estate. She also demanded that all costs relating to Wills and Harry, including their education, clothing and holidays should be met by Charles. More important, she demanded the settlement be guaranteed for her lifetime, whether she remarried or not.

Diana accepted that the question of custody of Wills and Harry was quite different than any other British children caught up in their parents' divorce settlement as heirs to the throne. They are the responsibility of the monarch who has jurisdiction over them. However, Charles and Diana agreed that the arrangement for access to the children, which had been in effect since their 1992 separation, should continue.

The queen forced the divorce in an effort to sideline Diana by removing her from the House of Windsor. That way, the full focus of attention could once again be trained solely on Prince Charles, as it had been before Diana came onto the scene in 1980. The queen was well aware that

Diana was stealing the headlines not only from Prince Charles but also from the queen herself.

It was a tough decision for the queen to make. Since Diana's arrival on the scene, there was a great surge of pride and passion in the royal family not only in Britain, but throughout the world. The queen also recognized that since her public break from Charles in the late 1980s, Diana had inflicted untold damage on the monarchy. At the time of Diana's divorce from Charles in 1996, only one-third of British voters believed the monarchy was relevant and more than half demanded less pomp, ceremony and lavish lifestyles from the monarch and her family.

For almost six years, the raging standoff between Charles and Diana and their respective advisers had played out beneath the surface in Buckingham Palace, Kensington Palace, St. James's Palace and Charles' country residence, Highgrove. Both the press and the general public knew that something was mighty wrong with the royal marriage, but they had no concrete evidence, no definitive signs that such a dramatic guerrilla war was going on.

On one side, there were the massed ranks of the royal House of Windsor, the most powerful and wealthy royal family in the world whose determination that their family should remain head of

state of Great Britain was of paramount importance. As allies, the royal family could rightly
claim the Establishment, the Church of England,
the government and the Armed Forces. Ranged
against this phalanx of power, prestige, position
and wealth was one person — Diana, Princess of
Wales, who had no power, no wealth, no influence and no allies. But she did have an idea, a
brilliant idea which, if it succeeded, would cement
her growing popularity with the British public.

It was in the late 1980s that Diana considered
writing a book. Every day, the tabloids, and sometimes the more reputable newspapers, were
writing stories about her and the No. 1 topic was
the state of the royal marriage. Whether the origi-
nal idea to write a book was Diana's, a friend's, an
adviser's or a publishers is not known, but Diana
thought long and hard about the suggestion before
deciding to go ahead. The more she thought of the
plan, the more she liked it because she could then
tell her story exclusively from her viewpoint. Of
course, she would need to write this book in secret,
away from the prying eyes of her advisers, her
staff, Prince Charles or anyone employed by the
royal family. She knew that if any of them had an
inkling that Diana was writing a book about the
royal marriage, she would be stopped dead in her
tracks and forbidden to continue.

But what if someone else wrote it?

For some months, Diana considered the possibility of hiring a writer, but she realized that could never work. She knew that she couldn't ask someone to write her autobiography because that would seem like it was all her idea. But if the book was seen to be written by another individual, always referring to Diana in the third person, and never quoting her, there was a real possibility that the public would accept the book as authentic and she would escape censure from the royal family.

One of her close friends, Dr. James Colthurst, a consultant at London's St. Thomas's Hospital, was seen by *News of The World* royal reporter, Andrew Morton, chatting amicably to Diana when she toured the hospital on an official royal visit. Morton played squash at the same club as Dr. Colthurst. One thing led to another and Colthurst agreed to become the secret go-between, providing Morton with tapes and written material given to him by Diana, which he passed to Morton to use freely in a book about Diana's life within the royal family. In other words, it would indeed be Diana's own true story.

During this time, Diana was feeling particularly low. As she put it, "I felt demons in my head." Her marriage to Charles had been over in all but name for nearly nine years; her serious love affair with James Hewitt was over — she firmly laid that to rest as soon as he returned from the Gulf War; her dear, beloved father was near death and her mother was living on a remote island off the north of Scotland. She felt alone and miserable, unwanted and unloved. But she also felt anger. She was convinced that the queen and the royal family were about to move against her, but in what way she wasn't sure. That gave her sleepless nights. Diana wondered to what lengths the royal family would go to be rid of her once and for all.

Diana knew that the book she was planning would cause Charles and the royal family untold harm. But she also knew that she had little or nothing to lose. She hoped and suspected that by revealing so much of her marriage, detailing the way she was treated by Charles and the family, she would not only win the support of the nation but she might also make it difficult, if not impossible, for the family to move against her. In moments of deep anxiety, Diana came to believe that publishing the book might be the difference between life and death.

When the book went on sale, the stores ran out of copies within days. And the more the people read of Diana's dreadful plight, her anorexia and the details of her miserable marriage the more they warmed to her and the more loathing and anger they felt toward Charles in particular and the royal family in general.

Now, she had the people on her side. And, more importantly, she knew it. As a result of her choice to let Andrew Morton publish *Diana: Her True Story*, the numbers of people who turned out to see, cheer and demonstrate their support for her grew to an extraordinary degree. "We love you, Diana," and "We're with you, darling" and "You can trust us" and "God bless you, Diana" would ring out from the crowds who would go to see and cheer her wherever she went. It was mainly the women who rushed to her support, showing their love and affection for her at every opportunity.

In contrast, shortly after the book's publication, some people actually booed Prince Charles when he made public appearances — which no member of the royal family had ever before experienced. The situation had sunk to such a worrying degree that the royal family seemed to have no idea what they could do to counteract the nation's extraordinary love affair with Diana.

In the late 1980s, I was approached by two senior courtiers and asked to write a book about the royal couple. As a polo player, like Prince Charles, I had long been accepted in the polo set and I knew some of their friends and one or two royal courtiers whose job it was to advise and counsel Charles and Diana. I was asked to write a straight, honest, objective book about their life together, the real facts of their marriage in an effort to put an end to the speculation and ill-informed gossip. I readily agreed. Having completed the book, my agent took the manuscript to five or six British publishers during 1989, but not one would publish it.

The publishers were simply incredulous, refusing to believe that the Prince of Wales was having an affair with his old flame Camilla Parker Bowles, the wife of Brigadier Andrew Parker Bowles and a woman of whom they had never heard. They accused me of fabricating an affair between the chaste Diana and some unheard of young Guards officer by the name of James Hewitt. They considered my allegation that the royal marriage was nothing more than a sham libel on both Charles and Diana, and they branded the manuscript a bunch of lies that they had no intention of publishing. After spending a year trying to sell the book in Britain, my agent went to New York, where the manuscript was snapped up and *Diana: A Princess and Her Troubled Marriage* finally reached the bookshelves in the spring of 1992.

At the same time, Andrew Morton's book

Diana, Her True Story hit the stores and instantly became a best seller with its stories of suicide attempts and marital violence that shook the British Establishment and the royal family to its foundations. The book told Diana's extraordinary story that behind her public smiles and glamorous image was a young woman who was enduring a loveless marriage, living on her own in London while Prince Charles had been enjoying a raging affair with his former girlfriend Camilla almost since their wedding day.

The world knows that *Diana, Her True Story* was written by Andrew Morton, but what the nation did not know was that most of the contents which related to Diana and Charles had been provided — and in some cases actually written and edited — by Diana herself. And the level of hate Diana felt toward Charles is revealed in the writing. Such intimate details of Charles' alleged involvement and adultery with Camilla from the very beginning of the marriage could ruin Charles' life and, hopefully, destroy his relationship with Camilla. As a byproduct, she understood that such revelations would seriously embarrass the queen and still further undermine the nation's love and respect for the royal family. Diana also hoped that her revelations might drive a wedge between Charles and his two sons.

She decided that the book should pull no punches and would allegedly reveal the true story of her life, her marriage, her husband's indiscretions and the dramatic effect the failed marriage and Charles' extramarital affair had on her health, driving her in desperation to undertake seven separate suicide attempts.

The publication of the Morton book was greeted with a hail of abuse by the Establishment. They wanted the public to believe that the book flagrantly exaggerated the facts. But the great majority of the British public was convinced the facts revealed in the book were totally true. The book was an instant success, a best seller, and the public voraciously read every juicy detail — and believed every word.

Chapter 6

A Book of Fabrications

*I*n many respects, *Diana: Her True Story* was a stranger to the truth. Much of what Diana wrote can now be revealed as invention, fabrication, gross exaggeration and lies. Perhaps the most dramatic fact that appalled and horrified most readers were the stories of Diana's alleged suicide attempts. The British public had no idea whatsoever that her life had been such hell that she had actually tried to take her own life on seven separate occasions over a number of years. Understandably, this piece of information sent shockwaves through Britain and, at a stroke, Diana had not only won the nation to her cause but had also succeeded in destroying Charles' reputation.

Because the seven suicide attempts made such a dramatic impact on the reading public, those attempts by Diana to kill herself were closely scrutinized. On close examination, the details of her seven separate suicide attempts revealed them to be not very convincing; indeed, some sounded positively improbable and others were unbelievable. No one had ever heard of anyone attempting suicide by walking into a display cabinet; no one had heard of a suicide attempt using a lemon grater, and the alleged attempts of suicide by slashing her wrists on two occasions were so halfhearted that, apparently, there were no marks. On one dramatic occasion, the book alleged, Diana picked up a penknife in Charles' presence and stabbed herself in her chest and thighs in a bid to kill herself. But there was no blood and barely a scratch on her body.

In one heart-rending claim detailed in the book, Diana, three months pregnant with William, tried to kill herself by "hurling herself down a wooden staircase" and it shocked people to the core. An excerpt from the book reads: *"Diana felt absolutely wretched ... Charles seemed incapable of understanding or wishing to comprehend the turmoil in Diana's life. She was suffering dreadfully from morning sickness, she was haunted by Camilla Parker Bowles and she was desperately trying to accommodate herself to her new position and new family ... On that January day in 1982, her first New Year with the royal family, she now threatened to take her own life. He accused her of crying wolf and prepared to go riding on the Sandringham estate. She was as good as her word. Standing on top of the wooden staircase she hurled herself to the ground, landing in a heap at the bottom."*

That dramatic description of that particular suicide attempt was, in fact, a total fabrication. In reality, Diana accidentally slipped on the last step of a three-step staircase and half-stumbled to the floor. Slightly shaken, but unhurt, Diana's immediate concern was for her unborn baby, but the fall was so insignificant that she insisted there was no need for a doctor or to go to the hospital. She didn't even want to lie down and rest, saying she felt fine.

It seems extraordinary that Diana should have included that suicide bid in the book. It is incredulous that the pregnant Diana would have risked killing her own unborn baby by deliberately throwing herself down the stairs. And yet, this possibly deadly consequence of her suicide attempt was not mentioned or even referred to in the book — despite the fact that during her pregnancy Diana was so concerned for the well-being of her unborn baby that she refused to take any drugs, fearing that the child might be born with a deformity.

I was told that Diana once claimed she had taken an overdose of tablets. A doctor was called and, after talking to her in private, came back to report that there was no need to pump her stomach or take her to the hospital for observation. It was his opinion that it was most unlikely that she had taken an overdose. He deduced that this alleged attempt had simply been a cry for help, a craving for attention.

It is this closer examination of the book's reports surrounding Diana's alleged suicide attempts that not only tend to negate her suicide claims but, unfortunately for her, raised many other questions which should have been examined and answered at the time of publication. However, people were so carried away by the horror of what they read and the anxiety they felt for poor Diana, that they took nearly everything at face value. Even those who doubted that she would ever intentionally commit suicide interpreted the events as a desperate cry for help by a young woman who had been severely wronged by her adulterous husband and treated disgracefully by her in-laws.

In many respects, writing the book gave Diana a chance to reveal her shrewd, innate intelligence because the facts she revealed to the reader were cleverly and skillfully managed. Many events described in the book had, in fact, occurred, but Diana showed them in a different light. In some cases she grossly exaggerated a happening, portrayed a fact dishonestly or lied about events, sometimes turning them around to suit her dramatic story line.

She wrote, for example, how the weight "dropped off her" after moving to Buckingham Palace before the wedding "because she was so miserable." The fact that she lost weight was accurate but not the reason she gave for losing the weight. In reality, on the advice of her friends at *Vogue* magazine who were helping to re-invent the plump, rather dowdy Diana, she enthusiastically and deliberately dieted like crazy, reducing her waistline from 29 inches to 23 inches in four months to make sure she would look slim and beautiful for her wedding day. Indeed, immediately before the wedding, Diana proudly told her friends of her weight loss. She was justifiably proud of the achievement of losing so much weight in such a short time.

There was also the heartrending story of the gift Charles sent to Camilla a week before the wedding. In the book, Diana made much of that gift because she claimed the highly personal present — a gold chain bracelet with a blue enamel disc with the initials G and F entwined — proved that only seven days before the wedding, Charles was still deeply involved with his beloved Camilla. Diana claimed the initials stood for "Fred" and "Gladys" — the nicknames Charles and Camilla called each other.

The book claimed that an angry and upset Diana immediately ran to the prince's office and the staff stopped work as she "confronted her husband-to-be about his proposed gift."

The book continues, *"In spite of her angry and tearful protests, Charles insisted on giving the token to the woman who had haunted their courtship and has since cast a long shadow over their married life."*

Again, it was mostly untrue. Diana had indeed gone to see Charles about the gift, but the meeting was in private, not in front of staff. And instead of a "confrontation," Charles put her mind at rest by explaining that the initials G and F stood for "Girl Friday," the nickname Charles had always called Camilla because of the number of errands and little jobs she had carried out on Charles' behalf. The book also failed to mention that at the same time Charles was giving identical gold bracelets — with initials — as presents to nine other women who had helped and supported him during his bachelor years, some of whom had been former girlfriends with whom he had enjoyed full-blown sexual affairs.

On the same subject, Diana claimed in the book that one week before the wedding, she was seriously thinking of calling a halt to the whole affair because at that precise moment she knew that Charles was handing over the gold bracelet to Camilla. He wasn't. All 10 bracelets were sent by mail to the 10 women.

Prince Charles was rather unusual in that he liked to keep in contact with many of his former girlfriends and still does so today. Charles hardly ever seemed to become involved with girls for purely sexual pleasure, but once he had met and enjoyed the company of a young woman he would want her as a friend, a confidant with whom he could relax — whether they went to bed together or not. Even today, for example, Charles is close friends with the British actress Susan George, star of the movie *Straw Dogs*, some 27 years or so after they first dated. Today, they correspond regularly with each other and sometimes meet as friends for a coffee, a meal or simply to chat.

Within a week or so of the book being published, Diana would admit to her close friends a rather different story about her suicide attempts, saying, "My suicide attempts were really only cries for help. I didn't really mean to do anything silly. I knew that I just needed time to adjust to my new role as a princess but I didn't receive any help or advice from anyone at the palace. I was just expected to get on with the job."

That statement, which Diana repeated over and over to most of her friends, was also untrue. In fact, the opposite was the truth. Diana had been given considerable help to adjust to her new role as the Princess of Wales and future queen. Unusual in royal circles, the queen gave Diana permission to ask her own close friends from her bachelor-girl days if they would like to be her ladies-in-waiting. Their job is to not only accompany the princess whenever she traveled or went on official royal visits, but also to advise and befriend her.

Diana also had guidance on form and etiquette from the queen's own ladies-in-waiting, including Lady Susan Hussey, the queen's experienced senior lady-in-waiting. She was advised on protocol by courtiers and advisers and received free advice from fashion designers as well as gurus from *Vogue* magazine. And when her unhappiness and personal problems, her black moods and doubts, her bulimia, anorexia and eating problems arose, she had London's most respected doctors, analysts, psychiatrists and professional counselors at her beck and call, only too willing to help her.

Indeed, Michael Colborne, an old navy colleague of Prince Charles' in the early 1970s, who also served as personal secretary to Diana for two years in the 1980s, commented, "At one time and another, the doors of Kensington Palace were busier than during Christmas shopping in the West End, with the number of professional medical people coming in and out to see the princess." And, to her credit, Diana, who called Colborne her "surrogate uncle" because of the help and advice he gave her, also admitted that during the early days of the marriage, Charles was helpful and kind, advising her on what to do and what not to do on royal visits, at royal banquets, at cocktail and dinner parties and even when out walking in public.

On occasions, Diana would publicly confess to official duties being "a nightmare" because she was so painfully shy, fearing she might say the wrong thing. But advisers, like Colborne, were always on hand to tell her how to behave, what to say to strangers, how to dress for the varied occasions and what protocol had to be followed. Diana received a personal briefing before every royal event, telling her whom she would be meeting or chatting with and what their jobs were. She was sometimes advised what topics to discuss with the people sitting on either side of her when attending dinners or banquets and what topics to steer clear of. And to her credit, she never did say the wrong thing and she was recognized by courtiers as a "fast learner," who had picked up the technique of going about visits and meeting people as though born a royal. That was praise, indeed.

Much of the book ran contrary to what was going on in private in Kensington Palace – in fact, even during those first tentative years, Diana was no shy violet. She showed not an ounce of nervousness or weakness when dealing with the staff running her affairs or working in their 28-room apartment at Kensington Palace. Indeed, she showed an unknown and surprising tough aspect to her character when dealing with the staff responsible for looking after her and Prince Charles.

In retrospect, it was extraordinary that Diana should have such strength of character that she even fired some of Prince Charles' most loyal and highly respected members of staff. Charles was the Prince of Wales and heir to the throne, but that didn't matter to Diana once she decided that, come what may, she was going to get rid of those people on whom Charles had relied ever since leaving the Royal Navy, some four years before.

Throughout his bachelor years, Charles gathered a team of people whom he liked and respected for the work they carried out on his behalf and, of course, his key staff and senior advisers were men who understood him and wanted everything to be shipshape. He acted as captain of the ship and his officers and men understood that every one of them had a role to play to make the ship efficient, well-run and basically a happy place to work. They all respected him and he respected the work they carried out.

Understandably, when Diana arrived on the scene she wanted some changes in the staff organizing and running Charles' household. Over the years, his staff had all come to know exactly what Charles liked and disliked, what was important to him and what was not. There was, naturally, apprehension among the staff at the arrival of a young woman into the household. None of them was certain what changes she might request or demand. None of them knew whether they would get along with their new boss, who also happened to be an enchanting and beautiful young woman. Initially, they all felt confident that things would, more or less, continue as before because Diana seemed delightful, charming and friendly. Little did they know, there was trouble ahead.

Diana was not happy with the staff from the start. She felt some of them treated her as a young, inexperienced interloper who didn't know how to handle royal servants or behave in the best traditions of the royal family. To a great extent, of course, that was true, but Diana didn't like that the staff continued to organize everything the way they had always done without consulting her or asking if she wanted any changes made.

After just a few weeks, Diana demanded things be done differently and most of the staff rebelled. They wanted to keep the cozy existence they had enjoyed for a number of years.

It was unfortunate, to say the least, that Diana did not get along, either, with the most important royal servant in the household — Charles' highly intelligent private secretary, Sir Edward Adeane. Right from the start, there was enmity between the two. Adeane, whose great-grandfather had been private secretary to Queen Victoria and whose father, Lord Michael Adeane, had been private secretary to the queen for many years, believed that Charles' duty to the nation must always come before his family life and that included Diana.

The problem arose shortly after Diana and Charles returned from their honeymoon. One day, in the month following their disastrous visit to Balmoral, Diana entered Sir Edward's office and headed toward Charles' study. Sir Edward jumped to his feet, "Can I help you, Ma'am?" he inquired.

"No, thank you," replied Diana. "I'm just going to see my husband for a moment."

"I'm afraid he's busy," replied Sir Edward. "Is it urgent? If not, shall I phone you when he's free?"

Furious, Diana glared at Sir Edward and made no reply. She turned on her heel and walked quickly out of his office.

This solitary confrontation persuaded Diana that there would need to be changes in the staff. She had no intention of permitting any flunky, no matter how important he thought he was, to stand between her and her husband.

An hour later, still smarting from the rebuke from Sir Edward, Diana demanded to Charles that Sir Edward be fired immediately for "gross insubordination." Charles explained that was not possible and Diana immediately formed the impression that Charles was taking Sir Edward's side against her — his wife of just seven weeks.

After more arguments, Charles told Diana that he would have a word with Sir Edward and explained that on some occasions it might not be possible for him to talk to Diana at a moment's notice because he might be involved in a meeting. To Diana's annoyance, Charles then said that some meetings were very important and he could not be seen breaking off discussions simply because his wife wanted a word.

Later, Charles organized a chat between the three of them in order to get everything out in the open once and for all. Diana told Sir Edward that as the Princess of Wales she should have immediate access to Charles at any time. Adeane strongly disagreed.

Whether Diana was trying to see how far her power extended or whether she, as a newlywed wife, just wanted to be around her new husband is unknown. Whatever the case, Diana did not like the outcome of the meeting, as Charles ruled that she simply could not have immediate access to him at any time she pleased, but that his study door was open to her "nearly all the time."

As one of Diana's friends commented, "When Sir Edward and Diana were in a room together you could cut the atmosphere with a knife."

Whether it caused tension or not, Diana continued to push the point home that she was in command of her husband and not Sir Edward. When William was a baby, Diana insisted that both she and Charles should spend an hour together with William in his nursery feeding and playing with him most every morning. Sometimes, when urgent matters arose, Sir Edward would knock at the nursery door, saying he needed speak to His Royal Highness.

Diana would open the door and say, "His Royal Highness cannot see you at the moment; you will have to wait until we are finished."

Sir Edward would hold his ground, explaining, "But, Ma'am, this is a most important matter. I really do need to speak to him urgently."

Diana would reply, "Well, it will just have to wait." And, without another word, she would close the door in his face.

Charles didn't know what to do, but he was certain that this could not continue. Diana believed that if Charles gave in to Sir Edward it would be a dereliction of duty as a father to young William and as a husband to her. Sir Edward believed Charles was showing a dereliction of his royal duties.

Charles asked Adeane to be patient, believing that, in time, things would calm down. Charles thought maybe it would take a year or two. Adeane said he was prepared to be patient, but it seemed like Diana was trying his patience on purpose. It is important to mention that the birth of William had given Diana a privileged place within the royal establishment as the mother of a future king. It had also given her a determination and a strong will that she never realized she possessed. Diana had matured, almost overnight.

It was that newfound determination that enabled Diana to push for the changes she wanted. Staff began leaving at an alarming rate. The first to go was Stephen Barry, Charles' gay valet, who knew many of his secrets and had known most of Charles' lovers and girlfriends. Diana believed that Stephen was too close to Charles — closer than she would ever be — so she decided he must go. She told Barry that now that they were married, she would be carrying out many of the little tasks that he had done over the years and that he would not be needed.

It was, of course, untrue. And Barry knew it. Stephen Barry would say later, "Diana was just jealous of me. I knew far more about Charles than she would ever know and she didn't like that. I knew exactly what clothes Charles wanted and needed for every occasion. I would only need to look at his schedule for the following day and I could lay out all his clothes, including the tie he would want to wear. I knew Diana had little or no idea what Charles liked to wear for all the different functions and occasions he had to attend. In reality, of course, she wanted total control over Charles and was prepared to do everything to maintain that position of power over him."

Diana was pushing her luck, saying that she could replace a valet. Someone in Charles' position, who sometimes needs to change his clothes four times a day, really does need a full-time valet — not simply to arrange his clothes for the day and the week ahead but also to keep them pressed

and in immaculate order, down to the last detail.
And that, of course, would include all his various
uniforms for the Royal Navy, for different regiments of the Army and the Royal Air Force,
which in total numbered some 20 different forms
of dress.

Barry also realized that the arrival of a wife
on the scene had fundamentally altered his
relationship with Charles and it was better if he
quietly slipped away to find another job. Diana
felt that she had won a major victory — a valet
was closer to Charles than any other member of
his staff. Now that position was hers. Diana's
next goal was to remove as many members of
Charles' bachelor days staff as she could.

In the first six years of their marriage, Diana got
rid of 24 members of staff. Not just the old royal
fuddy-duddies, but also one or two of the young,
less experienced members of staff whom Diana
herself had hired. Understandably, these dis-
missals were not improving Diana's standing or
popularity with the royal courtiers and servants at
any level. The House of Windsor has always
prided itself on caring for their staff, being kind to
them and keeping them for decades. That they
paid them dreadfully low wages didn't seem to
bother the royal family and never had. The royals
liked to think that courtiers and servants were

privileged to work and be accepted inside their palaces and homes — wages were of little importance. As a result of Diana's firing and hiring policy, the talk among both the lowest servants as well as the privileged, titled courtiers was of Diana being unable to cope with her position as the Princess of Wales.

At first, Charles would ask Diana why she wanted to be rid of whoever she was planning to fire but, in the end, Charles just went along with her wishes, hoping for a more peaceful, less abrasive atmosphere. From her wedding to the time of her death in 1997, Diana had arranged for the removal of or out-and-out fired some 40 members of staff. It was not a record to be proud of, yet those decisions to fire staff — some of whom had become almost close friends — never appeared to worry her or, seemingly, even caused her to lose a moment's sleep.

Those figures reveal what a remarkable change had come over Diana within weeks of her marriage. Staff at her family home in Norfolk, where she grew up, always remembered the young Diana being kind and thoughtful, even giving them little presents on their birthdays. She loved visiting the kitchens — helping the cook and the maids prepare food, helping to make cakes and biscuits. She would inquire about their families and sit and chat with them. All that changed the moment she became the Princess of Wales. It seemed that Diana's natural warmth, friendliness, kindness and endearing qualities had disappeared almost overnight.

Indeed, her life had changed overnight and she came to that realization in a flash. She was able to pinpoint the exact moment when life became too much for her and from which she would never be able to recover until she had split irrevocably from Charles. It was the moment that she came down to dinner at Balmoral, immediately following her sunshine honeymoon sailing and swimming in the warm blue waters of the Mediterranean. As her mother-in-law the queen greeted her with a wan smile and Prince Philip cracked some weak joke, she sat down and looked around at her new family.

During various chats with her friend Caroline, a young woman her own age, Diana would tell her, "At that moment my heart froze as I realized what I had let myself in for in marrying Charles. I looked around the table and everyone was so starchy, strait-aced and boring. That evening there were the queen and Prince Philip, Princess Anne, Prince Andrew and Prince Edward and, of course, Charles as well as some older guests I didn't recognize. I looked at the expressions on their faces; I saw the false smiles and heard the weak jokes ... They all treated the queen as though she was unreal, even the children behaved as though they had to be on their very best behavior because she was sitting among them ... There was no joy, no fun, no *joie de vivre* but just boring people of all ages making polite, boring conversation. I realized as I sat there that this would now be my existence for the rest of my life and I wanted to scream, leave the table and walk out of the dining room, the castle and the family. I just knew that it wasn't me and would never be me ... I wasn't royal and I didn't want to be royal but stupidly, stupidly, I had been carried along with the thrill and pride of being Prince Charles' girlfriend, something that I had dreamed of since I was 10 years old. I simply hadn't thought it through properly, what it would really mean being his wife.

"I remember sitting through my first dinner with the family as though it was yesterday. I don't remember the conversation really except that they talked about shooting and riding and I hated both those subjects. I just sat there and realized I had made the most awful, terrible mistake and I didn't see how I could escape ... I was trapped and I felt helpless and I looked at Charles being so correct and dutiful to the queen as though she wasn't really his mother and I felt a fit of the horrors knowing this was my life, and it would continue like this until the day I died."

Michael Colborne, the adviser to whom Diana frequently turned to for advice and guidance, would say later, "Charles and Diana should never have gone to Balmoral for that dreadful initiation. Diana wasn't ready for it; she couldn't cope with the strict observance of royal protocol, which dictates how everyone must behave when in the presence of the queen, even when they are all supposedly on holiday. It never alters and the realization of her future life in the royal family must have frightened the wits out of poor Diana. It is totally understandable that she should have reacted in such a negative way. Any young woman would have done the same in such a fraught situation. The formality of dinner at Balmoral was strict and precise and never varied. For Diana, more used to eating a snack on her knees while sitting in front of the television, those dinners must have been hellish."

From that moment, Diana's life deteriorated and her relationship with Charles went downhill. She was never to fully recover her love and admiration for Charles because she had seen how he behaved when in the presence of his own mother, simply because she was the queen. Diana could never rationalize that and never did. To Diana's straightforward, no nonsense, sensible, down-to-earth approach to life it seemed unbelievable that the man she married should treat his mother with such reverence and respect as though he was a mere servant in her presence. And, understandably, Diana would become angry with Charles when he sided with his mother in any discussion when Diana knew full well that Charles actually held the contrary opinion.

This trait in Charles shocked and disappointed Diana and undermined her respect for him. That loss of respect was perhaps the most crucial and fundamental reason for the collapse of the marriage because, until those two weeks in Scotland, Diana held Charles in the utmost esteem.

She would say later, "I can recall looking across the table at Charles during that first week at Balmoral and seeing not the man of action that I thought I had married but a bumbling, weak, sorrowful excuse for a man who buckled at the knees whenever in the presence of his mother."

On one occasion, Diana heard Charles and Sir Edward Adeane discussing the merits of employing some members of staff on a purely contract basis — hiring them for a specific time to carry out a specific task. Sir Edward was advocating this more modern approach because it saved money and avoided the problem of hiring and firing staff. Charles argued that he preferred to employ people on a permanent basis because he could then rely on their loyalty and, he believed, he could thus exercise greater control.

Some time later, Diana was present when the same subject was being discussed at Balmoral during dinner. The queen advocated the same proposal as Sir Edward and, much to her surprise, Charles totally agreed with his mother, never putting forward his argument of loyalty as he had done only a few weeks earlier.

To Diana, this showed great weakness in Charles' character and it was another reason why she found herself losing confidence in Charles and all he stood for. It seemed to her that Charles had no backbone when it came to holding any conversations with the family, as though he was scared of disagreeing with his mother for fear she would be angry with him. Diana simply couldn't understand it. She had never been like that with her parents and she had never known her friends to behave in such an obsequious, groveling way with their parents.

Almost overnight, Diana found herself reacting to Charles in a negative way. Until then, she looked forward to making love when they went to bed, but now she found herself less interested, even drawing back rather than enthusiastically taking part. Almost immediately, Charles realized that Diana seemed less than interested and, he, too, held back in deference to what he thought were her wishes. The physical side of the marriage was already beginning to disintegrate and they had only been married three or four weeks.

It is also necessary to understand what personal problems Charles brought to the marriage and what problems he had faced when growing up. To a great extent, his first seven years seemed more like the life of a child growing up in the Victoria era rather than the 1950s. But Charles had many larger problems, caused by his upbringing and his disastrous relationship with his father. Undoubtedly, Prince Philip bears a great responsibility for the disastrous relationships of the dysfunctional family – after all, he was the head. Because of the queen's role as head of state, Philip had taken over total responsibility for the upbringing of the four children and he made a poor fist of it.

Prince Philip is regarded by many as a rude, selfish, arrogant man. Indeed, even the quiet, amiable and highly respected former Archbishop of Canterbury, Dr. Michael Ramsey, summed up Prince Philip with a withering comment: "When I met Prince Philip, I thought he was very boorish, and he is."

However, to the queen, Prince Charles and his two brothers Prince Andrew and Prince Edward, the loudmouthed Philip was always seen as a bully. And he was. From the beginning of his marriage to the queen, Philip assumed the role of the archetypal Victorian husband who believed that a man was the more important in any marriage and that the woman must love, honor and, importantly, obey her husband. It never seemed to occur to Philip that because his wife was the queen, he would forever be second in importance to her. The fact that he walked two paces behind her made no difference whatsoever when they were alone together or with friends or relations.

Philip's treatment of Charles, in particular, verged on the brutish — almost cruel. Philip beat Charles for the most minor misdemeanors, such as forgetting to say "please" or "thank you" — and always if he did not obey his father in an instant. The frequent beatings became a ritual — ordering Charles to his study, making him bend over and then administering the punishment, usually six smacks on the backside with a tennis shoe or a slipper. This was before he was 6 years old.

Prince Philip continued to bully his eldest son at every opportunity. Mountbatten believed Philip's behavior toward Charles was driven by jealousy because, from the moment of his birth,

Charles was a far more important person than his father ever could, or would, be. Philip knew that and didn't like it — he always wanted to be top dog. Philip was also tough on Andrew and the more frail Edward but not to the same degree. He admired his daughter Anne and doted on her.

It was not surprising that Charles became a nervous little boy, frightened of his father. As Charles' first governess, Miss Catherine Peebles, observed, "Charles was nervous of coming forward, afraid to say anything for fear of the retribution he would receive from his father. If you raised your voice to Charles he would draw back into his shell and for a time you would be able to do nothing with him."

Such treatment from his father was not conducive to Charles enjoying easygoing relationships with others throughout his formative years. It also meant that he was nervous and hesitant when dealing with young women, which made life very difficult not only for Charles but more so for the girls he dated. They were never sure that he had sufficient self-confidence to enjoy a natural, loving relationship.

John Barratt was Earl Mountbatten's personal and private secretary for 20 years and Mountbatten would talk to him about the various relationships within the royal family, particularly, what he described as the "difficult" relationship between the queen and Philip. Barratt told me, "Elizabeth would frequently want to see Mountbatten privately and she would seek his advice as to how best to deal with Philip.

"I witnessed Philip telling the queen 'to shut up' during conversations in a rude and abrupt manner; tell her when it was time for her to go to bed, on occasions dictating what she should and should not eat during a meal. In discussions, Philip would always insist on silence while he made a point, interrupt the queen when she was speaking and rubbish her argument and points of view, sometimes telling her 'not to behave like a silly woman.' "

Barratt added, "Philip had a rather unpleasant way of putting down his wife, making her feel small, and such comments were often made in front of the family. It was as if Philip got some pleasure from treating his wife like that, deriding her, telling her she didn't know what she was talking about, ridiculing her views and her opinions. He intimidated her. He always did. And most of the time she accepted the admonishments he threw at her. As far as I can recall she always did as he said."

Charles also found settling down to married life far more difficult than he imagined. Since leaving

Cambridge University at age 23, with a creditable B.A. honors degree, Charles enjoyed his bachelorhood and his total freedom. He enjoyed the six months he spent learning to fly with the Royal Air Force and loved the six years in the Royal Navy, where he achieved his ambition of captaining his own Royal Navy ship. Life after the Royal Navy was very different, but Charles knew that he had a duty to the nation and to his mother, removing some of the burden from her shoulders and carrying out his share of royal engagements. The next few years Charles was happy playing the bachelor prince, enjoyed being a man's man, playing polo and skiing, hunting, shooting, fishing, sailing and piloting his own plane and helicopter and earning the nickname "Action Man," though he hated the sobriquet. He also enjoyed a string of girlfriends.

Charles first met Camilla Parker Bowles in 1972, only a few months before he was to go to sea with the Royal Navy. Her name was Camilla Shand, then age 23, but so very different from Charles' customary girlfriends, who tended to be tall, leggy blondes. Camilla was dark, animated and bright. She had a quick mind and, more importantly, she understood Charles. She quickly came to know what made him smile or laugh, and she encouraged him to open his mind to her and talk without constraint. Whenever they met they enjoyed lively discussions, chatting as if they had known each other for years. Rather, Camilla was a real *friend*, a woman with whom he could relax and be himself. He had never before felt like that with a young woman.

But Camilla was no girlfriend in the accepted sense of the word. They enjoyed lunches together in those few months but they never dated as such — never kissed passionately, never made love. And, as Charles admitted later, though there was a special chemistry between them he hadn't really fancied her. Indeed, Camilla's friendship with Charles began some nine months after she had been dating Andrew Parker Bowles, whom Charles also knew. In February 1973, Camilla and Charles said a fond farewell to each other at a private dinner in Charles' apartment at Buckingham Palace with champagne and much laughter. Then, Charles went to sea for the next six months. One month later, the engagement of Camilla Shand to Major Andrew Parker Bowles of the Household Cavalry was announced in *The Times*.

Charles kept in touch with Camilla, as she had offered to become his penpal while he was at sea and they kept up a steady stream of, apparently, chatty-type letters even after her marriage. In 1975, Charles was thrilled to be asked to be the godfather of Camilla and Andrew's firstborn, a son, Thomas.

Unfortunately, Charles never found that deep affection with any other woman — certainly not with Diana. In many respects, Diana was the antithesis of Camilla, despite the fact that Diana had a great sense of fun and, on occasion, a wonderful and wicked sense of humor that Charles admired and often enjoyed.

Diana had felt excited, exhilarated, overcome with love and devotion to Charles even before their first date. She had always felt that way toward him and had secretly been quite jealous of her sister Sarah during her 12-month relationship with Charles. But Diana's sense of exhilaration and love toward Charles didn't even last until the wedding day. The gloss had vanished from the romance and Charles was having difficulty balancing his duty to the crown and his mother and his duty to his young fiancée. From there it was nearly all downhill.

The deep regard and esteem that so attracted Diana to Charles had all but disappeared within the first weeks of their marriage. She discovered to her shock and horror that she had married a man whose duty was first and foremost to his country, then his mother the queen, then to the crown and the job that came with the position.

Last on Charles' list of priorities came duty to his wife and, understandably, Diana didn't like that one bit. The omens were not good — things would become far worse.

Chapter 7

Diana Unmasked

*T*he marriage of Charles and Diana was the result of a well-intentioned conspiracy by the queen, the Queen Mother and Diana's grandmother, Lady Fermoy. During Christmas week 1979, out of the blue, Diana received an invitation to join a shooting party at Sandringham taking place two months later. The invitation surprised her. The hunt was organized by the three ladies who decided that if Charles couldn't find a suitable bride for himself then they had better find one for him. They knew that Charles had taken out some 20 or 30 girls during the previous few years and yet he hadn't wanted to marry one of them.

The pressure was also mounting from Prince Philip, who would upbraid Charles for being selfish in remaining single because it was his duty to make certain that there were at least one or two heirs to the throne in case Charles met with an accident. This pressure from his father annoyed Charles because he believed it was none of his business to urge him to find a bride until he wanted to settle down. "All in good time," Charles would tell his father, who would then walk away making comments such as "Well, you'd better get a move on, your mother's concerned."

It was, of course, true. By the late 1970s, everyone except Earl Mountbatten wanted Charles to set about finding the "right" young woman, marry her and produce a few children to make certain the House of Windsor would not simply fade away. A "find a bride" quest had become a national pastime. The queen and the Queen Mother were concerned that Charles was so enjoying his bachelor life with his polo mates, his hunting, shooting and fishing that he had no desire to marry.

Mountbatten, however, advised Charles to do nothing hasty unless he was certain he had found the right girl. Charles took Mountbatten's advice until that fateful day in August 1979, when Mountbatten was assassinated by the Provisional IRA, along with other members of his family.

Mountbatten's violent death shocked the British people and devastated Prince Charles. Indeed, Charles was so angry that the IRA could have committed such a dastardly act against a man and his family out sailing on holiday that he went so far as to suggest in a strongly worded letter to the British government that he wanted to raise an army that he would lead to hunt down, and capture or kill as many members of the Provisional IRA they could unearth. And Charles was deadly serious. The government replied that they did not think it a very good idea.

Mountbatten's death, however, provided Charles with a very good reason why he should marry and soon. Now that the IRA were targeting and killing members of the royal family, the queen and Prince Charles were the most likely targets, according to MI5 and the Special Branch in Northern Ireland. And Prince Charles had no offspring.

Out hunting in November 1979, Charles met a dashing, attractive, blond young woman Anna Wallace, a good horsewoman and the daughter of a Scottish landowner. Charles fell for her almost overnight. Never had Charles experienced such a fiery, passionate young woman in the bedroom and she took his breath away. Known as "Whiplash Wallace," a nickname she was proud of, Anna was so different from every other girl Charles had bedded. Swept off his feet, Charles asked her to marry him. She refused, but Charles was not deterred and he continued to date her, but not for long.

In *Diana, Her True Story*, it is claimed that at a ball celebrating the Queen Mother's 80th birthday, Charles ignored Anna and spent the night dancing with Camilla Parker Bowles. But that was untrue. In such circumstances, Charles is bound by duty and protocol to dance with the majority of the women, married and unmarried, as he did on that occasion. But Diana used this fallacious story as another example of Charles' love for Camilla even before Diana was dating Charles.

At that same ball, Anna also failed to understand Charles' role as Prince of Wales and the protocol that meant he had no alternative but to dance with most of the women present. The fiery Anna exploded in anger, yelling at him in front of guests, "Don't ignore me like that again. I've never been treated so badly in my life. No one treats me like that, not even you." Within a month, Anna had married another member of the aristocracy, Johnny Hesketh.

Charles licked his wounds and wondered if he would ever find a suitable young woman to marry him. He looked at his rapidly balding pate and wondered if it was already too late. With the beautiful but demanding Anna Wallace out of the way, the three conspirators — the queen, her mother and Diana's godmother — set about their task with renewed urgency. They wanted to find a girl of good breeding, preferably from an aristocratic family who, naturally, had to appeal to Charles' preferences, meaning she should be tall, but not too tall, blonde with long legs, good-looking and fun. After many discussions, their choice was Diana Spencer. She matched the physical criteria, but they didn't really know about her character or personality. They knew she was shy, not highly intelligent but seemed kind and sensitive, nothing like her more red-blooded elder sister Sarah, whom Charles had recently dumped after eating problems caused her to become irrational and too emotional.

The three watched from a distance to see how the two would get along. None of them was too concerned about Diana — Charles was the important one in these marriage stakes. They hoped the two of them would get along well and enjoy a happy married life, but they were realists. They knew that the majority of aristocratic marriages ended in failure, but only after two or three children had been born, ensuring the family name would continue for at least another generation. Frequently, instead of protracted, hard-fought divorces, which were damaging to the children and to their estates, most couples continued to live in the same house but carried on separate lives while purporting to be happily married. Occasionally, they would appear together at church and attend local fetes. They stayed married, but made separate friends and, more often than not, took lovers. Such goings-on were always conducted discreetly and never in front of the children or the staff. It had come to be accepted practice and considered rather civilized. As evidenced by so many other aristocratic marriages in Britain, most couples were able to enjoy relatively happy relationships while living virtually separate lives.

The ladies could tell from the very beginning that Charles was quite taken with the immature, teenage Diana even though she was somewhat plump and lacked sophistication. They noted that Charles seemed attracted to her, especially when she laughed or smiled broadly. The Queen Mother, whom Charles always respected and admired, broached the subject of Diana with Charles, and received quite a positive reply. Invitations to informal royal gatherings took off. That summer, Diana was invited to informal lunches at Windsor Castle and she would accompany the family to watch Charles play polo in the afternoon. Soon, Charles asked Diana for a date — dinner in his private quarters at Buckingham Palace. That dinner date was so successful that within a few weeks it had become obvious that the couple were happy together.

The three ladies congratulated themselves and the wedding was one of the most extravagant royal events for a generation, the first royal wedding watched live by millions around the world. Yet within a matter of only a couple of years, the three women acknowledged that their conspiracy had failed. Charles and Diana were simply not suited. They weren't happy; indeed Diana was so miserable that shortly after the birth of William she had taken a lover. And Charles had become sullen and angry. It hadn't worked — failure was staring all of them in the eye.

The blame for the failure was placed at Diana's feet. The three wise women all conceded that it was the immaturity, the independence and the lack of discipline in Diana that caused the rift. They sensed that without a mother at home to guide and discipline her, Diana had grown up almost running wild with no one, including her dear father, prepared to take on such responsibilities. Instead, all four children were packed off to boarding schools.

Now, the three women didn't know how they could put the marriage back on track. This was the 1980s and young women were becoming far more independent. It seemed English women's newfound independence had spread to the royal family. New divorce laws had been introduced with "no blame" clauses and women were divorcing their husbands in far greater numbers than ever, some refusing to live with a man who treated them badly while others simply wanted the freedom of living on their own. Diana belonged to that generation.

In royal circles, it was hoped that Charles and Diana would understand that they had to stay together for the sake of the children, the royal family, the crown, the church and the nation. When Charles finally turned to Camilla and took her to his home in the country, the three women hoped Charles had decided to get on with his life. The marriage hadn't worked, but so what. Diana had done her duty, bearing two sons, famously commenting she had produced "an heir and a spare."

But Diana didn't want to acknowledge that the failure of the marriage had anything to do with her. Like tens of thousands of other women wanting to escape from unhappy marriages, she wanted to tell the world that she was the wronged party and the blame fell fair and square on the adulterous Charles and his long-time mistress Camilla.

But that wasn't how it happened. When the marriage fell apart, Charles tried to placate Diana, tried to please her, help her, guide her and, in his strange way, to love her. But Charles simply had little or no idea how to handle Diana. With every other girl he had ever dated, Charles had done whatever he wanted when he wanted and the girl had been happy to go along with his wishes. Some girls hadn't enjoyed playing that role and had gone their own way. But this time it was different — Charles was married and he was at a loss to know how to handle his wife's demands. And, sadly, there was no Mountbatten to advise him.

Charles desperately needed advice. He turned to his friend Camilla, a woman his own age. If Lord Mountbatten had been alive, Charles would have gone straight to him, not to Camilla. Indeed, Charles would have taken Diana to Mountbatten to seek his views as to whether he considered her a suitable bride before even thinking about marriage. Charles had enjoyed a remarkable relationship with Mountbatten, who had become the father figure he needed.

Following the assassination of Mountbatten in August 1979, Charles renewed his friendship with Camilla and her husband Andrew. Charles was the godfather of their firstborn and he would occasionally drive down to their Gloucestershire home to see young Tom and have a meal with the Parker Bowles. Their house in the country had become a second home to him, a place where he was welcome, where he could relax and chat with a family, so different from a lonely room in a cold, uninviting palace or castle with long, dark passages, vast rooms, flunkies and outdated plumbing.

Camilla volunteered to help Charles decorate and furnish Highgrove and he readily accepted her offer. They saw more of each other and he came to rely on her as a friend who would offer sound, down-to-earth advice. He even, famously, took Diana to see Camilla and asked her to see whether she thought Diana would make a suitable wife and companion for him. It was in the cabbage patch at the Parker Bowles home where Charles asked Diana to marry him — and she had been thrilled and delighted.

In the hope that Camilla — being a woman and a mother — would be able to advise him where he had gone wrong, Charles turned to her, pouring out his problems while they sat around the kitchen table drinking tea. He told Camilla everything. including that Diana had taken a lover and that, for all intents and purposes, it seemed their marriage was over. He wanted to know how he could win back Diana and mend his broken marriage. He revealed they no longer shared a bed, made love, kissed or even held hands and they barely talked except to fight and argue over petty, ridiculous things.

Camilla gave Charles the only piece of advice she could, knowing there was not the slightest possibility of Charles and Diana being given permission by the queen to separate or divorce. Camilla told Charles that he had no other choice but to put on a brave face, find out why Diana had turned to another man and try to mend the broken fences. Charles returned to Kensington Palace and tried to carry out Camilla's advice, but it didn't work. Nothing seemed to work. Diana made it plain to him that she just didn't want to know. She wanted out of the marriage, out of the royal family and she never wanted to carry out anymore royal duties, never wanted to attend anymore lunches and dinners where she was forced to make polite conversation with boring old people whom she didn't know and never wanted to see again. And she wanted the freedom to go wherever she wanted, when she wanted, with no questions asked, just like every other young married woman of the '80s.

Charles always explained that there was no question of separation or divorce because the queen simply would not permit it under any circumstances. During these discussions, which nearly always became arguments and frequently deteriorated into swearing matches, Charles often became angry and Diana would erupt in tears. It was during these early years of the marriage that Charles became increasingly frustrated and that frustration would, invariably, turn to anger. And when in such a fury, Charles would kick chairs and tables, knock things off tables, thump walls and doors with his bare fists and all the time screaming abuse at Diana. She was terrified that he would hit her, but he never did. On one occasion, he picked up a wooden bootjack and hurled it at the wall — just missing Diana's head and frightening the wits out of her.

During another furious row, Diana threw a heavy glass paperweight at Charles' head and she felled him — the paperweight hit the back of his head as he turned away. Silence followed as Charles collapsed on the floor. Diana looked down at him lying inert at her feet, turned white with terror fearing that she had killed him and she stared at his prone figure, not knowing what to do. Seconds later, Charles stirred, sat up and wondered what had happened. He was OK.

Charles has had problems coming to terms with his bursts of incredible anger and it alarms him. This author has seen Charles at polo turn angry at something that went wrong on the field of play. He would jump off his pony, throw the reins toward his groom, hurl his helmet, his whip and his stick to the ground and stand in front of a large, mature tree thumping away at the tree trunk with his fists and swearing. And suddenly he would stop, shake his head and go and pick up everything.

There have been other incidences. During one occasion, a new Range Rover was delivered to Balmoral. Charles had asked that no carpet should be fitted in the back because the vehicle would be used for throwing recently shot carcasses of deer in the back and the carpet would be soon bloodstained and ruined. Instead, the car company put in a carpet with press-studs so it could be easily taken up whenever necessary. Charles walked out of the castle and looked around the new vehicle admiringly and then he looked through the rear window and saw the carpet on the floor.

"Does no one take any f***ing notice of what I say?" he screamed at the five or six members of staff standing around him. Still yelling, his face red with fury, he shouted, "I told them I didn't want any f***ing carpet in the back and there it is … what the hell do I have to do to make my words understood? … Jesus Christ; will no one obey an order anymore?"

For almost an entire hour, Charles continued in this vein, sometimes stopping for breath, at other times remaining silent for a minute or so before launching into a fresh attack on all, swearing and hurling abuse at everyone and anyone for not carrying out his request. Time and again, those around him tried to point out that the carpet could be removed in a minute or so by simply releasing the press-studs. But he didn't and wouldn't listen. Those around him were amazed at the extraordinary outburst and many thoughts Charles had lost all control.

After such an abusive outburst, Charles would calm down and then worry that he had lost his temper so badly that he had lost control of himself. It was in the late 1970s that Charles came across a book entitled *George III and the Mad Business*, a serious, intelligent work published in 1969 and written by Ida MacAlpine and Richard Hunter. Together, they researched the nature of George III's mental illness and the possible causes for his deranged mind.

George III's madness was well-known during his long reign from 1760 to 1820 — his problematic behavior was discussed in private, in public, in Parliament, in the press, by doctors, laymen and indeed by the king himself. It was of course King George III who famously "lost" the North American colonies in 1789. However, after his death at age 82, a conspiracy of silence descended on the subject in deference to Queen Victoria, who was sensitive about her grandfather's derangement.

The lore of "the mad king" gained in popularity and became somewhat of a legend. George had his first attack at age 26 and although he was suffering a debilitating illness at the time, there was no evidence that his mind was affected. In fact, it is now accepted that King George was 50 years old when he first became deranged and all periods of derangement added together hardly amounted to six months in all. In his final illness from 1810 to 1820, when the Regency was established, it was said at the time that permanent madness had closed on him. But that was a convenient fable. In reality, he suffered a series of accessions and remissions before he was overtaken by senility, then blindness and ultimately deafness.

MacAlpine and Hunter scoured all the medical records of the king's illnesses and derangement, the published letters between the king and his prime ministers and physicians about his illnesses, faithfully recording them in their account and investigation of the reasons behind his alleged madness. They concluded from their research, from the king's medical history records and examining the symptoms of his illnesses that George III suffered from a recurrent, widespread and severe disorder of the nervous system, now called porphyria. In extreme cases, as the king experienced, such effects attacked the central nervous system and eventually the brain, causing giddiness, mounting agitation, non-stop rambling, persistent sleeplessness and confusion which, in turn, produced delirium, tremors, stupor and convulsions.

Prince Charles was even more interested in the research carried out by MacAlpine and Hunter in tracing any subsequent family history of the disease in the second part of the book, for porphyria can be handed down through the generations. The condition may also be latent for a generation or two and transmitted by someone who shows no symptoms or only inconspicuous ones. The research confirmed that close and distant relations of King George III had probably suffered porphyria at one time or another during the previous 400 years. They discovered the likelihood of the disease in James I of England, who lived from 1566-1625 and through his daughter Sophia to both the English and German royal lines.

Research also showed that George III's son, George IV who lived from 1762 to 1830, and Frederick the Great of Prussia, who lived from 1712 to 1786, suffered from the disease, as well as other family members. And within the present British royal family, the queen is descended from Queen

Victoria through both the blood line of George III and the German blood line. Prince Philip, of course, is German and his distant relations reach back to Frederick the Great. Recent medical research has shown that porphyria is basically an inborn error of metabolism and it can most certainly be inherited.

For more than 20 years, Prince Charles was seriously obsessed with the disease, reading a number of books on the subject and discussing with Earl Mountbatten the possibility that he might have inherited porphyria. And every time Charles lost his temper and resorted to violent language and violent behavior, he would wonder whether he was suffering from similar disorders that other porphyria victims suffer.

Even today, Charles occasionally loses his temper. He still kicks chairs and tables, smashes things on the floor and swears. He knows he loses control but he doesn't know why. Two recent explosions of anger involved his young brother Prince Edward and the second was a moment of fury at a dinner party he was hosting at Highgrove.

The first outburst occurred after his brother Prince Edward ordered a camera team from his film production company to shoot footage of Prince William's first days at St. Andrews University in autumn 2001. In an effort to protect William's privacy, all film, TV and photographers, as well as journalists, were banned from entry to the university campus. But Edward apparently ordered his team to go onto the campus and film William, explaining to those in charge that this venture had been agreed upon by St. James's Palace. When Charles heard what had happened he immediately phoned Edward and went berserk shouting, swearing and using a string of four-letter words in his fury at his brother's stupidity. Charles could not understand how his brother Edward could have given such an instruction when every effort was being made to protect William from film crews and the paparazzi.

In January 2003, Charles was enjoying a private dinner party at Highgrove when a joke was made by one of the male guests about the BBC's poll of listeners that voted Charles fourth person they would like to boot out of Britain. Charles leapt to his feet in a fury, picked up a piece of china and hurled it to the floor in front of the astonished dozen guests at the table, shouting that the poll was a "bloody stupid stunt" by the BBC.

However, the servants in attendance hardly blinked an eye at Charles' furious outburst because during the past few years Charles has shown all the appearances of a troubled man, losing his temper at the slightest provocation.

This was one of the demons Charles was battling as Diana was realizing that she would never fit in with the royal family.

When she returned from her honeymoon and discovered to her horror how her life had changed forever, Diana wrote that she was drowning in a world turned upside down.

Diana eventually sought solace in her children while she continued her affairs with Hewitt and others. Through Andrew Morton in *Diana: Her True Story*, she made it clear that the children were a point of stability and sanity in a topsy-turvy world: *"She loved them unconditionally and absolutely, working with a singleness of purpose to ensure that they did not suffer the same kind of childhood that she did."*

According to the book, it was Diana who chose their schools, their clothes and planned their outings. They came foremost in her life. But to those friends who had known the young Diana, it was surprising that she made the decision to send both William and Harry away to boarding school at such a young age. As a single girl, Diana had taken work as a kindergarten assistant because of her love for children. Diana herself did not attend boarding school until she was a teenager and she wasn't happy at being sent away. Wills and Harry were only 8 years old when Diana sent them to board at Ludgrove Preparatory School in Berkshire, some 30 miles from Kensington Palace. She did so even when there were many first-class day schools in London where Wills and Harry could have been educated while at Kensington Palace with their mother.

When Harry began boarding school in September 1990, Diana had discovered a new-found freedom in London. She was all-but single, fancy-free and enjoying a number of lovers while Charles was away in the country enjoying life with Camilla and what Diana dismissively referred to as "the Highgrove Set." Some of her friends said that Diana was happy to have her days, evenings and nights free to do whatever she wanted with no children around.

Also according to *Diana: Her True Story*, the Highgrove Set centered around Camilla, whom Diana maintained was never simply a confidant of Charles, maintaining the two had fallen in love when they met in 1972, just a few months before Camilla married Andrew Parker Bowles. Once again, that was simply not true.

Michael Colborne, who was in the Royal Navy with Charles in 1972, has said, "The suggestion that Charles was in love with Camilla at that time is plain wrong. At the time, he was on leave from the Royal Navy. They met perhaps a dozen times, got on well and became good friends. But in 1972, Camilla was engaged to Andrew and very happy. They were married six months after Charles met Camilla and, as I understand it, they were happy together for a number of years."

Princess Diana fully realized that her book, with all its inaccuracies, deceptions and false-hoods, would attract the wrath of the royal estab-lishment, including the queen and Prince Philip, so she was careful to portray her relationship with the queen as being cordial and friendly. Diana wrote that her relationship with the queen became "much friendlier in 1990 and 1991," and that they "developed a more relaxed and cordial relationship" and Diana ventured that the queen was becoming more critical of Charles, finding "the direction of his life unfocused and his behavior odd and erratic."

The book stated that Diana "had a deep respect for the manner in which the queen had conducted herself during her reign" and claimed she told the queen, "I will never let you down." In fact, Diana and the queen rarely met from the moment she was introduced to the queen in 1980 until her death. Diana admitted to being "simply quite terrified" in the presence of the queen and remained so most of her life.

Diana was aware that the queen would have

been informed of her affair with Hewitt and of the very serious likelihood that Harry was his son. This author understands that the matters of James Hewitt or Harry's parentage were never discussed or even mentioned in any conversations between the two women. On occasion, the queen commented that taking tea with Diana was always difficult because the conversation usually dried up within minutes of pleasantries being exchanged and they would often sit in silence, discreetly looking around the room but making sure their eyes never met. That was the main reason why the queen hardly ever invited her daughter-in-law to take tea or any other meal unless it was a formal family occasion.

Despite her lack of bonding relationships with anyone in the royal family, one important aspect of Diana's life called for sympathy. From 1980, when she was first recognized as a possible girlfriend of Prince Charles until her death in 1997, Diana was the prime target of innumerable photographers, cameramen and filmmakers. For 17 years, Diana was subjected to the most incredible onslaught by photographers keen to make their mark in the cutthroat world of royal photography. To the great majority of these photographers it didn't matter whether Diana sought their attention or not. They wanted a picture come what may and any pleas by Diana for restraint were invariably ignored.

One must wonder whether the great mass of the public, who loved seeing pictures of Diana whether laughing or crying, looking glamorous or rain-soaked, ever stopped to think of her feelings at being bombarded, chased and frequently insulted by the men and women taking those pictures. The photographers quickly came to realize that a picture of Diana in tears earned them more money than a happy, smiling picture. As a result, Diana became subjected to heavy-handed aggravation, cursing and threatening behavior by the paparazzi the longer she remained the center of world attention. At times, it wasn't a pretty sight.

This author can recall one such incident one dark, wet, winter afternoon in London in 1994 after Diana had dispensed with her police bodyguards. She came out of her London gym and was making her way to her car dressed in a tracksuit, trainers, a ski jacket and a baseball cap. Two paparazzi stood in her way as she walked along the sidewalk to her car, while two other photographers took up positions in the road. Diana walked with her face down to stop them getting any face shots. She tried to squeeze past the two men, but they stood shoulder to shoulder. "Please," she said. "I want to pass."

The two men stood still and, as Diana attempted to walk into the road to pass them, one flipped her baseball cap off her head. The cameras immediately began to flash. As she bent down to retrieve her cap, pictures were taken of her rear end. "You bastards," she said and, as she spoke, the flashes fired once more. Their planned ruse had worked because they had gotten a photograph of an unglamorous, unhappy, tearful Diana. These pictures would sell.

"Come on, give us a smile, lady!" one shouted and she looked at him in anger. "Now may I pass?" she asked after picking up her cap. "Not till you smile," he replied. "F**k off," she said.

I told the photographers to let Diana through. They looked at me disdainfully, not sure who I was or what authority I might have, and Diana took the opportunity to push past them and run to her car.

Of course, Diana also used the press and the photographers to her advantage. She knew that for the most part the press, the photographers and the public were on her side in the great marital battle of the 20th century that often seemed to be fought out on the pages of the tabloid press.

One of Diana's favorite tricks was to telephone national newspapers — mostly the tabloids — speak in a cockney accent and tip them off that Princess Diana would be at a particular place at a particular time. Diana was a good mimic. She famously mimicked the queen one evening as she and guests were waiting for her to arrive in the dining room. Unfortunately, Diana didn't notice the queen arrive, and she blushed bright red as her audience of guests fell silent and all looked to see the queen standing, staring at Diana. She must have heard everything but made no comment. Diana never made that mistake again.

Diana rather enjoyed giving tips of her whereabouts to the press, but it wasn't long before the photographers realized that the person giving these fantastic and accurate tips was Diana herself, though she never admitted it. Diana also had some contacts in the tabloid press and, without doubt, her favorite was Richard Kay, the highly rated royal correspondent of the *Daily Mail*, to whom Diana gave many a first-rate exclusive story — much to the annoyance of the royal reporters on rival papers.

So, of course, there were numerous occasions when Diana was very happy that the "ratpack," as she nicknamed the photographers, were around: the famous Taj Mahal photograph, the royal kiss that "missed" because Diana turned her head away as Charles went to kiss her cheek, and the summer evening in June 1994 when Charles was on television giving the fullest and frankest two-hour interview of his life. Diana stole the next day's front pages by appearing in a sensational, breathtaking off-the-shoulder, above the knee, black chiffon Christina Stambolian dress at a gala banquet in Kensington Gardens.

It is only fair that the death of Diana, following the chase through the streets of Paris by a large gang of photographers on motorcycles and scooters, meant that a share of the blame for the tragic car crash would have to be shouldered by the tabloid press and the paparazzi. One British newspaper, *The Daily Telegraph* wrote in a leading article that some tabloids treated Diana "with bestial cruelty." It went on, "The fact that they also published many articles of slavish adoration of the princess makes their cruelty only more refined, more cynical. It is almost past belief that organs which harried her and defiled her now claim to be guardians of her flame."

Diana's brother, Earl Charles Spencer, was so angry at the press that he withdrew the editors' invitations to her funeral, believing that Diana would not have wanted them there. All agreed to stay away.

In an interview with the French newspaper *Le Monde* only months before her death, Diana said, "The press in Britain has always misrepresented me in my attempts to help people. I can think of any number of occasions when I have been attacked by the press because I dared to help other people. They attacked me for hugging AIDS victims, for my visits to Imran Khan's (the Pakistan cricket captain turned politician) cancer hospital in Lahore and for wearing makeup during a visit to a hospital operating room during a heart transplant operation.

"The press is ferocious. It gives nothing, it only hunts for mistakes. Every good intention is twisted, every gesture criticized. I believe that abroad it is different. I'm welcomed with kindness when I'm overseas. I'm taken for what I am, without prior judgments, without looking for blunders. In Britain, it's the opposite. And I believe in my position, anyone sane would have left a long time ago.

"Over the years, I've had to learn to rise above criticism. But the irony is that it's been useful to me in giving me strength which I did not think I had. That's not to say the criticism hasn't hurt me. It has. But it has given me the strength to continue along the path I've chosen."

Yet, ironically, it would be the photographers, and in particular the paparazzi, feeding the demands of the tabloid press, who would be crucially instrumental in creating the scenario that led directly to the killing of Diana.

It was Diana herself who had unwittingly and

naively made the task so much more simple and straightforward for those planning to take her life, by making the rash decision in the summer of 1994 to dispense with her police bodyguards, except at public engagements. Even at that time this was a dangerous move for Diana to make against the advice of everyone she asked. Diana had her reasons, but they were not very well thought out. She wanted more personal privacy and she wanted to operate without the fear that what she did in her private life would automatically be reported back to Buckingham Palace. Diana knew that from the moment she became engaged to Prince Charles that every move she ever made, every person she ever met, every tiny part of her private life would be known and, if thought necessary, referred to senior police officers and palace courtiers. She hated that.

There were two other reasons. She wished to appear different from her in-laws and other members of the extended royal family, who often retained their personal bodyguards as status symbols, even though they were under very little threat. She wanted to demonstrate that she was the one high-profile royal who didn't need police protection because she had the protection of the entire British people. "Nobody's going to hurt me," she would say.

Her faithful private secretary, Patrick Jephson, wrote in his book *Shadows of a Princess*: "She seemed to be indulging her death wish. I could think of no other explanation for the whole series of decisions which marked her descent into self-destruction."

Jephson went on, "This apparent appetite for self-destruction was inextricably linked with a craving to be noticed. When — as was inevitable in the absence of a police protection officer — photographers got too close, crowds too insistent or even parking wardens too zealous, the inconvenience and occasional alarm she suffered could be borne as something akin to the wounds of martyrdom. The experience was painful but somehow holy and suffered in the cause of reminding the world not only that she was there but also that she was defenseless and occasionally at least potentially in danger."

Chapter 8

The Magical Princess

*I*t seems the world will never forget Princess Diana. Her engaging, sunny appearance, the spring in her step, the joy in her eyes — her sheer presence will be remembered for a generation. Those who never met Diana speak of her natural attraction and her devastating smile; those fortunate people who knew Diana well also speak of her sense of fun, her mischievous nature, her spontaneous laughter and her naughty jokes.

To many, Diana, Princess of Wales, was a remarkable young woman. To some she was a ministering angel, to others a comforter in their time of need, to still more she was the person who gave them hope in times of despair but to all she was one person who brought something special into their lives.

Diana left behind an extraordinary sense of loss.

As day dawned that autumn morning in 1997 and people heard the tragic news, mothers wept openly as though they had lost a daughter; fathers felt they had failed her; young women felt they had lost a best friend who understood them. People wept openly at the realization that someone they had grown to love should have been snatched from them so abruptly, so finally, so tragically. Yet her death brought together millions of people in shared compassion and heartrending grief, which circled the globe. Hundreds of thousands of people from across Britain headed for London in the following few days, wanting to be close to where Diana had lived and breathed, and there resided a deep-seated yearning to share their sense of loss and despair with total strangers who shared a common love for one remarkable person.

Throughout that long period of mourning, people's thoughts turned to William and Harry, the teenage boys who would now grow up without the mother who had so obviously and so openly adored them. Those thoughts brought forth more heartbreak, more pain and more tears and yet most of those who mourned had never set eyes on Diana or the boys, let alone met them.

But for all the pain and heartache that Diana suffered from childhood until her untimely death, it is not why she is remembered. It is everything else that Diana did, frequently against the will of the queen and her phalanx of advisers, for which people will long remember her. Her heroic AIDS campaign, as much against prejudice as the disease itself, transformed the way many people came to understand this killer disease. Indisputably, it was Diana who was responsible for people becoming far more compassionate and sympathetic to those suffering and dying from AIDS.

Diana's decision to throw her full weight behind an AIDS campaign in Britain began as a direct result of a friend of hers, Adrian Ward-Jackson, an art dealer and a governor of the Royal Ballet, who had contracted the disease. In the late 1980s, Ward-Jackson, who became deputy Chairman of the AIDS Crisis Trust in Britain, persuaded Diana to join the Trust and help their efforts to "de-demonize" the disease to the public. Ward-Jackson was responsible for helping Diana launch her public crusade for a better understanding of the disease that he had contracted. Indeed, it was the rapidly worsening condition of the dying Ward-Jackson that gave Diana the incentive to wake up the world to the AIDS crisis.

Diana's determination to highlight the needs of those people unfortunate enough to contract HIV and AIDS was both brave and bold. In her single-minded decision to face down the queen and her

courtiers and at the same time display her compassion, Diana showed a side of her character
that most had no idea she possessed.

Let there be no mistake. Diana was "invited" —
in royal parlance that means "ordered" — to see
Sir Robert Fellowes, then the queen's private secretary and, of course Diana's brother-in-law, and
he tried, in a smooth and gentle way, to persuade
Diana to drop her support for AIDS victims,
although he knew there was no point in simply
ordering her to do anything – Diana wasn't going
to be bullied. He knew Diana would have left the
room immediately and held him in contempt for
even suggesting such a thing. So Fellowes
"suggested" that an AIDS organization "might
not be suitable" charitable work befitting the
Princess of Wales because "the image" wasn't
positive for her or the royal family.

During that conversation, Diana became
increasingly angry, but somehow managed to
contain herself throughout most of her brother-in-
law's diplomatic attempts at persuasion. Finally,
after some 10 minutes, Diana could contain
herself no longer and, as she said later, "I was raging inside at what he was saying. In effect, I was
being told that the royal family considered AIDS a
'dirty' disease and that those suffering from its
effect were not deserving of royal patronage. I was

told that I should concentrate on other charities that would be more acceptable to the family."

At the end of the discussion, Diana said to Sir Robert, "So you are telling me that the royal family should take no notice of people dying from a particular disease and should have nothing to do with charities involved with killer diseases. Well, I will decide what charities I shall support and I fully intend to continue supporting those people dying from AIDS come what may."

To her great credit, Diana did just that. Until that moment in her life, Diana never knew that she had such determination, inner strength and courage to defy the wishes of the royal family and their bureaucrat messengers. She did it and it made her feel good. Now, she would go about her charitable work with greater gusto then ever. The royals didn't like her sudden streak of independence, however — it worried them.

Diana set about breaking down the prejudice that surrounded AIDS and her personal commitment to the task was primarily responsible for ordinary people, charities and the British government adopting a more relaxed and understanding attitude to the disease.

That was one reason behind Diana's decision to open Britain's first ward for AIDS patients at London's Middlesex Hospital. Newspaper columnists were amazed that a royal such as the pristine Princess Diana, the mother of two young sons, would take such an enormous risk as meeting AIDS patients "without wearing protective clothing." Shocked and dismayed, many people thought that Diana's decision to shake the hand of a man who was dying of AIDS was foolhardy at best and stupid at worst.

As Pamela Harlech, a British AIDS fund-raiser said, "One cannot overestimate the importance of what Diana did the day she touched an AIDS patient with her bare hand. At a stroke, it changed people's conception of the disease."

When in New York during a visit to an AIDS clinic, Diana picked up a baby with the disease and cuddled her. By doing this, she took the stigma out of the disease, changing people's perception of the dangers of AIDS. For months and years doctors and clinicians had been searching in vain for a way to lift the taboo, which many held against AIDS patients. Diana did it in an instant and earned the heartfelt and sincere admiration of not only everyone suffering from AIDS, but of all their relatives and friends.

For Diana, AIDS was one of the diseases that remained at the forefront of her charitable work until the end of her life. Nick Partridge, director of the Terence Higgins Trust, a major British AIDS charity, has revealed that Diana asked to be kept abreast of the scientific and medical advances being made in the search for a cure. Every two or three months, Partridge would brief her, informing her of the progress medical investigations were making and of the latest up-to-the-minute treatments for sufferers. She never lost interest.

One of the principal reasons Diana became involved in the cause was not only because of her concern to help those who had contracted the disease, but also because of her subconscious need to be closely involved with sufferers, particularly those whose diseases made them outcasts from society. Diana wanted to help these people because they were victims rejected by society, and she shared their feeling of rejection because she had been cast aside by her mother, her husband and the royal family. Diana felt strongly that the more involved she became with those rejected by society the more appreciated and loved she felt in return.

This feeling of rejection remained with Diana all her adult life. As she told patients at an AIDS clinic in London in 1987, when the subject was almost taboo in many social circles in Britain, "I understand the rejection you feel because I feel the same rejection."

Pamela Harlech explained Diana's remarkable

empathy with AIDS sufferers, saying, "Diana really does believe that she understands the rejection they feel better than anyone because she feels she is one of them."

But AIDS was only one of the prime examples of the way in which Diana acted as an agent of compassion to those in need and, at the same time, forcing people to face unpalatable and fearsome truths. To Diana, it was paramount to help the sufferers and she wanted to bring some peace and understanding to the victims and their families. She also wanted to get a better deal for the sufferers, many of whom were feeling ostracized and rejected by society.

There was also leprosy, the highly infectious bacterial disease that results in severe physical deformities. Diana realized that, like AIDS victims, lepers were being shunned across the world, rejected by the societies in which they lived by people who were frightened of coming into contact with them or even touching them. She understood that, unlike AIDS, this was no new disease, but something which poverty-stricken societies had lived with for centuries.

Baptist Minister Tony Lloyd, executive director of the Leprosy Mission in Britain, accompanied Diana on trips to Africa. "Our first trip was to Harare in Zimbabwe in 1993 and I noticed that

The future Princess of Wales, Lady Diana Spencer at age 3 (above), with younger brother Charles (above right) and during a summer holiday in 1971 (right). Warm but shy, Diana would attract Prince Charles with her natural beauty, but she would be unprepared for a new life in the public eye.

A young Prince Charles with his great-uncle Earl Mountbatten, whom he loved and adored. Mountbatten was assassinated by the IRA in August 1979.

Charles dated Sarah Spencer, Diana's elder sister.

Camilla Parker Bowles and Diana in 1980.
Camilla befriended Diana at Charles' request.

After the most celebrated wedding of the 20th century, the bride and groom share a kiss on the balcony of Buckingham Palace (above) and then honeymooned on the British royal yacht, Britannia, cruising the Mediterranean (left).

*In 1981 at Balmoral — a place the royals
loved and Diana found deadly dull.*

The royal couple leaves St. Mary's Hospital in London after the birth of their first son, Prince William.

Prince William and Prince Harry playing in 1985.

The princess, shockingly thin as her weight plunged to 100 pounds, suffered from anorexia and bulimia.

*Princess Diana and Prince Charles pose
for an official royal portrait in 1987.*

Sarah Ferguson and Diana enjoy a light moment at a formal event. Both women would later embarrass Buckingham Palace by speaking out on what it was like to marry into "The Firm," as the royal family calls themselves.

Diana brings William and Harry to review the troops – with Major James Hewitt.

Charles Spencer celebrates his 21st birthday with his three sisters – Princess Diana, Lady Jane Fellowes and Lady Sarah McCorquodale – and Prince Charles.

"It's all so dreadfully embarrassing," said Princess Diana of her life in the spotlight after marrying Prince Charles.

Princess Diana and Queen Elizabeth celebrate the Queen Mother's 87th birthday. Although the two maintained a public friendship, the queen complained to Prince Charles about her daughter-in-law's behavior.

A happy front – Princess Diana and Prince Charles pose with their two sons, Prince Harry and Prince William. Behind the scenes, the royal couple fought bitterly.

*Breaking apart – Diana and Charles
shortly before their divorce.*

The princess awards a polo trophy to Major James Hewitt in 1991, with Prince William looking on.

Paul Burrell, Diana's faithful butler and the man whom she affectionately called her "rock," poses with the princess.

A rare moment of solitude – Princess Diana takes a walk alone in the countryside.

Dressed to thrill — The same night Charles was on television giving the most revealing interview of his life, Diana appeared in this Christina Stambolian dress and bumped Charles right off the next day's front pages.

Diana with Prince Philip, who once wrote a letter to Diana in which he called her a "harlot."

Hasnat Khan

Oliver Hoare

Will Carling

James Gilbey

Ambassador of Goodwill – Diana visits Angola in 1997 during her personal crusade against the use of land mines.

Mother Teresa and the princess visit the poor. As Diana committed herself to humanitarian causes, comparisons between the two were inevitably drawn.

Diana enjoys a vacation in Barbuda in April 1997, only months before her tragic death.

Dodi Fayed and Diana share an intimate moment on his yacht and then stroll on the French Riviera.

00:19:23 3__/97 12HR

Minutes before the fatal crash, driver Henri Paul, bodyguard Trevor Rees-Jones and Dodi Fayed, pictured with his arm around Princess Diana, at the Ritz Hotel in Paris.

21:50:34 24H
30-8-97

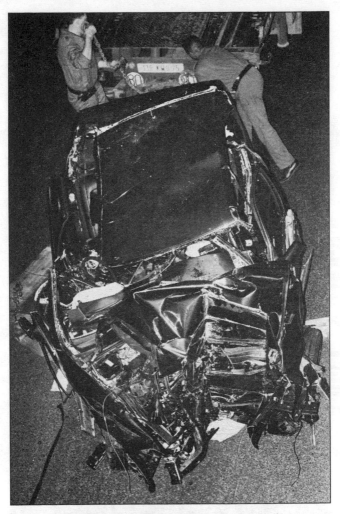

Workers prepare to remove the crushed Mercedes sedan from the crash scene.

Diana's casket is removed from the Pitie-Salpetriere Hospital in Paris.

Queen Elizabeth pays a public tribute to Princess Diana.

*From left: Charles Spencer, Prince William,
Prince Harry and Prince Charles
at the funeral for Princess Diana.*

*Diana's coffin is adorned with flowers and
a card from her sons addressed to Mummy.*

A royal procession leads the casket of Princess Diana from the church after her funeral.

Althorp, the ancestral home of the Spencer family, is the final resting place of Diana, who is buried on the island in the oval pond.

Diana was looking at a woman with no fingers. After a short while, Diana went behind a partition in the hospital and I saw she was crying, unable to control her sobbing. When she had composed herself, Diana told me that she wasn't only crying for the woman but because she was now getting proper treatment.

"Diana was without racial prejudice. She would talk to blacks and whites in the same way and was completely fearless for herself in the middle of a leper colony."

Before Diana left Britain, some tabloid news-papers ran headlines screaming, "Don't Do It" and doctors wrote articles curdling the readers' blood with details of disfigurement and loss of limbs that might occur if Diana shook hands with a leper patient. Little did the public know that Diana not only shook hands with AIDS patients and lepers but, when out of view of the cameras, she would take the opportunity to cuddle babies, hold AIDS sufferers in her arms and hug anyone that she believed needed to be hugged by anoth-er human being.

Lloyd related another story: "We flew to a refugee camp near the Mozambique border and she shook hands with everyone and those people who had no hands, she shook their wrists instead as though that was perfectly normal. With all of them she laughed and joked and chatted, listening to whatever they had to say.

"But what I noticed was that when Diana walked into the tent where they were all sitting, she simply looked around the room at everyone and smiled to them all, as though she was really happy to be among them. It was like a ray of sunshine coming to visit them because she had this incredible charisma and, I have to say, I was in awe of it.

"I believe she sympathized with lepers because she realized they had been both rejected and cast out from society, forced to live like outsiders forever, until they eventually died — alone, unloved and often despised. It seemed to me that in her care for lepers Diana was searching for a spiritual dimension. The more I came to know her and work with her the more I felt, in the last couple of years, that she had found her place in the world, helping and inspiring the outcasts of the world and this brought her a sort of peace to her life. As a result, she seemed much clearer in her life's work. She had found herself."

Lloyd explained that Diana had brought three things to the leprosy cause: "First, a high profile; second, money, including tens of thousands of pounds from her own bank account that no one ever knew about, and third, she helped people around the world to overcome the stigma of leprosy as she had with AIDS. Diana touched lepers, cradled children dying of leprosy in her arms, kissed them and joked with them. No one in her position had ever done anything like that before and, even today, we thank God for what Diana brought to those suffering from leprosy. I can understand why some people called her a saint."

And though some people disparaged the charity work Diana did with AIDS victims and lepers, suggesting she only involved herself with these charities for publicity or headline-grabbing photo opportunities, much of the work Diana carried out with victims of both those diseases she carried out in secret, with no photographers or media people in attendance. Indeed, for most of the time, the media had no idea Diana was carrying out such compassionate visits.

During another African visit, Diana found herself deep in the south African bush at the Mazerera Red Cross center feeding hundreds of children who had walked for hours in the hope they would be given a bowl of bean soup. With tears in her eyes, Diana ladled out the soup from a huge iron cooking pot to the children of the Karanga tribe, many of them suffering from severe malnutrition. She stood for three hours in intense heat handing out the soup until every child had been fed. With sweat pouring down her

face, neck and arms and her dress wet with per-
spiration Diana managed a smile for every child
who stood in line waiting for the food. As Diana
flew back from the bush, she sat in the helicopter
with tears streaming down her face because she
knew she was returning to a life of luxury and
plenty and the children were returning home on
foot with no idea where the next meal would
come from.

As a result, Diana came to love her work
with lepers and came to understand the disease
remarkably well. She also admired and applauded
not only the extraordinary courage of the
victims, but also the nurses and helpers who
defied so much prejudice to help them. She
would confess, "Whenever I think of those poor,
deprived lepers, particularly the children, I can't
stop the tears because I feel so ashamed."

Patrick Jephson, Diana's private secretary and
most influential adviser from 1988 to 1996, wrote
in his memoirs, *Shadows of a Princess*: "To me,
the princess's work with lepers stands out as her
greatest monument. It would be impossible to
find a better example of her ability to transform
attitudes, to help the ignorant accept the
untouchable. There were no moral overtones
to distract from the central message, as there
sometimes were in the case of AIDS. This was

goodness in a rare form and if it also made a good photo opportunity, I should really only have been glad."

Diana had become an angel of hope and not only in championing major, high-profile diseases. She never forgot those at home. Every so often, the postman delivered to Emma May's home in Copthorne, West Sussex, some 50 miles from London, a letter from Kensington Palace. The postman knew they were personal letters from Diana. He also knew that Emma May was a girl of quite exceptional courage. She had been born with a rare chromosome disorder called Turner's Syndrome, which not only caused heart and kidney problems in young children but also stunts their growth. As a result, Emma had to make regular visits to Great Ormond Street Hospital for Children in London, staying there while she underwent difficult and painful stretching surgery. Doctors and nurses see many brave youngsters, but Emma May was exceptional.

Bright, blue-eyed Emma would lie in the hospital for months at a time, wondering what the future held for her. She had always been a sickly child, unable to enjoy the normal rigors and rough-and-tumble of childhood. Whenever she went into the hospital, she knew it would mean pain, sometimes extreme, and always physical discomfort. When Emma was 10 years old, the doctors and nurses at the hospital had become so overwhelmed by her courage that, in 1992, she was awarded the annual bravery prize for children who had triumphed over adversity.

As always, Diana, Princess of Wales, the hospital's patron, came to present the award and it was then that she first met Emma. After that first meeting, Diana asked the doctors, "Her eyes are so bright; she seems a remarkable child. How can she take such pain and still smile? She makes me feel ashamed." Until the day of her death, some five years later, Diana never forgot Emma. Young Emma, now age 21, recalls their meetings through the years. "Diana told me that I was her special friend. She would come and sit on my bed and talk to me. After a while I didn't call her 'princess,' just Diana, and she called me Emma. That's because Diana told me we were friends.

"So much of what happened to me is down to Diana. She was my inspiration throughout some traumatic times when I would lie in bed feeling rotten with the continuous pain. I would think of her and smile. During the first meeting, Diana told me to keep in touch and write to her, telling her how I was getting on. I felt a bit silly writing to her because I knew I would never get a letter back. But she wrote back immediately telling me how lovely it was to hear from me and asked me to keep writing. She seemed really interested.

"Diana gave me hope. She gave me the courage to face all my operations and the strength to face the future. She kept telling me that one day everything would be fine and because she told me I believed her. She was such a wonderful, extraordinary person and she was right. Now, basically I'm fine and never a day goes by without me thinking of her."

Emma May was not the only child to have faith in Diana. All over the world there are children who have met Diana in similar, disturbing situations and, somehow, she would encourage them to believe in themselves and have faith in the future. She gave them hope, which they never forgot.

On many occasions when Diana carried out her charity work, it was a high-profile event, meaning headline-grabbing photo opportunities. The photographers and television crews needed their pictures and the journalists wrote their pieces, encouraging people who saw the good works the charities were carrying out to contribute desperately needed money. As a patron of these charities, Diana was only too happy to pose for such activities. Toward the end of her life, however, some journalists began to carp, exclaiming that she only appeared at such charitable functions when she knew the cameras would be present. That was a slur on Diana's good name and totally untrue.

In fact, Diana saw far more ill, sick and dying patients, particularly children, when there were no cameras present to record the scene. And Diana preferred it that way because she discovered that on a one-to-one basis, particularly with children, they would relax more easily and become more open and confident with her.

The case of Bonnie Hendel was typical. Diana had met Bonnie at St. Mary's Hospital, Paddington, London, where she was lying desperately ill, looking miserable and lethargic, suffering from AIDS. Doctors warned Diana that they feared Bonnie was close to death. When Diana arrived at her bedside she could see the child had eaten no food, so slowly and patiently Diana fed her the food until she had eaten every morsel.

After Diana left, after chatting to Bonnie's parents and asking to be kept informed of her progress, Bonnie told the doctors, "I don't need any more medicine, just lunch with Diana every day. She makes me feel better."

A few days later, Diana sent Bonnie a letter wishing her well and enclosing a photograph of herself for Bonnie to keep by her bed and kiss every morning and every night. Within a matter of weeks, doctors at St. Mary's phoned Kensington Palace to tell Diana that Bonnie was only hours away from death. Diana immediately canceled her next engagement, jumped in her car and raced to the hospital. But she arrived too late; Bonnie was dead.

Diana joined Bonnie's grieving parents, and for 15 minutes the three stood together clasping each other, tears running down their cheeks. When Diana left the hospital she was still holding a handkerchief to her eyes, trying to stem the tears. There was not a photographer or journalist in sight. Diana had not taken the trouble to rush to Bonnie's bedside because she thought it might provide a photo for the next day's papers but simply out of her love and concern for a helpless child.

In the great majority of her private visits to hospitals, Diana would arrive alone, usually driving herself. Unlike any other member of the royal family, she preferred to arrive with no police protection, no armed bodyguard, lady-in-waiting or secretary. She preferred to chat with patients one-on-one, especially with children with no one else standing around the bed. She wanted the occasion to be personal, intimate and totally informal, which is why she usually dressed in jeans and a sweater.

As Anne Houston, director of ChildLine

Scotland, commented, "We were all struck by Diana's understanding of children's problems when she visited us in Glasgow. She had an amazing empathy with children."

Joy Bradbury, 11, woke up in the London's Royal Brompton Hospital after open-heart surgery. She was critically ill, hovering between life and death, and doctors weren't sure whether she would survive the trauma of the operation. She was still on a ventilator and unable to speak. She had drifted in and out of consciousness, watched by doctors and nurses who kept her under constant supervision. Then she awoke and looked up to see a woman with blond hair and dressed in a sweater and jeans smiling down at her. Instantly, Joy recognized Diana. A smile crossed her lips and her eyes lit up.

"It was a wonderful, magical moment," said her mother Doreen who was also at the bedside. "Diana gave her the will to live because she showed she cared for Joy. Diana's presence made Joy feel special. And Diana never lost contact. The following Christmas, Joy received a card from Diana wishing her well. That's the sort of person she was, always thinking of other people, putting ordinary people first, caring for them. That's why everyone was so distraught at her death."

In a similar story, Diana met Paul and Jo

Thompson during one of hundreds of private visits to the Pediatric Intensive Care Unit at St. Mary's Hospital in London. Their son Harry, only 12 months old, was suffering from a rare disease that destroys the lungs.

Jo explained, "Diana came to comfort us shortly after she heard it was Harry's first birthday. We were sitting by his cot praying he would recover when, to our surprise, Diana walked into the ward, came over to the bed and began to chat to us about Harry. She held his hand and talked as though she was one of the family. She was so sincere — you could tell she was genuine. She had a compassionate aura about her."

A month later, Harry's condition began to deteriorate and he was given only days to live. As Diana had requested, the doctors wrote a letter to her informing Diana that young Harry was at the point of death. An hour later, Diana had handwritten a note to Harry's parents expressing her concern and sympathy. She had immediately sent the letter by car to the hospital. Jo said later, "She had no need to write — no one knew about what was going on — and yet she took the trouble to do so."

Amazingly, within 24 hours after receiving Diana's letter, Harry began to improve. Jo said, "It is a miracle that Harry is still here. That's what the doctors say. They thought he only had days to live but somehow he pulled though. I just wish that Diana could see him now. Sometimes I really do believe that Diana was an angel of mercy."

Dr. Parviz Habibi, director of the Pediatric Intensive Care Unit, said, "Harry was just one example of Diana's caring nature. Once she had pledged her support to a patient, she did so in style. We knew she was a genuine and honest person — she proved it time and again. Harry's parents had gone through hell with worry and she gave them moral support when they so desperately needed it. That was why she was such a remarkable person."

However, there were very few people who realized the extraordinary toll those secret hospital visits took on Diana. Frequently, she would arrive back at Kensington Palace, walk up to her bedroom on the second floor, throw herself on her bed and lie there, face down, crying and distraught at the suffering of the children she had seen that day. She felt their pain and wretchedness and would frequently castigate herself for living such an indulgent life and having the nerve to complain about her situation. But throughout her visits, Diana would always be the smiling, upbeat, happy princess, though the distress she witnessed week in and week out drained her and left her physically exhausted.

An example of the pressure Diana was under

and the trauma of her marriage problems was illustrated in yet another secret initiative that Diana undertook when she was alerted that an 18-year-old girl, Louise Woolcock from Poulton-le-Fylde, Lancashire, was dying from terminal cancer.

Social worker Philip Woolcock told the story of the remarkable friendship that grew out of the relationship that Diana began with his daughter Louise in 1992: "Louise was looking forward to university when she was diagnosed as having a virulent form of cancer. My wife Judy and I made the decision to protect her from the knowledge that she was dying, trying instead to help her through a traumatic course of chemotherapy.

"But Louise was so wonderfully brave that she began raising money for a cancer charity to help others. Diana heard of her efforts and came to see her. That first meeting was magic. They had lunch together, talking for an hour and both giggling like schoolgirls. Louise was always incredibly loquacious and bubbly and I think Diana was moved because she felt Louise should have her whole life ahead of her."

At the end of that first meeting, Philip Woolcock asked Diana if she would open the local day hospice in honor of his daughter. Diana told him to write, but could promise nothing. Diana did eventually come to open the hospice but Louise had not come out of remission and was close to death.

Philip continued, "By any normal scale, Louise should not have been alive for that visit but the thought of meeting the princess again instilled in her a newfound strength and determination. Even though she was full of morphine, Louise forced herself into a wheelchair and out into the reception area. When Diana arrived she almost bounded up to Louise, hugging her and soon they were giggling and laughing as they had a year before. It was wonderful to see. But one week later Louise was dead."

Diana was informed of her death by the hospital and the Woolcocks received a letter of condolence from her. Shortly afterward, Diana phoned and asked if she could come and see them.

Diana arrived at their house at the appointed time. Philip told the story: "We spent quite a time just sitting and chatting. It was about this time that the newspapers were full of Diana's marriage problems and she looked pale and distraught. Her knuckles were white, her eyes full of tears.

"Eventually, I asked her how she was about everything and suddenly it all came spilling out ... about her marriage, her distress, her loneliness. 'I've had 11 years of this,' Diana said, 'and I'm getting out. I can't take anymore.'"

From 1992 until a few days before her death, Diana kept in touch with the Woolcocks, primarily through long phone calls. Judy recalls, "My son Sam had had his navel pierced and his hair bleached and I told Diana about it and she laughed, saying, 'Gosh, I don't know what my mother-in-law would do if William did that!'

"She also told me that she didn't know how she would cope with the situation when William found his first girlfriend. She said, 'I don't think there's anyone on the scene at the moment ... I hope!' "

During her last phone call to the Woolcocks in August 1997, Diana sounded bubbly and happy. Philip said, "She spent 15 minutes chatting away to us about everything — children, holidays, work. She sounded so happy and we both felt happy for her. When we woke on that Sunday morning and heard the news of her death, we were devastated, speechless. Now that we are over the pain of her death, we feel we were privileged to have known Diana so well — but we do miss her. I just want people to know what a wonderful difference Diana made to our lives and to countless others."

Diana relied on the teams of doctors, surgeons, consultants and nurses at various hospitals to keep her informed if there was a child whom they believed would benefit from one of her personal visits. And Diana never forgot that it was those teams who carried out the day-to-day work that really mattered and not a quick visit from her. She simply hoped that her visits might provide something memorable to cheer up a child after weeks and months of hospitalization. To Diana, it did not matter whether the child was black or white, rich or poor, British or foreign; only that there was a possibility that her presence might prove positive to the youngster.

Robert Creighton, chief executive of the Great Ormond Street Hospital, gave an example. "For 18 months we had cared for a poor little Bosnian girl, Irma, age 8, who had been seriously injured when a bomb exploded near her during the fighting in 1993. Irma was paralyzed from the head down and we tried to make her life easier. Diana came to visit her once or twice and she would sit and stroke her forehead and would encourage the little girl to smile, trying to give some encouragement to this child who, for so long, hovered between life and death. And then, on March 31, 1995, little Irma died and all of us who had fought long and hard to save her life were truly devastated. We felt we had failed her, all of us.

"We phoned Diana and told her of Irma's death and she asked me if I could gather the team who had looked after Irma throughout her long illness so that she could meet and chat to us. There was probably a core of about a dozen doctors and nurses who had been closely involved with Irma and Diana came, chatted to us all and thanked everyone of us for the effort and devotion that we had all put in for Irma. It was a sad, moving experience for all of us, including Diana, and I think that on that day there were tears in all our eyes, including Diana's. But the team really appreciated that Diana wanted to come and say 'thank you' to them for all the care and nursing of the little Bosnian girl that no one in England knew anything about.

"There were no cameras, no journalists present. There was only Diana and us. It was typical of her. She felt for people, understood them like no one ever had before. I often witnessed Diana meeting parents and sick children, and I must tell you it was always a remarkably moving experience. Both parents and children seemed to trust her instantly, to gravitate toward her as though they had known her for ages. Usually, in the hospitals, children take time to adapt to a stranger, but not to Diana. She had an instant rapport with them that was warm and natural, and children responded to her. It was wonderful to see. I can honestly say that Diana's presence will be impossible to replace. She was simply unique."

Diana also found great benefit in her hospital

visits. She confessed to Dr. Habibi, "It's not only one way. I believe that I gain from these visits, too. These visits to the children give me a warm feeling of well-being, that I'm giving something of myself to others far less fortunate than me. I know that I'm living a privileged life and I feel that visiting the sick and disadvantaged children is a personal duty that I have grown to love."

Later, Diana would tell her friend Sarah Ferguson, "I began these hospital visits after years of feeling sorry for myself, wallowing in my own misery because of what I believed was a pointless existence in a failed, loveless marriage. I believe that for some unknown reason I had an extraordinary capacity for unhappiness, which is why I wanted to encourage others to overcome their sadness. Fortunately, it seemed to work and that brought me great inner happiness.

"When I began visiting children in hospitals, it was a form of therapy for myself. And when I saw them suffering, often fighting for their very lives, it hit me hard and made me realize that my troubles were nothing compared to theirs. The more private hospital visits I made, the more I realized that my own unhappiness was of little or no consequence. It also stopped me returning to the dark days when I was unable to control my eating habits because I was so wrapped up in my own wretchedness.

Those poor children gave me a feeling that my life could be useful and I found the children responded to me no matter how ill they were. Finally, I was doing something positive and it made me feel a different person. I could hold my head up."

Diana also understood that she had a very important public role, getting people to dig deep into their pockets and contribute to worthy causes. She recognized the charities needed the money to carry on their wonderful work and Diana was of the mind that if her presence would give their coffers a boost, she was happy to take part. That was the reason she was only too happy to make high-profile visits to hospitals in front of ranks of photographers and television crews, but she didn't enjoy these occasions half as much as her private visits.

As a result, Diana came to wonder whether she might actually possess a form of healing power. This developed in her mind because some people came to believe that Diana enjoyed a form of saintliness and, as a result, she became only too happy to touch, hold or shake hands with people not only suffering from AIDS or leprosy but other ailments as well. So many matrons and doctors in hospital wards all over the world would tell Diana that her mere presence in a ward full of patients had a more beneficial effect on the patients than any amount of medicine. It is accepted that so much healing of many patients, particularly in Third World hospitals, takes place in the mind of the patient and Diana came to believe that perhaps she was actually capable of making people recover faster than if she had not visited them.

Her private secretary, Patrick Jephson, wrote in his autobiography, *"The idea that Diana had some kind of gift of healing remains very much an open question, of course. If she did possess such a gift, then it was completely unrefined, undisciplined and undirected. Had it been recognized and developed as the talent it sometimes seemed to be, I believe that her round of compassionate visiting would not have taken the toll it did on her emotional stamina. Sadly, the lack of any appropriate direction and discipline forfeited for her any chance to explore or use a gift for which she seemed otherwise so eminently qualified. After all, as many believe, it is a gift which requires a level of personal spiritual development that I do not think she would ever have claimed to have reached."*

Jephson, who studied Diana closely for nearly a decade, noticed that the more charity work, both private and public, that Diana undertook, the more desperate Diana became for personal fulfillment. He wrote in his book: *"However cynical, manipulative or self-indulgent her motives might sometimes have been for doing some of the good things for which she received such credit, in the act of doing them there was no cynicism at all ... People who had no knowledge of her other than as recipients of her concern or gratitude were in no doubt about what they felt she gave to them. It is the same quality we can see now, years later, in contemporary news photographs of the princess doing her routine work of bringing hope and comfort to people in need. It was given and received at a level beyond speech and I do not think it can ever be explained properly in simply human terms.*

"In my time with her, however, she never found the faith that might have given her strength in moments of real doubt and loneliness. It was probably the only way in which she could have gained genuine satisfaction and happiness from the good that was so often laid at her door ... In the absence of a solid faith that could comfort her, she took refuge in impulsive bouts of mysticism and psychology. Without a reliable framework of knowledge and support, or wise guidance she was prepared to trust, these, too, were bound to fail her."

But in the last few years of Diana's life, the public image that the press had created for her — a cross between Mother Teresa and a supermodel — faded as Diana preferred to direct her energies toward her secret, more private visits to young hospital patients. She preferred that work — she was tired of the cameras and TV crews. She had also become angry and upset at the cruel sniping by some in the media who had come to the conclusion, incorrectly as it happened, that Diana only undertook her hospital visits for the publicity it gave her.

When Diana was invited to become involved in high-profile matters of major international importance, such as the campaign to rid the world of antipersonnel mines, she was only too happy to help. The new Diana wanted to become more involved in humanitarian issues on an international level. AP mines was the first cause for which she earned praise for her contributions and, at the time of her death, she was planning her next major international campaign, fighting for the rights of refugees.

Chapter 9

Philip, the Bully Prince

iana really did believe that she had found her "handsome prince" when Prince Charles started treating her as a serious girlfriend rather than just another young, blond, long-legged girl joining the list of young women with whom he had enjoyed dalliances, affairs, long-term relationships or one-night stands. In a matter of months, Charles told Diana that he was infatuated by her and wanted her to become his one-and-only girlfriend. It seems they first made love on the day Charles turned 32, when he invited her to celebrate with him alone at a small house on the Sandringham estate in Norfolk, only a stone's throw from her family home.

The dream, however, would deteriorate into a nightmare within a matter of months. The final details of the fabulous, historic wedding day in the most glittering royal marriage for a generation had not even been confirmed before Diana started to have second thoughts. Despite heroic efforts on her behalf, countless intimate conversations with her sisters and girlfriends and frequent tears, Diana stood at the altar at St. Paul's Cathedral declaring her marriage vows to the world, knowing in her heart that she was making the most terrible mistake.

The marriage never recovered from that wretched beginning. Diana struggled to come to terms with her new life as the Princess of Wales. Unfortunately, Diana's character and temperament were of little help to her — she was an incredibly shy, modest and private young woman who had always shunned the limelight.

And yet this was the woman whom her father-in-law, Prince Philip, the Duke of Edinburgh and the husband of Queen Elizabeth II would call a "harlot" and a "trollop" in letters he wrote to her after the marriage broke down. These letters were seen by Simone Simmons, a friend and confidant of Diana's, whom she knew in the 1990s.

Shortly after this shocking revelation was printed in newspapers in 2002, Philip issued a statement in which he denied ever using such terms in letters to Diana, claiming the letters were friendly attempts to resolve a number of family issues. The statement added, "He regards the suggestion that he used such derogatory terms as a gross misrepresentation of his relations with his daughter-in-law and hurtful to his grandsons." Philip claimed that far from signing these letters simply "Philip," which Ms. Simmons read in the letters Diana showed her, Philip allegedly signed them, "With love from Pa." However, he refused to reveal the contents of the letters to verify his denial.

It was Philip who, by accident, began the series of events that ended with Diana's butler Paul Burrell appearing in court on charges of stealing 310 items that had belonged to Diana following her death. Philip was concerned that his letters to Diana might be made public and asked MI5 to visit Burrell at his home to ask if he had any knowledge as to the whereabouts of letters Prince Philip had written to his daughter-in-law. Under questioning during MI5's visit, Burrell admitted taking hundreds of items that had belonged to Diana but claimed in court that he only took them to "look after them for William and Harry." Skeptics asked why should Philip go to such lengths to retrieve those letters if they were not disparaging when the world knew that Diana never liked her father-in-law?

If Prince Philip's claim of writing warm and

loving letters to Diana is accurate, it seems odd that Diana should have for years felt such alienation, aversion and hostility toward Philip that she usually referred to him as "Hitler." Diana must have felt some serious antipathy toward her father-in-law — she never had such an implacable loathing for any other member of the royal family. Unlike Charles, Prince Andrew or Prince Edward, who all experienced their father's domineering character as well as the lash of his tongue, Prince Philip's hostile criticism and occasional reprimands failed to upset Diana. One reason was that Diana knew she held the upper hand with Philip. As her marriage crumbled, Diana felt that her father-in-law was becoming rather overattentive and overfamiliar toward her. At first, Diana wondered why Philip had become more pleasant when he was with her; cracking jokes, making the odd remark, giving compliments and smiling more than he had before. This made Diana feel uneasy and a little later she found her father-in-law's attention so disconcerting she became nauseous whenever he came too close.

In an effort to put an end to his unwelcome attention, Diana began dropping hints, keeping her distance from him at family gatherings and making sure that she was never alone with him. She made it obvious that she no longer wanted his close attention, leaving Philip in little doubt that his interest was not reciprocated and was certainly not welcome.

It seems extraordinary that Prince Philip, a serial adulterer throughout his married life, could have had the audacity and hubris to suggest in a personal and private letter to Diana that she was prostituting herself by dating a number of men after her marriage to Prince Charles was legally over.

Ironically, it was Earl Mountbatten, Prince Philip's uncle, the man who urged his nephew to date and propose marriage to the young, innocent Princess Elizabeth at the end of World War II, who came to realize that Philip was little more than a selfish cad and a physical and moral bully.

Philip's disgraceful treatment of his wife and his sons over a period of decades would have remained secret but for Earl Mountbatten. He told John Barratt, his faithful private secretary for some 20 years, to make sure that before he died he had to let the nation know what a dreadful husband and father Philip had been to Elizabeth and to their three sons, Charles, Andrew and Edward. Some years later, I was introduced to John Barratt who urged me to help carry out the wishes of Earl Mountbatten and inform the world of the true facts of Philip's relationships with

Elizabeth and their sons. Over a period of several months I met with Barratt and he briefed me on the family secrets Mountbatten had entrusted to him.

I was told of the way in which Prince Philip had treated Elizabeth from the day she became queen, some five years after their wedding. Until then, Philip enjoyed his life in the Royal Navy, advancing up the promotion ladder, showing his determination to succeed — even if it meant driving his naval ratings beyond their capabilities. But as soon as Elizabeth became queen, he was forever doomed to be nothing but her shadow, forced to walk two paces behind her, stand whenever she entered the room and treat her in public as the monarch and not as his wife. He couldn't take it.

So, in private, the bullying began. At first, Philip was simply ordering his wife about when they were off-duty at home or staying with friends or relations — telling her what to do, what to wear, what to eat, what to drink, when to go to bed, interrupting her conversations, and ridiculing her arguments or discussions with others.

Those who witnessed such scenes would be deeply embarrassed, but Philip took delight in his behavior. When friends and relations were present they saw that though Elizabeth might be the queen, he was "the boss," and she had to obey his orders or face the consequences of looking foolish. Mountbatten would tell John Barratt: "It is pathetic behavior, but then I have come to realize that Philip is nothing more than a bully."

Charles was, perhaps, Philip's favorite to bully. From the moment of Charles' birth in 1948, Philip was demoted to a far lesser role in royal circles, since there was an heir to the throne to take precedence. Philip couldn't handle his inferior status, so he began to take out his frustrations on his young son, humiliating him, deflating his confidence, making him feel small, silly and incompetent — all designed to crush the young lad's confidence. And from age 4, Philip began the beatings, using slippers and canes, for the most trivial offenses.

Throughout his early life, Charles tried everything to please his father, but praise was rare. Criticism, fault-finding and condemnation were Philip's principal weapons in bringing up his son and, whether by design or not, they succeeded in reducing Charles' confidence to near zero. John Barratt commented, "It was fortunate for Charles that he found in Lord Mountbatten another father figure to replace the bully that was his father. Mountbatten knew how Philip treated Charles and he provided a home and an environment where Charles could find friendship, security, encouragement and some paternal love."

Barratt also described Philip's nefarious and disreputable life outside the marriage. He told me of the Thursday Club, officially little more than a gentlemen's lunch club, where a number of wealthy, influential, aristocrats and friends — including Philip — met in London's Soho to eat, drink and chat. But, unknown to Elizabeth and the rest of the world, the Thursday Club would sometimes adjourn to an apartment after an afternoon of drinking, where the fun would begin. They were joined by seven or eight young women and all would drink, listen to music and play card games that frequently ended with bizarre sex games, often involving sadomasochism and sometimes group sex. Most of the card games would result in two or more of the men selecting women to take off to a bedroom for half an hour or so.

Prince Philip can also attribute his love of polo to his womanizing ways. A keen polo player for some 20 years, the sport brought him into contact with many beautiful women, both married and single. As a result, his name became linked with numerous society women. A wealthy patron of a number of polo teams during those years recalled, "Philip attracted and was attracted by a number of polo wives. How many I don't know, but at least a dozen or more during those 20 years. It was a well-known fact. I would watch him chatting to them after play, perhaps over champagne or a beer. He had them eating out of his hand. They were attracted to the macho image of the game and Philip was always a strikingly handsome man, especially in his polo gear. These matters were well known but to his credit, he was most discreet and, it must be said, the women behaved impeccably, never kissing and telling."

Philip's favorite polo tournaments, however, did not take place in Britain, but in France. They were held each year at St. Memse near Orly Airport, usually at the end of May. The tournaments took place in a stunning chateau owned by Robert de Balkany, a millionaire Rumanian of humble origins who, after a Yale education, made a fortune from real estate. Once married to Maria Gabriello, daughter of Italy's ex-King Umberto, Robert de Balkany had built a great polo arena on the estate with stabling for 50 ponies and accommodation for some 30 grooms.

A multimillionaire who attended several of these annual tournaments at St. Memse said: "Four or five teams and their patrons would be invited for the weekend and I saw Prince Philip there on several occasions. For those players not bringing a lady with them, no one seemed to bring their wives, there were a number of very attractive young women imported for the weekend. I cannot recall Philip ever bringing a young lady and, certainly, the queen never accompanied him. He would just take potluck with one or more of the imported young women."

In his bid to enjoy life with as little risk of discovery as possible, Philip sought to be invited overseas, where he could behave with more freedom and indulge in more overt sexual adventures. One of his favorite annual jaunts was to the famous Bohemian Grove in the California redwoods, where a thousand or more VIPs of America's male power elite — the decision-makers and opinion-molders of the Western world — would meet in mid-July to relax, attend lectures and debates and enjoy themselves for three weeks. No women were permitted entry to the 2,700-acre grove on the banks of the Russian River during those three weeks. But many members would "jump the river" and quietly leave their sacred enclave in favor of a trek to nearby Guerneville, where a number of young women would entertain the renegades.

Barratt revealed another overseas venue frequented by both Mountbatten and Philip on occasions. "Occasionally, I went to this club in Nassau in the Bahamas with Mountbatten. He liked to go and let his hair down. He rather enjoyed the raunchy atmosphere. So did Philip. It was a place for wealthy as well as famous people, where everyone was discreet. One had to be a member or an invited guest. In reality, it was a high-class dive with lots of heavy drinking, drugs and, of course, high-class whores. The girls waiting for wealthy clients were all very good-looking, mostly white but there were some coffee-colored girls as well."

Prince Philip also enjoyed affairs with some high-profile women like the beautiful actress Merle Oberon. Their affair went on for a number of years. Philip fell for Merle in a big way and considered her one of the most beautiful women he ever met. Philip even managed to enjoy a two-week holiday with Merle at her beautiful Acapulco home. Without her, Philip enjoyed a trip through South America, visiting more than a dozen countries, officially sanctioned to "stimulate British commercial relations." Philip managed to take part in a number of polo matches and most evenings he was entertained at parties attended by beautiful women. During the Argentine part of the trip, Philip spent three days with the beautiful, stylish widow Malena Blaquier, the social megastar of Buenos Aires who enjoyed an outrageous reputation.

After this historic trip, a British newspaper editorial wrote of Philip, "His enemies say he is arrogant, overbearing and has an exaggerated idea of his role in the monarchy. His friends describe him as loyal, highly intelligent, hardworking, with a deep desire to do the job to the very best of his ability. His friends say he has traveled the world showing the flag. His enemies regard these trips as junkets, highly relished by someone they still regard as an extravagant playboy."

One point that can be made in Philip's defense is that for the most part he has tried to be discreet, not wishing to embarrass the queen in any way, though the risks he sometimes took were foolish. Despite Philip's vigilant awareness of the need for prudent behavior, he has nevertheless been involved with a succession of married women throughout his life.

Perhaps Philip's most scandalous affair and the best-kept secret in the hearts of most members of the royal family was his 20-year long adulterous affair with the queen's cousin, the lovely Princess Alexandra of Kent. From the queen's standpoint it was also his most insulting liaison. With her warm, enchanting smile and fun-loving personality, Princess Alexandra is perhaps the most natural of all the royals and undoubtedly one of the nation's favorites.

The affair began sometime in the 1950s, when Alexandra was in her 20s and Philip in his late 30s. A retainer, who worked for the royal family for a generation, said, "You could set your watch on a Thursday afternoon because at 2:30 p.m. precisely, Princess Alexandra would arrive at the palace in her car for her weekly swim with Prince Philip. The pool was always reserved for Philip at that time every Thursday afternoon and the entrance to the pool was locked whenever they were in there together. No one else was permitted entry until 3:30 p.m."

Mountbatten knew what was going on. He wrote to Philip advising, "I do hope you will be more discreet in your relationship with Alexandra ... If news of this affair should enter the public domain you must realize the reflection this would have on the whole family and especially on Lilibet."

It does seem extraordinary that Prince Philip should have led such a licentious life and yet had the audacity to describe Diana as a harlot. Diana's affairs were, for the most part, genuine attempts to chase the rainbow, simply searching for the man of her dreams. Before she married Charles the young Diana believed she met the man with whom she would spend the rest of her life — but it was not to be.

After the collapse of her marriage, Diana's love life would follow a remarkably topsy-turvy pattern where she would fall in and out of love with at least half a dozen men of different backgrounds, different religions, diverse characters, personalities and appearances and she would sometimes find herself in love with different men at the same time! Far from being in love only with Hewitt, the art expert Oliver Hoare and the heart surgeon Hasnat Khan, the more one examines Diana's love affairs during the last 15 years of her life the more extraordinary and complicated they become. Indeed, in some respects it seems Diana had a penchant for falling in and out of love as frequently as many women change their hairstyles.

Chapter 10

Hewitt

In fact, it was an accident of fate when Diana first met James Hewitt. At first, she saw him as a young man who could entertain her, someone with whom she could escape the confines of Kensington Palace and the royal family with their retinue of advisers and servants. Hewitt was a breath of fresh air in the stuffy royal environment. Over time, Diana found Hewitt as someone to whom she could talk, confide in and later he became her shoulder to cry on, someone in whom she could confide her fears and her worries. Within months, Diana came to rely on Hewitt as a confidant and close friend.

In his autobiography, Hewitt wrote: *"I was genuinely sorry for her, for both of them. Their marriage was going through a bad patch. I always thought they made a good couple and I didn't really want to hear otherwise. But sometimes she could hardly bring herself to refer to her husband by name."*

Hewitt is not a bad man, as the newspapers claimed – calling him evil — but he is weak and suffers from a false understanding of his own character. Within a matter of months of meeting Diana, the irrepressible Hewitt admitted that he was becoming obsessed with Diana. He wrote: *"I lived from week to week. I couldn't wait to see her again. It was just a complete joy ... And from her phone calls and her conversation she gave every indication of just wanting to be with me."*

It was totally understandable that their relationship would become a full-blown affair — Diana desperately needed someone to depend on and to provide a respite from her prison life at Kensington Palace, an escape from the husband she no longer loved and no longer respected.

The affair gave Diana an opportunity to unload all her emotional baggage. Hewitt wrote, *"Diana was emotionally fragile ... She was a woman deeply damaged by rejection. Whether it was true or not, she saw herself as being wholly alone in a hostile world, with no one to turn to share her problems with or give her guidance."*

But Diana was to face rejection yet again when Hewitt's regiment was posted to Germany. Not until almost the last day did Hewitt tell Diana that he was leaving England and, more importantly, leaving her for a two-year tour of duty. She wasn't at all pleased. In his book, Hewitt related how resentful and bitter Diana became, telling him, *"You promised you'd always be here for me and now you've broken that promise."*

Hewitt left for Germany and did not hear another word from Diana for three months. Hewitt and his regiment were transferred to the Gulf in late 1991 to form The Life Guards Squadron part of the 4th Armoured Brigade. Diana reeled at the danger facing her former lover, the man whom she believed was the father of her beloved young Harry, and she followed the war with as much enthusiasm and nervousness as any woman with a loved one in that war. She lit candles for Hewitt and wrote many letters.

One letter from Diana to Hewitt contained the following, *"God the worry is simply dreadful — bordering on agony for you all. I do hope that you're home soon ... I think of you constantly and I've got the youngest son (Harry) doing the same now and every tank on the news contains you as far as he's concerned."*

But Diana's relationship with Hewitt had already reached the end of the line and, in his book, Hewitt hardly makes mention as to how and why the affair broke down. Little did Hewitt

know, however, that Diana had not been faithful
to him for a good number of years. In turn, Hewitt
betrayed Diana. He boasted to journalists and the
few remaining friends of Diana's sexual secrets,
telling of her demands, sexual appetite, her sex
life with Charles and of her intense pleasure when
making love to Hewitt. It was sickening, stomach-
churning stuff and the mark of an old-fashioned
English "bounder," a man guilty of ungentlemanly
behavior, discussing intimate details of a sexual
relationship. The tabloid press described him
variously as "vermin" and a "cad."

There were, in fact, two separate love affairs
that Diana enjoyed with Hewitt. The first was
fierce, passionate and furtive; the second beginning some 12 months after Harry's arrival, was
more open and relaxed. At first, Diana wanted the
excitement of an illicit extramarital relationship
and Hewitt provided the heights of ecstasy which
she craved, while Hewitt simply loved the fact
that Diana wanted him. But during her second
relationship with Hewitt, the more world-wise
Diana happily accepted that Hewitt enjoyed bed-
ding other women and she would cross-examine
him about them, indulging her prurient interest,
asking details of the lovemaking, the sexual preferences and the reactions of the other women.

In some ways, it was most fortunate that the

dashing, flirtatious, confident Hewitt appeared on the scene at that moment in 1983, when Diana was desperate to meet people outside the cloistered confines of Kensington Palace. Hewitt's offer to teach her to ride was a great opportunity to escape from her gilded prison. It was unfortunate, however, that Diana was still a naive, almost innocent, young woman who had never practiced birth control and had never needed to. Except for those few months of love with Charles at the time of their engagement, Diana had never really enjoyed a full-blooded, passionate relationship with any man. But Hewitt changed all that and Diana reveled in the passion, the sexual craving, the desire and the all-consuming lust she had never before experienced. She felt deep physical attraction for this man who took her to heights she never before experienced. In those first few years with Hewitt, Diana believed that she had met the man with whom she wanted to spend the rest of her life, especially after Harry arrived.

It was after the birth of Harry in September 1984 that Hewitt gave Diana his signet ring to place in safekeeping for the day when Harry reached his 18th birthday. At the time, both he and Diana believed they were destined one day to live openly together and maybe even marry.

Diana was not absolutely certain that Harry

was Hewitt's child, but she was fairly confident that he was. At one stage she toyed with the idea of a DNA check, but decided against it. She didn't want to remove all doubt, preferring to live with the faint possibility that Harry might, in fact, be Charles' son.

When Diana discovered that she was pregnant with Harry, she decided that she had to cool her relationship with Hewitt. Although he did occasionally visit her at Kensington Palace, their trysts were put on hold. Diana was scared that someone might discover that she was having an adulterous affair and because she had convinced herself that Charles had rekindled his interest in Camilla Parker Bowles, she was keen not to be seen as the pot calling the kettle black.

Diana confessed some two years after their first meeting that although she had, at first, loved that she and Hewitt would drive down to Devon to their love nest — his mother's small, cramped cottage in the quiet of the Devon countryside — she had come to realize that she could never live in such a place or in such surroundings. She had been brought up in her father's ancestral home in Norfolk, a grand country mansion, and, except for a brief time spent in her London apartment with three other girls, her only other home had been a royal palace. She realized all too soon that Hewitt's parents had very little money, no wealthy family background and that he was only a young officer who couldn't even afford to dress himself on his army pay!

Diana said during one of her breakups with Hewitt, "I've spent a fortune buying that man all the clothes he owns." And, according to her bodyguard of 10 years, Police Inspector Ken Wharfe, she also generously gave Hewitt $24,000 in cash for a sports car. Diana also gave him a tie-pin with a fox's head in diamonds, a gold fob watch with the words *"I will love you always"* inscribed on it, as well as cuff links and a gold cross that bore the inscription, *"I shall love you forever."*

Diana enjoyed being generous to Hewitt and looking after his every need, but in her heart she knew she could never settle down with a man who could not keep her in the style to which she had become accustomed. In a matter of a year or so after her wedding, Diana had taken to the high life and found she really enjoyed it. She adored designer clothes, fabulous jewelry, servants at her beck and call and a palace to live in.

When Inspector Wharfe became one of Diana's police bodyguards in 1986, he was briefed by senior officers about her relationship with Captain James Hewitt. He was also informed that Diana had become involved with Hewitt because "though no one had confirmed the relationship,

Diana knew in her heart that Charles was seeing Camilla Parker Bowles."

Diana's announcement that she was pregnant for the second time surprised Charles and he wondered whether he or his wife's lover was the father. Apparently, Diana said nothing that could shed light on the baby's paternity and Charles discussed the matter with Camilla. She advised that Charles had no option but to assume that he was the father of the unborn child and Charles vowed to accept the baby as his own and treat the child in exactly the same way as if he was the father. To his credit, Charles has always done so.

As a result, Charles turned more and more to Camilla for advice when he was in the most dreadful quandary. He profoundly believed his mother would never agree to a separation or a divorce and, for the sake of the two children, he had no wish to separate from Diana and cause the children heartache and pain. He knew that any separation or divorce might have the most disastrous effect on the monarchy, on the royal family and the nation. Charles had no wish to hurl the country into a crisis similar to that caused by his uncle, King Edward VIII, when in 1937 he chose to marry the love of his life, the American divorcée Mrs. Wallis Simpson, and abdicate the throne of England, rather than give up the woman he loved.

By the mid-1980s, Charles reached the conclusion that there was little chance that he could patch up the marriage — Diana's actions and words left him no doubt that she wanted nothing whatsoever to do with him or the royal family. He made the decision to move to Highgrove on a more or less permanent basis while Diana and the children lived at Kensington Palace. As a result of that move, Charles began seeing Camilla on a daily basis.

This arrangement is verified by Hewitt himself, who commented in his book that it was during the mid-1980s that Camilla came more onto the scene. The two had always got along well together, enjoying the country life of horses, hunting, shooting and dogs, listening to opera and classical music and reading. Charles had always found Camilla's intelligence, as well as her sense of humor, remarkably refreshing. Camilla told Charles that her marriage to Brigadier Andrew Parker Bowles, one of Charles' polo pals, was nearing the end of its natural life and eventually Charles and Camilla became lovers.

Andrew Parker Bowles was a man I came to know during his time serving as aide-de-camp to Lord Soames during the 1979 transfer of power in Rhodesia from white minority to black majority rule. During his six-month stint in Rhodesia, I noticed that Andrew seemed to lead a bachelor-style life and did not appear to be pining for his wife back in Britain. He thoroughly enjoyed dinner parties, dances, cocktail parties and was a most sociable member of the Soames set in Rhodesia, nearly always accompanied by a young woman. The Parker Bowles' separation and eventual divorce in January 1995 was amicable on both sides and they agreed the marriage had run its course.

The facts reveal, however, that Diana's claims that Charles had been in love with Camilla throughout his adult life, that he was still madly in love with her at the time of their marriage, that he had kept in contact with her while on honeymoon and that he had, in effect, ditched Diana as soon as William was born simply are not true. But the arrival of James Hewitt and then young Harry put Diana in a most difficult situation because she feared that she would be seen as the guilty party — the adulteress, the homewrecker. This weighed heavily on Diana's mind. She couldn't face the prospect of the nation, who now adored her, turning against her in condemnation of her philandering so soon after the fairytale wedding. She also suffered from a gut-wrenching feeling of guilt that she had difficulty coping with.

These were the real reasons why Diana's health deteriorated so rapidly before Harry was born and continued to decline afterward. These were the reasons she became bulimic and suffered anorexia. And it wasn't only physical. Mentally, as her lack of educational qualifications illustrates, the young Diana was not a strong woman and she simply could not cope with the trauma going on in her personal life as well as the fear that at any time her most intimate secret — adultery — might be splashed over the front pages of every newspaper in Britain. Those fears tore her apart and she suffered dreadfully.

These thoughts never left her mind and, in some desperation, she decided to banish Hewitt from Kensington Palace, at least for a while, even though she believed she was in love with him. Hewitt agreed to her plan and, although he occasionally visited her at Kensington Palace, his visits were few and far between and he never stayed overnight. She would phone Hewitt and they would spend hours talking, but their distance during these crucial months of pregnancy and afterward made her depressed and miserable.

Some 12 months after Harry's birth, Diana decided that it would be safe to renew her relationship with Hewitt. It seemed that no paparazzi had seen them together, there were no incriminating photographs and no one had heard any rumors of their relationship. She felt there was no reason why they should not rekindle their wonderful weekends together. Diana, however, did not want to take too many risks and Hewitt, once again, began visiting Diana at Kensington Palace, usually arriving for dinner and disappearing sometime in the early hours of the morning.

Their relationship continued for some years and Diana always hoped at the back of her mind that there was a possibility that the man she believed was Harry's father might be the man she would eventually settle down with and, one day, marry.

The affair continued off and on until after the Gulf War of January 1991. It was during that war, where Hewitt served as commander of a tank squadron, that Diana became once again emotionally involved with Hewitt because she feared there was a real possibility that the man who was Harry's father might be killed in action. Hewitt served with distinction during that short, sharp war in the deserts of Kuwait and Iraq.

For Hewitt, that war will always serve as a memory of the support he received from Diana. She wrote to him frequently, mailed him presents and Hewitt would sometimes phone her from the desert, one time stupidly borrowing the phone from a tabloid journalist who knew exactly who he was calling. Diana would sign her love letters "Julia," and the name on the back of the envelope — which was required by the army — was Evelyn Dagley, Diana's personal dresser.

However, there was little or no passion or declarations of everlasting love in those letters she sent to the Gulf. The letters appeared to reveal a new side to Diana's character, showing how caring and supportive she could be in one-to-one relationships. She wanted Hewitt to understand that there was at least one person back home in Britain who was thinking of him in his hour of danger. Despite that, most of the letters were simply friendly, chatty, sometimes even jokey and flippant. Diana would tease Hewitt, often with obvious sexual connotations and references, asking him, for example, how many women he had laid since arriving in the Gulf, adding "all chicks look good with a tan." She also asked about Hewitt's personal well-being writing, "I'm glad to hear about my friend, let's hope he's OK" (a reference to Hewitt's penis).

Diana would send Hewitt top-shelf sex magazines and would lovingly add, "Take enormous care, I think of you a great deal and long for you to return. F***ing practice really needed."

At the same time, back in London, Diana was also enjoying the sexual attentions of other men, but it seems that she didn't want Hewitt to know. The new, adventurous, sexually confident Diana had become increasingly restless for new male companions and she would take great delight in attracting, seducing, enjoying and loving a number of other handsome men.

Chapter 11

Power and Glory

*P*rincess Diana made one of the most important decisions of her life some months before Prime Minister John Major officially announced her separation from Prince Charles in December 1992. She determined that she would branch out on her own and decide her own fate independent of Prince Charles and the rest of the royal family. She reached that conclusion as a result of the tremendous upsurge of love and affection toward her following the revelations in *Diana: Her True Story* portraying her life as so miserable and unbearable that she had resorted to numerous suicide attempts.

The tide of public opinion was flowing strongly in her favor for some years and the book cemented the bond between Diana and the great mass of the British public, particularly among women with young families. They had seen what a loving, good mother she had proved to be to Wills and Harry, and they knew that being married to a man who kept a mistress caused stress and despair, triggering other health problems like bulimia and anorexia. Diana's star burned brightly while Charles' reputation plummeted, almost overnight.

Diana would cement her relationship with the ordinary moms and dads of Britain by showing that she was one of them, taking Wills and Harry to public amusement parks, where newspaper photographers would be waiting to snap away. It was, however, no accident that the photographers were on hand. Diana, pretending to be a palace maid, phoned them beforehand, tipping them off about the next day's visit. In these theme parks, Diana would enjoy some of the rides with her lads, putting on a wonderful display of unstuffy modern motherhood so very different from the traditional ways royals were expected to rear their children. The nation loved it. In 1993, Diana went further, taking Wills and Harry on a holiday to Disney World in Florida. They loved it.

There was, however, a perceived negative element to such ordinary family entertainment. Patrick Jephson, her secretary, would write, "Such actions however also reinforced the contempt in which she was held by many of those who would never have dreamt of setting foot in such a place." To her eternal credit, Diana didn't care a damn what those "stuck-up old fossils" — the palace courtiers — thought.

Such excursions to amusement parks were signs that Diana was indeed no empty-headed numb-skull, but someone with a carefully thought-out strategy. Having secured her base at home, Diana could now target her true ambition — to capture the hearts and minds of people across the world so that she would be seen as the new embodiment of the British crown, at the same time casting Prince Charles and the queen into the shadows.

The queen finally agreed that Diana could conduct her first solo overseas visit in September 1991 and Diana was thrilled. A royal tour to Pakistan had been planned for some years, but members of the royal family had not been keen to undertake such a trip because some members of the Pakistani political elite still remembered the days of the Raj, when Britain ruled the entire subconti-nent. That fear didn't worry Diana one bit. She was different from any other member of the royal family. She had no historical political baggage to consider and she was confident that she would be quite capable of stepping into the queen's shoes.

She had been given the golden opportunity to prove herself and she was determined to show the doubters in the British Foreign Office that she was not only a capable ambassador for Britain, but someone who would show the world that the royal family had changed and that she embodied that new change. Now she faced her moment of truth.

Diana knew that if she failed, she would never again be permitted to travel overseas alone as the queen's ambassador. But if the tour was a success, her future role as a representative of the royal family was bright, indeed. She was playing for high stakes.

Back home in Britain, even Diana's private secretary and principal adviser, Patrick Jephson, recorded, "Opinion on the visit on the royal home front was at least neutral, if, I felt, rather watchful. Not too many tears would be shed if this groundbreaking solo tour disappeared in the inside pages of the tabloids."

In fact, Diana's first solo foreign tour was a triumph, far surpassing the critics who believed that she wasn't "royal enough" to carry out such a visit without the odd diplomatic gaffe or two. Her groundbreaking overseas visit even surprised the pro-Diana tabloid editors back home in London. The tour was splashed over the front pages of both the tabloids and even the skeptical broadsheets. Finally, after 10 years as a member of the royal family, she had earned her place.

In *Shadows of a Princess*, Jephson's account of life as Diana's private secretary, he noted after Diana's speech at the Pakistan prime minister's dinner, *"The princess proposed a toast and made a speech ... with an assurance that would have brought sorrow to all — and there were not a few — who would have liked her to be portrayed on her solo mission as an empty-headed lightweight, more accustomed to pop concerts and clothes shops than the volatile politics of the subcontinent."*

Diana returned in a blaze of glory and secretly wondered if she would represent the queen on future foreign tours. Diana knew that one day the queen would be forced to permit Charles a divorce, but right now she was enjoying living in the limelight, reveling in the escalating adoration of the nation. Whenever the media examined any aspect of her life, the verdict was always high praise whether it was her lifestyle, her fashion sense, her fitness, her beauty, her charitable work or the obvious love she showered on her two boys.

Diana did, however, have one frightening concern. She knew that one day the question that she so feared would be raised. As young Harry grew older and became a teenager and then an adult, there was every probability that he would look more and more like James Hewitt, the man she believed was his real father.

She believed she was living on borrowed time. She was certain that the queen and the entire royal family had been led to believe that Harry was not Charles' son, but she was keeping her fingers crossed that they would never want that fact revealed for fear of the damage that might cause to the House of Windsor. Diana understood she was conducting a high-risk strategy but rather enjoyed being able to live an entirely free life, taking as many lovers as she wished, while still being legally married to Charles. She was fully aware that the queen and the Queen Mother were adamantly opposed to divorce — particularly in their own family. She rather hoped that she would be permitted to continue with her married status as long as she kept her nose clean, didn't flaunt her lovers before the general public and didn't embarrass the royal family. Diana reasoned that the royal family had more reason to let the status quo continue rather than push for a divorce and cut her off, permitting her to pursue a life they could not control.

The queen and the Queen Mother realized Diana's power and it worried them. Their earlier instinct was to force through a divorce and rid themselves of Diana, but that moment had now past. They knew that if they forced a divorce at this time there was a real possibility that the monarchy itself might be put in peril and the deep-seated cause to which they had both dedicated their lives — the preservation of the House of Windsor — would be in jeopardy. They couldn't take that risk, so they decided to wait and see.

The "War of the Wales'" continued in print. The media were constantly on the watch to report any problems or difficulties between Charles and Diana. My book, *Diana: A Princess and Her Troubled Marriage* and *Diana: Her True Story* had both been avidly read and, it seemed, the entire nation was now riveted into this classic royal soap opera unfolding before their very eyes in the national press. The vast majority of the ordinary British people took Diana's side while the traditionalists, the monarchists, the Establishment and the wealthy classes supported Charles and the monarchy.

Throughout the 10 years of their separate lives within their marriage — 1982 to 1992 — many attempts were made to repair their relationship but all came to naught. Charles believed that Diana showed so much ill-temper and spite toward him that he could never forgive her. Charles could also never forgive that Diana had gone out of her way to lie to the world that it was he who had quit the marriage bed for another woman when, in fact, both he and she knew that she had been the one who fled into the arms of James Hewitt two years before he and Camilla had made the decision to become lovers.

Charles could not comprehend why Diana had become so vitriolic toward him, seemingly more so since they had been living separate lives. Charles never understood why Diana, who had so obviously loved him in their premarriage days, had so completely turned against him — venting her rage, blighting his reputation and insulting him in front of friends, relatives and even servants.

One such occasion was the death of her beloved father, Earl Spencer, in March 1992, while Diana and Charles were enjoying a skiing holiday together in Austria. On that ski trip, however, there wasn't that much togetherness. They resided in separate hotel suites, dined separately and skied on different mountains. They were rarely seen together throughout that holiday. When her bodyguard broke the news to Diana of her father's death, anticipated since he had been in ill health for quite some time, Inspector Wharfe reported that she broke down in a state of "terrible distress." She told him that she wanted to return to her dead father and the Spencer family — without Prince Charles at her side.

He quoted Diana as saying, *"I mean it Ken. I don't want him with me. He doesn't love me — he loves that woman. Why should I save his face? Why the bloody hell should I? It's my father who's gone. It's a bit bloody late for Charles to start playing the caring husband, don't you think?"*

Charles had always been his own worst enemy and was hopeless in such a situation. He had little idea how to comfort women in distress and virtually no idea how to humor, charm or cajole them. He was too gauche, too artless. Throughout his life, Charles had been in the company of only boys and men, from school to the armed services. He even felt awkward talking to women, even his mother or his sister Anne. And when Diana made it plain that her love for him was fading, he did little to persuade her otherwise. He simply had no idea what to say, what to do or how to act. So he froze her out, turned his back and walked away.

In private, Diana retaliated by freezing him out of her life. She was happy when Charles moved to Highgrove in the mid-1980s, leaving her alone at Kensington Palace with the boys. She preferred to be left alone to carry on her own life in her own way and let Charles carry out his royal duties without her. She simply wished to turn her back on the entire Windsor family.

Occasionally, Diana felt guilty for what she had done to blacken Charles' name in her bid to conceal the reasons for her own adultery, but she had no wish for a divorce. She had grown up in a family where her parents' acrimonious divorce had cast a blight on her life and the lives of her siblings. She hated the very idea of divorce because of the effect it had on children. Indeed, Relate, a British charity of which she was patron, studied the effects of broken marriages on children and she recognized it could be catastrophic for them. On a number of occasions, Diana would sit in during interviews when young women would pour out their problems to trained counselors who would offer advice. And, time and again, Diana would hear the professional advisers tell couples of the distress caused to children when their parents divorced.

This knowledge of the ill effects of divorce on children was one of the reasons Diana wanted to keep her marriage legally intact — she had somehow convinced herself that if she remained married to Charles, though living a totally separate life in separate homes 70 miles apart, it was far better for the children than the agonies and embarrassment of a very public divorce. It was, of course, an intellectually debatable argument, yet she clung to it. Throughout her life, Diana had always turned her back and run away from problems; from her Swiss finishing school, from dance lessons and from jobs and now she was running away from marriage. Though counseled and urged by family, friends and advisers to give the marriage another try, not once did Diana ever consider such a move.

She even refused to go on holiday with Charles and the boys, despite marriage counselors urging her to do so for the children's sake. One of their last suggestions to which she reluctantly agreed, after great pressure from the queen, was a 10-day Mediterranean cruise in summer 1992. Wills and Harry joined their mother and father. But Diana, unhappy at the idea, adamantly refused to enjoy herself and spent the holiday feeling miserable, deliberately ruining what should have been a holiday atmosphere. She demanded separate cabins and she ate at a separate time. The atmosphere was tense. After four days at sea, Diana disappeared and a frantic search of the yacht was carried out. Some feared that she might have jumped overboard, not to commit suicide — she was a good swimmer — but to draw attention to her unhappiness. She was discovered after two hours, hiding in a lifeboat under a tarpaulin, crying her eyes out.

Diana had come to enjoy her life as a single person, particularly after she had solved her bulimia and anorexia problems, not to mention her new sexual confidence. However, Diana appreciated the constant stream of media stories about her eating disorders and played up her suffering — she realized that the causes of these alleged disorders were always focused on her unhappy marriage and unfaithful husband. But there were some people who knew the truth. Hewitt himself alleged that Diana consistently overplayed her bulimia, exaggerated her miserable, unhappy life and he would tell how the two of them enjoyed many wonderful meals together without any sign of her eating problems. He also knew, better than Charles, of course, that by the mid-1980s Diana's body was slim, her muscles well-toned, her skin and hair in perfect condition. This would not have been the case if she had still been suffering from major eating disorders for so many years.

Diana had found herself and she was reaping the benefits with lovers at her beck and call, with the world's press salivating over her every deed, her every dress, her every appearance and the mass of the civilized world accepting that she was one of the most popular people in the entire world. She was a person who could persuade others to part with their cash for charities, sway governments, make grown men go weak at the knees in her presence — all with a stunning smile or a mischievous glance.

But despite her interesting love life and various affairs, Diana did not always enjoy her life. The men who refused her desire, choosing closer, more fulfilling relationships, really upset her and she found it hard to cope and very difficult to recover from being spurned by a man with whom she had fallen in love.

Her staff at Kensington Palace would frequently note the unhappy princess wondering around the place looking depressed. For no known reason, Diana would burst into tears, run to her bedroom, throw herself on the bed and stay there for an hour or more until she had composed herself. She would then return and chat away as though nothing whatsoever had occurred. Sometimes at small parties of 30 or so people, most of whom Diana knew, she looked like a lost and unhappy figure. She only seemed happy when there was a gaggle of people around her, smiling, giving her compliments and enjoying the chitchat. It was at these times that Diana would tell her very risqué jokes. Some of these jokes were so sexually oriented and so coarse that many listening didn't know whether to laugh or pretend they hadn't understood the punch line. Most of the women would blush and cover their faces in embarrassment, amazed that someone like Diana could crack such jokes. Diana took delight in shocking these people, who she thought were just being priggish and prudish.

In autumn 1992, Diana learned the queen would permit Charles to seek a legal separation from Diana, though not a divorce. She had been given no warning that the queen was planning such a decision, nor had her Secretary or any of her staff. Presumably, the Buckingham Palace senior advisers and the queen hoped the news would shock and intimidate Diana into fearing that she was about to be exiled entirely from the royal family, thrown out alone into the cold. They hoped such a move might "knock some sense" into her. On the other hand, they wondered whether such a move against her might encourage her to move away and begin a life of her own, far removed from the royal family. The queen took a dim view of such behavior, believing it would only lead to trouble. She had enough trouble within the family without wanting further embarrassments.

The queen was fully aware that the close relationship between Charles and Camilla Parker Bowles had now entered a serious phase but, nevertheless, she was adamant that divorce was out of the question. She discussed the matter with the Archbishop of Canterbury and other senior clergy as well as with her mother. All had reinforced her intention of never permitting the heir to the throne of divorcing. The message it would send to the churchgoers of Britain could be disastrous to the few faithful Church of England congregations still attending church every Sunday. The queen informed Charles in a letter that, if it was his wish, a legal separation could go ahead but she would not permit divorce. Within 24 hours, Charles issued a statement agreeing with his mother's suggestion.

Charles' immediate acquiescence surprised Diana because Charles never once mentioned to her the possibility that they should divorce, although they had discussed the possibility of a legal separation. It also unnerved her. However, Diana's reaction was more furious than nervous as she exclaimed to a friend, "If that's what he wants, he'll get everything he deserves. He behaved like a s**t to me during our marriage and I will never forgive him nor will I forgive that bitch Camilla."

Scathing mad, she raged, "Charles has never said no to his mother in his entire life and hardly ever said no to me either. It's typical of his character that even now he gets his mother to carry out his dirty work because he hasn't got the balls to do it himself."

Diana also wondered why the queen had suddenly permitted the separation because during one of their few chats together in the late 1980s the queen said that there should be no question of a separation or divorce for many years because of the affect it might have on Wills and Harry. Diana agreed. Now, it seemed, for some unknown reason, the queen had changed mind. That worried Diana.

One of the reasons the queen made the decision was to placate the bishops of the Protestant Church of England on the point that that the heir to the throne and the next titular head of the Church, by being formally separated from his wife, was not breaking church law by living in sin. It was in many ways a pathetic and empty gesture, but it had to suffice in the present delicate situation.

Her next solo trip, to Paris in November 1992, was another very important tour for Diana. She selected her wardrobe for those few days with meticulous care and much advice. She knew that Parisiennes were convinced that France was still the capital of haute couture and she was determined to show them that the Princess of Wales knew how to dress and, if necessary, dazzle her hosts. Diana understood that this trip could make or break her wish to become accepted by the royal family, that she was capable of doing a first-class job representing the family abroad and that she would never let the House of Windsor down. Before leaving Britain she told numerous people, including close friends and her officials,

"I'm going to show them. I'll bloody well show that family."

The French people and the all-important French media took Diana to their hearts, newspapers proclaiming, "Courage Princesse!" They had also followed the travails of the princess and her marriage problems. Diana glowed throughout the trip, giving her best, captivating the paparazzi and winning the hearts and minds of the French nation. More importantly, back home in Britain, the media reported the tour as a triumph.

Her private secretary, Patrick Jephson wrote in his account of their life together, *"For me, her Paris tour marked the princess's apogee ...To my eyes, knowing what she had already endured and what lay ahead in the immediate future, there was something heroic in her. Like much heroism, it was not without its flaws and may even have been the compensating flip side of some deep fear. Nonetheless, that night in Paris it sprang from a strength of spirit momentarily freed from accumulations of false sentiment in a simple bid for survival."*

Back in London, Diana knew from the newspapers she avidly scoured, that her solo trip had been a huge success and that she had won the laurels she so desperately wanted. Now she could represent the royal family and do a job which many of them would be envious of.

Challenging them on their terms and on their turf, she had scored a resounding victory. Now she would plan more trips and would hope to conquer more hearts and minds in the process. There was no stopping her. Her adrenaline was coursing through her veins. She felt fantastic. For the first time she had tasted power and she reveled in the confidence it gave her.

Six months later, in March 1993, Diana secured another foreign tour for herself — a working visit to see British aid projects in Nepal, accompanied by Lynda Chalker, the Minister of the Crown responsible for overseas aid. Once again it was a triumph. She not only looked stunning in designer dresses when pictured dining with the King of Nepal in the splendor of his palace in Katmandu, but she also won praise for visiting the poverty-stricken peasants living in ramshackle huts in a rural village high in the Himalayas and sympathizing, in her inimitable way, with the squalid life they were leading.

Diana continued her work with the British charities, winning praise from all. Her disarming, engaging charm captured the hearts and genuine admiration of all she met and, at the same time, secured approval from the all-important media that she was doing a wonderful job. The more headlines proclaiming her endeavors, the more charities asked for her assistance. The more success Diana achieved the more she was usurping the power and prestige of not only Prince Charles but also the queen herself. And she knew it.

Diana sought private, informal chats with Prime Minister John Major at No. 10 Downing Street, which were happily granted. Diana understood that if she could make the prime minister an ally, he would be very useful in persuading the queen that it was important for Britain that Diana conduct more foreign tours because of the prestige and popularity it would bring the nation.

During her visits with the prime minister, Diana flattered him in her inimitable way. He was charmed and thrilled that this beautiful princess would come to see him for advice and to seek his help in organizing her life and realizing her ambitions. John Major reveled in his new role and Diana came to trust him, confident that he would support her new, unofficial role as a roving ambassador for Britain.

At first, the prime minister tried to persuade Diana to concentrate her energies on British charities, suggesting that she consider promoting a national scheme of recognition for caregivers and helpers, which would bear her name and of which she would be the patron and guiding light. Diana told John Major that she would consider the project most seriously, but in reality she didn't want that. She wanted to target the wider world. She finally persuaded the prime minister to support her plan of action.

Having the support of the prime minister gave her planned tours the added impetus of political legitimacy. Diana then moved on to plan where she should visit to gain maximum publicity. As patron of British Red Cross Youth, Diana suggested that she would like to carry out overseas tours on behalf of the International Red Cross. Such high-profile, high-minded and serious work on the international stage was exactly the type of work Diana needed to propel her from being seen as a lightweight, empty-headed clotheshorse to being accepted as a serious-minded woman whose work for and on behalf of world-class humanitarian organizations was valued by governments.

She was convinced that she would get worldwide coverage for the International Red Cross and the Red Cross agreed. They were only too happy to have the celebrated Princess of Wales carrying out overseas trips on their behalf — such visits not only received press and TV coverage in Britain, but news organizations around the world were reporting the princess' activities wherever they took place. Diana was exactly the type of apolitical high-profile celebrity the IRC needed to conduct such tours, sometimes in highly sensitive political areas. She had become the world's most photographed and celebrated person — it seemed that everyone wanted to see her, meet her and read about her life, her problems, her children and her charity work. Diana was only too happy to oblige.

As Patrick Jephson wrote, *"In due course it became evident that the princess had only to express an interest in any of the Red Cross's activities for them to be made available for her patronage."*

But Princess Diana's ambition to become a celebrated and famous ambassador of world humanitarian organizations by undertaking headline-grabbing visits to the world's trouble spots would lead — in a few years — to her own tragic death. Unwittingly and unknowingly, Diana had ventured into political arenas where her work was not wanted and not respected. The politicians and powers-that-be had different political agendas and ambitions they did not want usurped or swept aside by some trumped-up princess who, in their eyes, was someone of no importance.

Diana, however, had come to believe her own sought-after publicity.

Was she not the crowned angel of mercy, the title bestowed on her by the media? Was she not the natural successor to the acclaimed octogenarian Mother Teresa? Was there nothing that Diana could not achieve with her personality, charm and effortless manner? She was about to find out.

Her first major trip on behalf of the International Red Cross was to visit Zimbabwe in May 1993. She was happy to carry out numerous inspecting projects in the depths of the African bush on behalf of the Red Cross, the Leprosy Mission and Help the Aged. That visit also gave fresh impetus to Africa's major emerging problem, the AIDS plight, which was threatening to engulf an entire generation of young Africans and their children.

Patrick Jephson, who accompanied Diana on the trip, wrote, *"Late one evening we visited a hospice for orphaned children with AIDS. None was over (age) 5. None was expected to reach the age of 6. The princess wept."*

Once again, Diana's trip was greeted with great applause from the traveling press and the photographs showed a quiet, introspective, concerned princess carrying out some harrowing, meaningful duties — not riding around in the back of an open limousine waving to masses of cheering, flag-waving children and their parents. She loved the image the television and the newspapers were portraying.

Diana also wanted to go solo on the overseas political stage to show that she wasn't just some mindless woman who was only capable of touchy-feely charitable work, but someone who had a brain. In September 1993, she enthusiastically carried out an official engagement in Luxembourg intended to boost British interests. Diana was informed that the Luxembourg royal family was connected to the House of Windsor through Europe's interrelated royal families. Officially, Diana was the guest of the Grand Duke, but she also attended a dinner hosted by Jacques Santer, Luxembourg's prime minister who, shortly afterward, became president of the European Union. Diana was happy that the prime minister wished her to attend the dinner — it proved to her that her endeavors to portray herself as a woman of intelligence and substance were paying off.

In November, Diana flew to Brussels, as patron of the Help the Aged charity, to promote the work of the international charity HelpAge. Once again, there was a political bonus in the trip — she was invited to give her views about organizing aid and projects for elderly people with the European Union's Commissioner for Social Affairs.

Patrick Jephson, who accompanied Diana on all of these overseas trips wrote, *"Diana's formidable combination of talents had the potential to be a vehicle for far greater causes — the grand, global welfare crusades for which she seemed outwardly so suited. As events were to show, however, in the end, she was tragically unable to prove herself a reliable standard-bearer for many of these."*

Diana now sought more high-level relationships with the powerful and influential. During these years, Diana entertained the United States Ambassador to Britain at Kensington Palace as well as the Russian, Chinese, Hungarian, Pakistani and Argentine ambassadors. It was obvious that these ambassadors believed the princess to be a serious-minded young woman of some powerful, even political potential, otherwise they would not have wasted their time attending informal private meetings over tea or lunch.

The queen and her advisers were becoming increasingly worried about the power and prestige that Diana was wielding as her popularity escalated throughout the 1990s. British ambassadors discovered that they might wait months for an invitation to see a head of state, but when Princess Diana even hinted at a possible visit, the red carpet was laid out immediately and she was given direct access. This was becoming hard for the queen and her advisers, as well as senior advisers at No. 10 Downing Street, to bear — they all saw that Diana was being invited to fly the flag for Britain over and above any other member of the royal family, including the queen. Diana had achieved her greatest ambition. She had become the world's most sought after personality whom kings, presidents and even emperors wanted to meet and wanted to be seen with on a personal level. Prince Charles wasn't even in the picture and Diana loved that. The taste of victory was sweet, indeed.

The time had come to clip Diana's wings, according to the men and women of influence who rule the corridors of power in both Buckingham Palace and No 10. Downing Street. The queen gave instructions that Princess Diana must never be permitted to represent her abroad, but it did not stop the invitations arriving each and every week at Kensington Palace.

A whispering campaign began throughout Buckingham Palace aimed, it seemed, at undermining and belittling Diana's overseas trips and suggesting that the only reason she was accepted by kings and presidents was because she was still, technically, a member of the House of Windsor since she was only separated from Prince Charles and not divorced from him.

It seemed that Diana would not be permitted to go overseas again as a representative of the House of Windsor, but there was little or nothing that

Buckingham Palace could do to prevent her from attending overseas invitations to whatever was offered. As a result, when foreign governments, organizations or charities wanted Diana to attend a function in their country, they would simply write a formal letter of invitation. And Diana would reply in the affirmative.

In an effort to put a stop, or at least put a brake on Diana's escalating foreign engagements and increasing popularity among governments across the globe, the royal courtiers decreed that the princess was no longer permitted to use an aircraft of the queen's flight to make such journeys. These queen's flight aircraft are for the specific use of the queen and, importantly, whomsoever the queen, with the advice of courtiers, decides should be permitted to use the planes. Until now, Diana had always been given permission to use the royal planes because they added prestige to the visit.

Informed of this latest restriction, Diana reacted with a wonderful pithy remark, "they'll be cutting off their noses next!"

To Diana, it was just another hurdle to overcome. It seemed the palace had failed to take into account Diana's stubbornness and determination. She saw the withdrawal of the royal aircraft as yet another deliberate ploy to cut her out of the royal family and make her life as difficult as possible. However, the facts were beyond contention. Throughout the 1990s, Princess Diana was almost alone among members of "The Firm" in garnering goodwill for the monarchy. The queen's crude attempts to stop Diana's remarkable success in winning the hearts and minds of foreign governments, charities and ordinary people was neither logical nor reasoned. It appeared that the queen was prepared to act against her daughter-in-law, risking the good name and reputation of the House of Windsor and the British people in the eyes of foreign governments, charities and their citizens.

It also demonstrated the desperate levels to which the British monarchy was prepared to sink in a bid to put an end to Diana's dramatic success overseas. Courtiers would argue that the queen was simply making sure that Diana was not usurping the power and authority of the British monarch.

Diana took the initiative and ordered her staff to contact wealthy individuals she had met and ask them if they had an aircraft the princess might borrow. Diana offered to pay for these flights at a reduced rate, but on virtually every occasion the wealthy owner happily offered the plane, plus crew, to her at no charge, believing it was a privilege to have been asked.

As a result of such bargaining, the queen, as a result of persuasion from the prime minister, agreed that Diana could visit Argentina. Diana's less formal relationship with the British monarch might make the visit less "tricky" than if the queen or Prince Charles undertook a tour of that country as Britain and Argentina had fought a bloody war over the Falkland Islands only 13 years before. Princess Diana had engineered an invitation from Argentina for her to carry out charitable work in Buenos Aires. She was also keen to visit South America, where she had never been. Wickedly, she saw this tour as a golden opportunity to conquer the country where Prince Charles was particularly popular and where he had enjoyed visiting. The Argentines had a passion for his favorite sport, polo.

Once again, the visit was a great success and once again Diana was invited to meet the country's head of state, President Menem who hosted a lunch for a few of his most important ministers and senior officials. Diana was impressed. She had chalked up another resounding success, causing even deeper furrowed brows back at Buckingham Palace. The Argentines loved her and turned out in thousands to give her a wonderful South American welcome. Diana beamed and waved, loving the adoration. The British press corps once again hailed her triumphant tour, emphasizing that Diana had done more to restore good relations with the Argentine nation in a couple of days than Foreign Office officials could in years.

Since the official separation, Prince Charles and his advisers at Highgrove were trying to marginalize the princess in the same way as the queen, Prince Philip and Buckingham Palace courtiers had been. Charles was certainly more than irritated to find Diana usurping his role in his beloved Argentina and more annoyed still to read in the papers that Diana had been received with such acclaim and affection. To Charles, it seemed that his estranged wife had virtually succeeded in sidelining him — the Prince of Wales and heir apparent — rather than the other way round.

"Every time I pick up a bloody newspaper," he was reported to have said in one outburst, "I see Diana disporting herself in some farflung part of the globe and receiving rave reviews in the papers while it seems no one is interested in seeing me at all. I'm meant to be the bloody Prince of Wales for God's sake."

Diana knew of none of these outbursts and continued her globe-trotting, often wondering what effect her travels and subsequent rave reviews was having on both Charles and the rest of the royals.

In early 1996, Princess Diana was invited to
Hong Kong by the multimillionaire socialite
David Tang, who had widespread business
interests in both Hong Kong and mainland
China. Tang was perhaps one of Hong Kong's
most famous entrepreneurs, who seemed to revel
in the limelight of glamour and fame. He was also
legendary in supporting numerous charitable
institutions, including the Leprosy Mission.

Once again, Diana was in her element, acting her
part as princess and fund-raiser extraordinaire in
stunning fashion, appearing happy and elated
throughout the three day tour. On all occasions she
was smiling, radiant and charming — the people
loved her. At a dinner attended by Hong Kong's
rich and famous, Diana managed to raise $500,000,
which was channeled through her Charities Trust,
mainly to the Leprosy Mission. During the day,
Diana worked, visiting hospitals and dealing with
the appalling social problems leprosy caused.
Once again, she showed her empathy with the sufferers as well as her professionalism in providing
photo opportunities, which only helped the cause
when they were published around the world.
Indeed, this Hong Kong visit should have been a
template for her own future as a semi-detached
royal, touring the world and persuading wealthy
people to part with their money for charitable

causes to benefit the poor, the sick, the hungry and the dispossessed. But it was not to be.

She was happy to perform the task as charity fund-raiser occasionally, but she wanted to be seen involved with more vital, important work where she could have a more dramatic, lasting effect on major issues.

The issue that Diana had been searching for to galvanize her life and give it real purpose arrived on her desk in the autumn of 1996, when her friend Mike Whitlam, Director-General of the International Red Cross asked her whether she wanted to become involved in the highly political issue of antipersonnel land mines. From that October day until her death some 11 months later, banning antipersonnel land mines became her great crusade. Diana was prepared to go anywhere, see anybody and use her influence in any way necessary to push through a worldwide ban.

Diana accepted the argument of those seeking a ban that AP mines were nothing less than an evil attack on the innocent of the developing world. What appalled and angered her was that she had been led to understand that nothing had been done to stop the production of AP mines, or their use, although politicians and generals were fully aware of the awesome facts — that a staggering 26,000 people, many of them children, were killed or maimed each year by such mines.

Diana's interest in the mine issue began a year earlier, on the 125th anniversary of the British Red Cross, of which she was patron. She was supposed to be taking a high-profile role in events being planned for the celebration, but Buckingham Palace frowned on the idea of Diana being the sole royal representative on such a high-profile anniversary. Palace officials argued that as Diana had decided to retire from official public duties, she should not be permitted to star in the Red Cross celebrations. Diana was livid, but there was little she could do. She talked over the issue with Mike Whitlam, who understood that Diana's involvement in the celebrations would give enormous impetus to the event and reach far greater public awareness for the charity than if any other royal took the leading role. So a compromise was reached.

It was decided that Diana would become involved in only one aspect of the current Red Cross campaign — the thorny issue of land mines. "That struck an immediate cord in her," Mike Whitlam said. "But because of the situation, it was decided that she would play no major part in our celebrations on the home front but would concentrate instead on the mines issue. She was delighted."

He went on, "We sent her videos, photographs and reading material. Some of the videos were truly horrifying, showing footage of children and adults who had lost an arm, a leg, a foot or half a face in AP mine accidents. The photographs pulled no punches. The videos also showed the excellent work being carried out by Red Cross volunteers, doctors and specialists who were carrying out wonderful work helping amputees."

It was after seeing such harrowing material that Diana told Mike, "I am prepared to do anything, anything at all, if I can help put a stop to the production and use of land mines. I will make speeches, attend meetings, travel wherever you like to highlight this grotesque trade which kills and maims so many innocent children."

Diana did not reveal to Whitlam that she had shown some of the gory photographs to her sons William, then age 14, and Harry, then age 12, and discussed the issue with them in some detail. Harry asked her with childlike innocence, "Mines kill children, don't they, Mummy?"

The concern of her sons motivated Diana even more to help in any way she could to rid the world of land mines. Here, at last, was an issue of great humanitarian interest that she totally believed in. She hoped it would bring her the credit she craved. Diana talked passionately whenever the issue was raised and she read and learned by heart all the arguments put forward why land mines should be banned.

She asked for more material and studied the papers and the details of the different types of land mines until she attained a good working knowledge. She also studied the worldwide problems involved in tracing, finding and destroying the mines. In many Third World countries, for example, searching for the misplaced mines sometimes began years after they had been laid. She understood the primary problem — no maps had been kept by the armies laying the mines and, as a result, no one knew precisely where they were buried. As a result, many people, including children, were being killed and maimed each year.

By a stroke of good fortune, the premiere of the film *In Love and War*, produced by Lord Richard Attenborough, was to be screened in London at the end of 1996. Attenborough approached Mike Whitlam, asking whether the Red Cross might be interested in highlighting the film. Whitlam immediately saw this as a golden opportunity to promote their campaign to ban land mines and discussed the idea with Diana, knowing that involving her at the film premiere would create extensive media attention. He wrote to her asking if she would be interested and she jumped at the idea. It was exactly the opportunity she had been waiting for.

The premiere was a great success and afterward Diana told Whitlam that she would be prepared to travel anywhere in the world if he thought it might help the cause. Her next trip was to Angola in the early part of 1997 to meet young victims of land mine incidents.

Diana was eager to make this trip. It meant a lot to her in terms of her own personal ambition to be accepted as a world player tackling serious issues. Whitlam explained, "She wanted her visit to Angola to be a working tour. She wanted no high-profile meetings with government ministers, no official dinners. She didn't want to pack any posh dresses. She wanted to travel light, taking only jeans and a few shirts."

As expected, press and television cameras followed. Emotive pictures of innocent, seriously injured children all but killed in land mine accidents made front-page news in the papers and heartrending footage on television screens around the world. Those pictures of Diana, Princess of Wales, comforting child victims propelled the land mine issue to the center of political agendas throughout the Western world.

In Angola, Diana saw for herself the extent to which land mines hindered aid and development and caused tragedy for thousands of refugees seeking to return to their villages. She met children and adults horrendously mutilated by anti-personnel mines and realized the desperate need for aid to enable the wounded to live normal lives.

Demands for a worldwide ban on the manufacture and use of antipersonnel land mines were slowly gathering supporters over the years, but the pictures of Diana holding mutilated young victims catapulted the issue into the living rooms of ordinary people. For the first time, the silent majority took note and demands for action on this issue forced governments to address it as a matter of urgency and promise action. Suddenly, banning land mines was an issue at the forefront of people's minds and the voters were not prepared to take "no" for an answer.

The Canadian government had been trying to persuade governments everywhere to address this issue for some years, so naturally they agreed with the ban. The Nordic countries also responded positively, as well as those developing nations whose people were suffering terrible injuries and loss of life from the exploding mines.

Throughout the developed world, however, the powerful arms lobbies and the military were fighting a rearguard action against such a ban. From a military viewpoint, the politicians accepted the arguments of their generals: The use of mines was a necessity in protecting their armies. The generals convinced their politicians that if anti-personnel mines were laid correctly, with every mine diligently recorded on a map, there was no danger to civilians because they could be removed by the army when the danger or the war was over.

The International Red Cross, however, pointed out that for some countries it was too late — many armies in Third World countries did not keep accurate records and maps. It was the manufacture and sale of mines to irresponsible governments and warring factions that caused the problems and the thousands of deaths and injuries each year. The Red Cross argued that laying antipersonnel mines had become an ethical issue, which the world's responsible governments now had a duty to face.

By 1996, many Western governments accepted that the laying of land mines had become a moral issue but many countries were not prepared to stop the production and sale of antipersonnel mines unless an internationally recognized worldwide ban was enforced.

The International Red Cross reported that deaths and injuries caused by land mines had escalated since the 1970s. Other nongovernment agencies have also noted the increase. From 1979

to 1997, the International Red Cross manufac-
tured 100,000 prostheses for 80,000 amputees in
22 countries. Much of that was for amputees in
Cambodia, Afghanistan and Angola. Since the
end of the Angolan civil war, when land mines
were laid randomly over a 20-year period, the
IRC fitted 1,550 new amputees with prostheses. It
gave Afghanistan 600 wheelchairs and 6,000
pairs of crutches. This covered only a fraction of
the number of victims who needed help.

The IRC insisted that nearly all of these
horrific injuries were occurring in countries with
very low incomes, so that those maimed could
never receive the help or treatment for their
injuries without outside assistance. As a result,
the vast majority of maimed people in developing
countries were condemned to a life of abject
poverty and wretchedness, unable to work or
care for themselves.

Across the developing world, voluntary organi-
zations have been at work for years clearing mines.
The Red Cross, the Cambodia Trust, Motivation,
Power, The Halo Trust and The Mines Advisory
Group have all been involved in the clearing of
mines and caring for the maimed and wounded in a
number of countries, including Afghanistan,
Angola, Bosnia, Cambodia, Chechnya, Laos,
Mozambique, Sri Lanka and the Sudan.

These voluntary organizations needed someone to highlight the plight and the appalling results of laying land mines indiscriminately. They were desperate for someone who could combine a high profile with compassion, bringing the attention of the world to the problem. No politician or organization had the image or the mass appeal necessary to grab the attention of the international media and demand action.

Even after Diana's Angolan visit, some nations continued to hold out against the Canadian government's efforts to persuade all nations to sign a draft treaty outlawing the use of antipersonnel mines. But the tide was turning against them. Across the world a total of 1,000 nongovernmental agencies in 60 countries joined the campaign to outlaw these indiscriminate weapons.

Six months after visiting Angola, Diana readily agreed to visit Bosnia, where the IRC reported increasing numbers of people, including many children, had become victims of land mines laid during the horrific ethnic wars in the former Yugoslavia during the 1990s. Once again, the photographs and the TV footage revealed the full horror of the effect of laying mines indiscriminately. On this visit Diana also heard some horrifying stories of wounded children related through interpreters.

Viewers were touched when they saw Diana sharing a birthday cake with a little boy named Hamic who lived outside Tuzla, one of the cities most affected by the war. Hamic had lost both feet when he stepped on a land mine. He had no idea who Diana was. She was just a young woman dressed in blue jeans and a white shirt, who came in, sat next to him, held his hand and cuddled him like his mother did. Hamic was fascinated by the television cameras, the photographers and their equipment.

Diana was deeply affected by this mission, fighting back tears as she spoke to widows and orphans, to parents who had lost their children as a direct result of anti-personnel mines. Through this mission Diana had found herself; found a cause that would give meaning to her new life outside the royal family, outside fundraising and outside Britain. When she flew back to Britain from Bosnia at the beginning of August 1997, Diana committed herself to helping the International Red Cross in any way she could to help bring about a worldwide ban on mines.

In fact, it was Diana's death some three weeks later that helped bring forward the treaty dedicated to banning the use of land mines. Two weeks after her death, representatives from 100 nations met in Oslo, the Norwegian capital, to sign the treaty. The final document was signed in Ottawa, the Canadian capital.

In October, some six weeks after her death, the campaign to ban land mines received the final accolade when it was awarded the Nobel Peace Prize. The Norwegian Nobel committee said the $1 million award would go in equal parts to the International Campaign to Ban Land mines and to Jody Williams, the campaign coordinator. They had, the Nobel committee said, "started a process which, in the space of a few years, changed a ban on antipersonnel mines from a vision to a feasible reality."

Diana had known before her death that the campaign was a success and that a treaty was about to be signed banning the future use of land mines. To Diana this was the most important and rewarding achievement of her entire life. But some powerful people were far from happy. Until Diana, Princess of Wales, had entered the arena, they believed it was possible to sideline the anti-mine campaign. But Diana inspired ordinary people who, in turn, created a furor in many Western capitals in support of the ban. She had demonstrated her remarkable power in the twinkling of an eye by appealing directly to voters over the heads of politicians and gaining their wholehearted support for a fundamental change of policy toward mine-laying.

In her naivete, Diana upset a number of factions that were taken aback by the speed which Diana's intervention had accelerated a mines ban. Jubilant Diana knew none of these problems. Now she determined to follow up this extraordinary success with a new challenge, a new project, another high-profile issue that would once again grab the world's attention. Unknown to nearly all of those around her, Diana had found that new project, one that would send shock waves through the capitals of the Western world. And once again she was keeping this secret to herself.

Chapter 12

The Day of Reckoning

 *T*he world knows how Diana spent the last day of her life. Waking on Mohamed al Fayed's luxury yacht the *Jonikal* with her lover Dodi Fayed, she decided to take one last swim in the warm blue waters of the Mediterranean before flying to Paris on the way back to London. They sped the *Jonikal* around to a nearby cove. But while splashing about and enjoying their privacy, a motor launch packed with paparazzi headed toward them. The Fayed bodyguards in another launch confronted the photographers and asked them to respect Diana's privacy and leave. They refused, using their customary lame excuse — that they were simply making their living and should be allowed to do so unhindered.

Les Wingfield, one of Dodi's trusted private bodyguards said, "We tried to appeal to their better nature but they didn't want to listen. They were determined to stick around and take pictures of Diana and Mr. Dodi together. There was nothing we could do."

Annoyed their swim had been interrupted, Diana and Dodi headed back to the *Jonikal* moored at the jetty of the exclusive Sardinian resort of Cala di Volpe on the Costa Smeralda. They showered and ate a light breakfast on deck. They had some time to spare and Diana lay around the deck sunbathing until lunch, keeping out of sight of the photographers who were kept out at sea away from the port.

Diana arranged to be back at Kensington Palace on the morning of Sunday, August 31, because William and Harry, who had been staying with their father at Balmoral, were due to fly to London that afternoon. On the spur of the moment, Dodi suggested to Diana that they fly to Paris so they could both do some shopping. Diana liked that idea and planned to buy some presents for her beloved boys. Little did Diana realize that the reason Dodi wanted to stop over in Paris was that he planned to buy Diana an expensive ring — an engagement ring — and propose to her that night. For weeks, his father Mohamed al Fayed had been urging his son to propose to Diana, despite the fact that Dodi had little or no reason to suppose Diana had ever contemplated marrying him.

Diana was enjoying herself with Dodi. She found him fun, upbeat and enjoyable company, happy to do whatever she wanted, when she wanted. Diana had first met Dodi, the 42-year-old playboy, erstwhile film producer and eldest son of Mohamed al Fayed, the owner of Harrods, the London store. On numerous occasions, Mohamed al Fayed had offered his villa in the South of France, the Castel Sainte Terese, to Diana for her to use, a place secluded from paparazzi and patrolled by Fayed's own bodyguards, where she could stay as long as she wished — in peace. Fayed thought it a perfect holiday home for Diana, William and Harry.

Fayed's invitations to Diana had first come through Raine, Earl Spencer's second wife, a director of Harrods International. Until the summer of 1997, Diana had always declined. But her beach holiday with Wills and Harry the previous year had been an unmitigated disaster, primarily due to the infuriating attentions of the paparazzi, who not only discovered the exact location of their holiday villa, but spent days and nights camped nearby, their intrusive lenses forever trained on the terrace leading from the villa to the swimming pool. During that holiday, Wills and Harry deliberately remained out of sight inside the villa because they did not want to give the photographers a chance to take any pictures. In the end, Diana cut the holiday short and returned to London, furious at the press intrusion.

Diana first met Dodi Fayed 10 years earlier, when Dodi's polo team, sponsored by his father, played the Prince of Wales' team in the final of the Harrods Cup at Windsor Great Park. It was Diana who presented the winner's trophy.

When Diana met Dodi again, she had no idea of his life or his background, except that his Egyptian father owned Harrods and his mother was Samira Khashoggi, sister of the billionaire international arms dealer Adnan Khashoggi. Dodi was a playboy who wanted to become a film producer and enjoy the company of beautiful young women aided by the financial muscle of his father. He led a typical Hollywood rich-kid lifestyle, trying to break into films, setting up his own film production company, Allied Stars, when he was only 23 years old. He flashed his money around, drove expensive cars and dated young starlets. He also became addicted to cocaine and was a steady drinker.

In the early months of 1997, Dodi, spurred on by his father, invited Diana to dinner. Dodi took her to his penthouse apartment in exclusive Mayfair only a few hundred yards from Buckingham Palace. Dinner was cooked and provided by his father's chefs, the meal served by a young waitress and the wine by a butler. Diana was impressed and she was once more enchanted by a Muslim man whom she found gentle, fun and, shortly afterward, an accomplished, passionate lover. As ever, Diana tried to keep this new relationship a secret from the ravenous British press and she succeeded. Diana came to appreciate that Dodi had the money, which she now recognized was absolutely necessary to ensure that she could enjoy a secluded existence, assisted by bodyguards, chauffeurs, blacked-out motor cars and all the necessities to ensure a quiet, secluded, peaceful life.

From the beginning, however, Diana felt uneasy with Dodi, feeling he lavished her with too many expensive gifts. It seemed that Dodi was trying to "buy" her love and that left an unpleasant taste in her mouth. Diana had never wanted anyone to own her. She decided that the cause was his experience with the young starlets of Hollywood, whom she believed were only too happy to receive presents from wealthy men.

Diana came to feel obliged that she had to buy Dodi presents in return to show her appreciation for his generosity. She preferred that they simply enjoyed each other's company, being together because they wanted to be together. She would usually give him the benefit of the doubt for a

somewhat quirky reason — his given name,
Emad, translated from the Arabic, means "someone you can depend on."

In the early summer of 1997, Mohamed al
Fayed offered his St. Tropez villa to Diana,
suggesting that his son Dodi would be on hand in
case of trouble from paparazzi. He would stay
in the fisherman's cottage on the beach some 200
yards from the villa. Diana jumped at the invitation. A way had been found for Diana to enjoy a
free and easy holiday with Wills and Harry in
privacy, while in the dead of night she could visit
her lover for a few hours before stealing back to
her bed in the villa as dawn was breaking.

Dodi had fun with Wills and Harry, though he
had never met them before. He was happy to play
rough-and-tumble games with them in the pool.
Occasionally, Diana would invite Dodi to take
lunch with her and her sons on the terrace and
occasionally he would dine with them. After the
boys had gone to sleep, Diana and Dodi sometimes
would take moonlit walks along the deserted
beach. Most evenings they sat and chatted on the
terrace over a bottle of wine. Sometimes they made
love at Dodi's cottage, at other times in Diana's bed
in the villa. On occasions, Diana wanted to make
love in the moonlight on the beach with the gentle
Mediterranean waves lapping nearby.

Diana and the boys also had the use of the *Jonikal*, al Fayeds' magnificent yacht, and the boys thoroughly enjoyed running all over it, inspecting the cabins and the crew quarters as well as taking turns at the wheel. The boys were allowed to roam the yacht at will, unlike the times they had spent aboard the royal yacht when they had to obey strict rules. Both Diana and the boys had a wonderful, carefree holiday, swimming in the warm Mediterranean, taking rides in the *Jonikal* and sunbathing back at the villa. Most important of all; there were no photographers about. When she returned home Diana pronounced, "That was the best holiday I have ever had in my entire life."

Three weeks later, and to everyone's surprise, Diana and Dodi flew from Stansted Airport near London on a Harrods Gulfstream jet for a six-day cruise aboard the *Jonikal*. They visited Monte Carlo and the island of Corsica. Their days were spent visiting quiet coves, swimming in private, lazing about the yacht and making love. In fact, this second holiday had been planned several months earlier. Once again, they enjoyed a quiet, peaceful time and only once did the paparazzi capture their quarry on film.

The happy couple was caught when an Italian photographer, Maro Brenna, snapped them with a long lens, producing the grainy, out-of-focus

photograph that has since been named "The
Kiss." It seemed from that picture that Diana was
becoming seriously involved with Dodi. In reality, she wasn't. She was simply enjoying a romantic summer with a generous, wealthy playboy
whose company she enjoyed and whom she had
discovered was quite a stud.

That single photograph set the tabloid press
speculating furiously about Diana's intentions
toward Dodi. Was Diana in love with him? Would
they marry? Where would they live? Would Diana
ever leave her children? Would there be any reli-
gious problems? After Diana's infatuation and
love affair with the heart surgeon Hasnat Khan,
Diana's friends were coming to the conclusion
that, for whatever reason, Diana decided that she
enjoyed the company of Muslim men.

For many years, Diana had a close friendship
with a woman who became almost a mother to
her, Lady Annabel Goldsmith, wife of the late
billionaire Sir Jimmy Goldsmith. During the
past 12 years, Diana enjoyed Lady Annabel's
hospitality at her beautiful Queen Anne home at
Ham, near Richmond, some 15 miles from
Kensington Palace. Diana loved taking Wills and
Harry there for a Saturday or Sunday lunch when
other children and their parents would also be
invited. Annabel's home was open house and the

meals were often taken in the lovely large kitchen with much chatter and noise as the children ate their food, watched over by their adoring mothers. After these meals, sometimes attended by 16 or more people, Diana would insist on doing the washing up, for example the pots and pans that wouldn't go in the dishwasher. Other mothers protested, but Diana would insist. "It'll do me good," she would say with a laugh as she pulled on the rubber gloves and set to work.

Lady Annabel's daughter Jemima, who was the apple of her father's eye, fell in love with Imran Khan, the former captain of the Pakistani cricket team. A tall, handsome, Oxford-educated intelligent young man, Imran had a well-earned reputation as a ladies' man. Most of his adult life he lived in Britain, except when playing cricket for Pakistan. Jemima and Imran fell in love and they married, though Sir Jimmy wasn't too happy that his beloved daughter had decided to marry a Muslim and live in Pakistan. But Annabel knew that Imran made her daughter happy and they enjoyed a wonderful, loving relationship. In Pakistan, Imran founded a hospital for cancer patients and decided to enter the troubled world of Pakistan politics.

Even after Jemima left Britain to live in Pakistan, Diana and Annabel frequently chatted on the phone and sometimes visited each other. Over the years they became close friends and Diana put great faith in Lady Annabel's judgment because she was so natural, honest, had common sense and gave sound advice.

Annabel warned Diana that she didn't believe Dodi was the right man for her. Diana knew that Dodi had become addicted to cocaine, which Diana certainly didn't like. She also didn't like that Dodi was a "Daddy's boy," obedient to everything his father suggested because he held the purse strings. Diana wasn't sure that the presents Dodi was giving her all the time were from him or his father. Sometimes Diana felt uneasy, suspecting that Mohamed al Fayed was using his fortune to try and "buy her" for his son. She also realized that if she ever married Dodi, the greatest beneficiary would be Mohamed himself, who might then believe he was on almost equal footing with the royal family. It made Diana feel uneasy. She had no intention of settling down with Dodi, as Lady Annabel confirmed, despite Mohammed al Fayed's contention that Diana and Dodi were on the point of becoming engaged.

At first, Diana had enjoyed Dodi's company, his jokes, his sense of fun and his ability to make her laugh. But Diana came to suspect that the jokes he was making and his patter were the same as he had used on other women. In time, Diana came to see him as a professional lover who took pride in seducing beautiful women with his charm, his humor and his father's money. Toward the end of their summer fling, Diana discovered that the more time she spent with Dodi, when they weren't having sex, the less interested she became in the relationship.

Throughout their time together, apparently, Dodi had not informed Diana that he had been married before, though the marriage had lasted only eight months. Nor had he told her that just before their summer holiday in St. Tropez with Wills and Harry, he had become engaged to a beautiful American model, Kelly Fisher, 31, who had also spent a holiday with him on the *Jonikal* a month before. As Dodi was romancing Diana, Kelly Fisher's lawyers issued a statement that Miss Fisher had met Dodi Fayed in Paris in 1996 and they traveled together — staying in London, Paris, California and New York. He agreed to pay her $500,000 in premarital support because she had abandoned her modeling career to be with him. Allegedly, Dodi promised to marry her the following year and buy her a house in Malibu Beach, California. He had also given her a check for $200,000, which bounced. Diana learned this from reading the British newspapers, just before her fateful journey to Sardinia.

Meanwhile, Diana's good friend Rosa Monckton, the president of Tiffany & Co., wife of Dominic Lawson, the editor of the *Sunday Telegraph*, invited Diana to accompany her on a short Mediterranean cruise only days after she returned from holiday with Dodi. Rosa Monckton confirmed after Diana's death that they discussed her relationship with Dodi and Diana had led her to understand that she had no plans whatsoever to marry her playboy lover — though she happily admitted to enjoying a wild, passionate summer with him.

But Dodi's father thought differently. He was convinced that Diana was seriously involved with her son. He pushed Dodi into buying a ring for her and suggested that while handing it to her Dodi should also make a proposal of marriage. Even if Diana said "no" to marriage, there was a possibility that she would have found the stunning and expensive ring irresistible and accepted it as a generous gift from her lover. Such outward signs of affection and commitment as accepting a ring from a lover can persuade people that their relationship has serious intent. It was not to be.

Diana's last hours began as the Harrods jet landed at Le Bourget at 3:20 p.m., after a 90-minute flight from Sardinia. Dodi was also on board, as well as a number of bodyguards, including Trevor Rees-Jones and Les Wingfield. Waiting on the tarmac was Gamma photographer Romauld Rat, a large, soft-spoken and respected photographer with five colleagues. They snapped away as Diana and Dodi disembarked and clambered into the black Mercedes 600SEL leased by the Ritz for ferrying VIPs around Paris. Henri Paul, deputy chief of security at the Ritz, a man well-known and trusted by Dodi Fayed, was also waiting to welcome his boss.

As is customary in Paris and Rome when high-profile celebrities make an appearance, the paparazzi gave chase on motorbikes and in cars. Bodyguard Les Wingfield described the journey: "A black Peugeot came from behind, overtook our vehicle and then slammed on the brakes, forcing us to slow down. The guys on the motorbikes then came up on either side of the Mercedes and began snapping away at the princess. The Peugeot then controlled the speed at which we could drive into Paris."

On the way to the Ritz they stopped off at the Villa Windsor, the house where the Duke and Duchess of Windsor had lived for many years before their deaths. Mohamed al Fayed had bought the lease on the substantial, detached French mansion in the exclusive Bois de Boulogne for $6 million and spent a further

$35 million modernizing, refurbishing and redecorating the beautiful house.

At the Ritz, they managed to evade photographers at the front of the hotel by driving to the service entrance at the back. They went to the prestigious Imperial Suite and Diana ordered tea and later had her hair done. Two hours after their arrival, Dodi slipped out, accompanied by two security guards, and crossed the Place Vendome to Repossi, the jewelers. Later, a diamond ring was delivered to Dodi at the Ritz.

At 7 p.m., Diana and Dodi left the Ritz, once again using the service entrance in the Rue Cambon, but this time the photographers were ready. Next, Diana and Dodi were driven to Dodi's private apartment just off the Champs Elysee. As the couple arrived, some 15 or more photographers moved toward them and a scuffle developed on the doorstep of the block of apartments. Punches were thrown, cameras knocked away. The paparazzi were objecting to being physically manhandled and prevented from taking their precious pictures and, in turn, the bodyguards didn't like being physically assaulted by the paparazzi. The atmosphere was heated and it would get much worse.

When they returned to the Ritz, Diana and Dodi were met by a phalanx of photographers —

perhaps 30 or so — as well as a swelling crowd of people, tourists and sightseers who heard Diana was staying at the Ritz and were curious to see her.

Les Wingfield later described the scene: "We unlocked the car doors and got the couple out. We were immediately surrounded by about a dozen photographers who jostled us, coming within a couple of feet of Diana, shooting away in her face. Some were aggressive, others were OK."

But behind the scenes, a secret intelligence operation that would end with the deaths of Diana, Dodi Fayed and their driver Henri Paul was professionally and meticulously being put into place. Discussions at the highest level had been held involving MI5 and the French D.S.T. — La Direction de la Surveillance du Territoire — the French equivalent of MI5. The U.S. Central Intelligence Agency was informed of the plot. An agreement was reached — Diana had become a dangerous liability to those whose duty and responsibility it was to protect their nations against any threat from any quarter, though usually such threats came from terrorism, espionage or subversion. The decision was made that since Diana was a British citizen, MI5 should take responsibility for organizing, planning and carrying out her death. Diana's alleged threat to the status quo of international relations came from the fact that she had become political dynamite, a naive, well-intentioned young woman innocently wielding great persuasive, personal power among the electors of the Western world.

Diana's involvement in the International Red Cross campaign for ridding the world of antipersonnel mines had been astonishingly successful. Pictures of Diana in mine fields in Angola and Bosnia, and further pictures of her chatting to children maimed by AP mines, had touched the hearts of the Western world and at the time of her death it was all but certain that a worldwide ban of those mines would come into force, despite fierce objection and opposition from defense chiefs from across the Western world.

Flushed with this extraordinary success, Diana decided to use her power to aid the plight of the world's refugees. It was almost certain that with the assistance of the International Red Cross and other agencies dealing with refugees the world over, Diana could move from one refugee problem to another, bringing her own, magical brand of political pressure to bear on nations of the developed world to sort out these intractable problems.

It was accepted and recognized that Diana's involvement in any particular refugee problem would bring enormous pressure on politicians from their electors and the media to alleviate whatever problem she highlighted. And there was real concern, if not dismay, among the three security intelligence agencies that if Diana was pictured with a group of wretched, poverty-stricken Palestinian children in a hovel of a refugee camp in Gaza or the West Bank, there was no telling what might be demanded by voters around the world. As always, security intelligence agencies were concerned with maintaining the status quo; Diana was concerned with the plight of refugees and her new ambition to become the world's No. 1 ambassador for humanitarian issues.

Diana let friends know that if the royal family refused to permit her to be a roving royal ambassador, she would seriously consider moving to another country, perhaps France or the United States, and setting up a permanent home there. Diana told friends, "I am deadly serious. This is no idle threat because I am determined to do the job for which I believe I am uniquely equipped. And if the royals won't let me carry out that work, then I will go and live where I can."

MI5 was well aware that Diana had become a serious liability and an increasing embarrassment to the British royal family. Without a doubt, she succeeded in becoming the nation's favorite royal, even supplanting the queen from her customary position as the most popular and respected royal. The British people loved her and they wholeheartedly supported anything and everything she said and did. The public enthusiastically endorsed the contentious issues Diana raised in her *Panorama* interview, where she overstepped the bounds of her position as a royal princess. In suggesting that some of the royal courtiers treated her as the "enemy"; in suggesting the Prince of Wales was unfit to be king, and, lastly and most importantly, in criticizing the queen for not changing and modernizing the monarchy and its relationship with the British people, Diana had gone too far. Some people, including her own private secretary Patrick Jephson, had described it as a "suicidal speech."

Diana didn't give a damn what critics had to say about the *Panorama* interview because the newspapers showed that the British public were right behind her, agreeing with all she had said. But there were others who had taken offense at her remarks and accusations. And there were still more who believed she had taken a step too far. What, they would ask, might she do for her next trick? It is little wonder, therefore, that the death of Princess Diana bore all the hallmarks and fingerprints of a classic security service operation.

MI5 was, of course, aware of Diana's ongoing affair with Dodi Fayed in the summer of '97, the information was supplied by the police and Special Branch. For some years MI5 had been kept informed as to Diana's whereabouts, her habits and, more important, the men in her life. At some point in the early part of the year, a decision had been made: if Diana continued in her ambitions to raise her international profile — and, in particular, to concentrate on the politically charged Palestinian refugee issue — there might be a necessity to take the ultimate action.

Until the late 1960s, Britain's intelligence and securities agencies,which had been set up before World War I, had a virtual carte blanche in the decision-making of people they believed should be removed from society. They did not have to seek advice or permission from the political establishment or the head of state when it came to making those decisions.

During the late 1960s, however, Britain's Labour Prime Minister, Harold Wilson, decided this practice had to cease and that in the future, reasons had to be argued and permission had to be sought from the home secretary or the prime minister before such action could be taken. That has remained the policy of all successive British governments. Crucially, however, the intelligence and securities agencies retained their decision-making privilege if, in their opinion and for whatever reason, they believed the security of the state was at risk.

The 1994 Intelligence Services Act placed the functions of the Secret Intelligence Service (SIS) and the Government Headquarters (GCHQ) on a statutory footing for the first time. It also established a group of senior parliamentarians, reporting to the prime minister, who looked into the expenditure, administration and policy of the intelligence and security agencies. Greater openness was also introduced and a new official committee was set up to examine the plans of the Security Service and review its work. Of course, this did not mean that MI5 and MI6 had to reveal top-secret information to the committee, nor have they done so.

With Britain's media renowned for their dogged pursuit of issues that gripped the nation and sold newspapers, MI5 was not keen to undertake such an operation in Britain. They were well aware that if there was the faintest whiff or suggestion of MI5 involvement in her death the media would pull out all stops in an effort to establish the truth. It was therefore preferable for such an operation to be undertaken overseas.

The fact that Dodi's father owned the Ritz in Paris as well as the Windsor's former home in the Bois de Boulogne led MI5 to the conclusion that there was every probability that Diana and Dodi would visit Paris from time to time to continue their affair in private — out of sight of the tenacious British press. After consultations with their counterparts in the D.S.T, the decision was made to make preparations for the operation in Paris. They needed a plan that could be put into action within days, if not hours. Over the years, security agencies have frequently used the fatal car crash as their most favored method of arranging the "accidental" death of those they want to target. Throughout Europe, a hundred people or more die every day in road accidents. The fact that people die in car crashes has come to be accepted in all Western civilizations and, as a result, raises fewer questions than any other method of removing unwanted citizens.

M15 contacted the D.S.T in Paris, saying that they needed a car for an operation they were planning. By pure chance, in the spring of 1997, the D.S.T. obtained a Mercedes, used on a regular basis by patrons of the Ritz. This car, leased to the Ritz by a car company called Etoile Limousine, was used to ferry guests to and from airports and, when required, for shopping and sightseeing. The D.S.T. was now using the vehicle to eavesdrop on the occasional distinguished visitor and also keep an eye on distinguished VIPs thought to be targets for terrorists.

They arranged for the Ritz's black Mercedes S280 — license number 688 LTV 75 — to be stolen by professional car thieves just in case someone was caught in the act. In return for their assistance, the thieves were given permission to take whatever they wanted from the vehicle and then dump it. On April 20, the car was stolen from outside the fashionable Taillevent Restaurant in Paris. Sixteen days later, it was discovered stripped and abandoned outside the city. The wheels and the tires were missing as well as the inner workings of the doors. Also stolen was the all-important electronic "brain," which controlled the car's vital functions, including the power steering, the electric windows, the speedometer, the antilock braking system and the six-cylinder 195 brake horsepower engine. Total cost of repairs: $20,000.

By June, the Mercedes was fully repaired and back in service. In the meantime, D.S.T. technicians secretly installed sophisticated tracking devices and transmitters. The tracking device transmitted detailed information of the car's exact whereabouts directly to a Visual Display Unit map back at headquarters. A voice-activated transmitting device had also been installed, which meant that all conversations inside the vehicle could be overheard and recorded back at base. A fail-safe tracking device — a backup mechanism — was also installed in case either of the other two failed.

It was decided that this Mercedes would be used for the operation. Meetings and discussions took place with D.S.T. officers and a plan of action was thrashed out. Officers visited the site of the proposed crash, approach routes were discussed, necessary speeds measured and dry runs made in another Mercedes S280. Experienced police drivers considered that the entrance to the chosen site — the Alma Tunnel — was such a narrow, awkward approach that driving at speeds in excess of 50 mph created problems for the driver. That was the reason why the Paris highway authorities had applied a speed limit of 37 mph on the approach to the tunnel beneath the Pont de l'Alma.

Back at the Ritz on that fateful night, Diana and Dodi made their way to the hotel's Espadon Restaurant, where Diana ordered her last meal — roast turbot garnished with dried seaweed and seasonal crispy vegetables. From the neighboring dimly lit bar, she could hear the pianist playing romantic melodies that included *You Must Remember This*. After finishing their main course, Diana and Dodi left and went upstairs to their suite. It was 10:15 p.m.

About the same time, Henri Paul arrived at the

hotel, alerted by a phone call asking him to
return because Diana and Dodi were planning to
leave the Ritz after dinner and drive to Dodi's
apartment off the Champs Elysee.

The MI5 team and their D.S.T. counterparts
had been alerted after Diana and Dodi arrived in
Paris, and they were informed to pre-arrange
their tasks for that night because it was believed
the operation would shortly take place. They
were also warned that if Diana and Dodi changed
their plans and did not spend the night at Dodi's
apartment the operation would be called off.

Officers from both MI5 and the D.S.T. took up
positions outside the Ritz, two or three posing as
photographers, others mingling with the excited
crowd eager to catch a glimpse of Diana. Their
task was to create a fuss, to excite the crowd, to
keep the photographers busy and to create an
atmosphere of confusion.

D.S.T. technicians were working on the
Mercedes S280 earlier in the evening. The world
has always been surprised, indeed taken aback by
the fact that neither Dodi nor Diana was wearing a
seat belt when they were found in the back of the
crashed Mercedes. Diana's friends, her former
police bodyguards and anyone who had ever
traveled with Diana in a car knew that she was
meticulous about "belting up" before each and

every car journey. Diana would insist on William and Harry "belting up" before the car they were traveling in had even started to move. And, when the lads were older, she would frequently check to see if they had secured their seat belts correctly.

It is beyond comprehension that as the Ritz security officer Henri Paul accelerated to speeds in excess of 100 mph, as he raced through the near-deserted streets of Paris, that Diana would have quietly sat back and not made any attempt whatsoever to secure her seat belt. Everyone who ever knew Diana well has never been able to provide a satisfactory answer to that conundrum.

Therefore it is highly likely, in fact highly probable, that Diana *did* fasten her seat belt on that fateful journey. The safety belts on Mercedes cars are made to the highest standards. The anchorage of those belts is tested to a remarkable degree. But Diana's seat belt failed that night — Dodi's also failed. The only conclusion that can be drawn is that someone tampered with those seat belts that night.

And there is more. As with all bodyguards, it is their duty to ensure that their VIP passengers are "belted up" before they commence any journey. Of course, it is possible in the heat of the moment that Trevor Rees-Jones forgot to tell them to secure their belts or, as has been suggested, Dodi may have told him that it didn't matter if they "belted up" that night. But the fact that Rees-Jones secured his own seat belt adds greater mystery to the fact that Diana never, apparently, secured her seat belt.

It is also an insult to Trevor Rees-Jones' professional reputation to suggest that if, as had been presumed, neither Dodi nor Diana "belted up" that night, he would not have warned Diana and Dodi to fasten their seat belts when he decided that he should secure his own belt, due to the fast speeds Henri Paul was driving.

Following Diana's tragic death, experts specializing in the causes of deaths and serious injuries suffered by car passengers in road accidents, were of the belief that if Diana had her seat belt on that night, there was every probability that she would have survived the crash, especially as she was sitting in the rear of the car and the furthest away from the front near-side of the vehicle that sustained the initial impact. Surgeons who deal with the broken bodies of car accident victims everyday are of the belief that despite the speed the Mercedes was traveling that night, it would have been very unlikely that Diana would have suffered the injury which was mainly responsible for her death — a torn pulmonary vein – if she had been wearing a seat belt.

The D.S.T. technicians who were working on the Mercedes that day, on orders from MI5, had been "fixing" the rear passenger seat belts. This process of "fixing" seat belts is well-known and frequently used, not only by those working for security agencies, but also by many personal bodyguards who spend much of their life sitting beside a driver in the front of a car while the person they are guarding sits in the back. The reason is that bodyguards may be called upon to take action within a split-second and having to undo a seat belt, which takes two hands, takes precious seconds.

The pin that secures the seat belt in position across the person's lap is filed down. In the event of a bodyguard wanting to take immediate action and leap out of the vehicle, he only needs to thrust his body toward the door and the seat belt breaks loose without the need for the bodyguard to even touch the belt. And this filing process, usually carried out with a power grinder, can be adjusted to any degree. If the person wants a rapid release, more of the pin is filed down and, conversely, if the person wants a little protection, the pin is only gently filed, which means a greater effort has to be made before the safety pin flies loose, but still with no need to use the hands.

This was the operation that the technicians were carrying out on the Mercedes that night.

Since the fatal crash, much of the blame has been attached to Henri Paul, the 41-year-old security officer who had worked for the al Fayeds for six years. Balding and stocky, the 5-foot-5-inch native of Brittany looked 10 years older. A former pilot in the French Air Force, Paul spent most of his evenings after work drinking and socializing in the bars and small clubs around the center of Paris where, as a gifted musician, he would happily play the piano in exchange for free drinks. Paul, who spoke fluent English and German, was also a paid informant for both the D.S.T. and the DGSE (Direction General de la Securite Exterieure), the French equivalent of MI6. His handlers asked him to keep an eye on certain guests at the Ritz and keep them informed if certain people they were interested in booked a room there. Henri Paul would frequently meet his French handlers in one of his Paris haunts and have a few drinks with them.

In 1988, he dated Laurence Pujol, a petite, young, blond secretary at the Ritz who had a 2-year-old daughter Samantha. A year later, they were married and the three set up home. Paul was happy and adored little Samantha. But in 1992, Laurence and Samantha moved out and a heartbroken Henri Paul turned to more serious drinking.

Following his death, there have been conflicting stories about Henri Paul and the part his drinking may have played in the crash that killed Diana. Some considered Paul to be a social drinker; others, that he was a heavy drinker and others claimed he was an alcoholic. His former wife, Laurence, insisted that she had never seen him drunk, claiming that he drank only one or two glasses of wine a night. Friends who knew him really well reported that Paul was a habitual drinker, but never showed any sign of inebriation.

In 1996, however, it became obvious that Henri Paul was worried about his drinking problem. After the fatal crash, Dr. Dominique Melo said that she prescribed medication — Aotal — to Henri Paul for alcohol abuse. He was later prescribed Tiapridal to combat aggression, as well as the antidepressant Prozac. Despite warnings to stop drinking, Henri Paul continued to do so.

Investigative journalists reported of friends and acquaintances confirming that Henri Paul had been drinking with them that evening. Staff at the Ritz also claimed that Henri Paul drank alcohol that night as he waited for Diana and Dodi to appear. Dodi's bodyguard Les Wingfield, however, stated that he had not seen Paul take a drink that evening. On the night of August 30, Paul was seen in a happy and excited mood, but no one reported that he looked drunk or acted as though he had been drinking.

That evening, Henri Paul was briefed at a meeting with one of his intelligence handlers. He was told that the *gendarmerie*, the Paris police force, had a plan that night to prevent photographers from following Diana and Dodi after they left the Ritz. He was told the police had been ordered to give the couple some privacy and save them from further harassment. Dodi was instructed to drive the Mercedes S280 while the other Mercedes, a much larger 600 model, would be used as a decoy. At that vital meeting, Henri Paul was also given precise instructions as to which route he was to take to Dodi's apartment. Importantly, it was not the usual or the fastest route. He was also informed that there would be no police patrol vehicles checking his speed and that he should drive as fast as possible in order to escape the photographers on their scooters and motorbikes. Henri Paul was told to phone Dodi in his suite, tell him of the plan and to impress upon him that the plan of escape from the Ritz and the route had been devised by the Paris police to prevent further harassment. From Dodi's actions and instructions that night it seems he agreed to the plan.

Despite the late hour, there were 30 to 40 people still mingling about, waiting for Diana to emerge, beside the 15 or so photographers who had waited patiently most of the evening. Parked by the door was the Mercedes 600, the driver and the body-guards. Hotel staff were also popping in and out of the main entrance. Some of those standing around in the cool of the summer evening and posing as pushy cameramen and eager spectators were British and French intelligence agents.

At 12:15 a.m., hotel staff announced to the wait-ing photographers that Diana and Dodi would be out in five minutes. Photographers and members of the crowd pushed forward toward the entrance, creating a sense of excitement and expectation. Bodyguards and Ritz staff stepped outside ready to prevent the photographers from getting too close to Diana as she took the short, five-yard walk to the waiting car. There had already been two scuffles between bodyguards and paparazzi, and the situation had become heated with much pushing, shoving, shouting and heated exchanges. The atmosphere was electric.

But Diana and Dodi didn't appear. Once again, they had used the hotel's back exit, where Henri Paul was sitting in the Mercedes S280. Only one photographer was there. In no time, staff helped Diana and Dodi into the car, Trevor Rees-Jones jumped into the front passenger seat and Henri Paul put his foot down hard on the accelerator.

Gamma photographer Romauld Rat recorded later, "As I arrived at the lights, which had been at red, I saw the Mercedes with Diana and Dodi inside pull away. As the Mercedes increased speed along the road beside the River Seine we all dropped back, unable to keep up. At that stage, I believe the Mercedes must have been doing in excess of 80 mph and it was accelerating farther away from us."

Drivers entering the Alma Tunnel veer slightly toward the right before the road dips down to the left and straightens out. The road has a slight camber and there are no crash barriers, just massive concrete columns some 3 feet in diameter on the driver's left side and a wall on the right.

It was at this moment that one or two of the chasing photographers saw a bright flash of a light coming from inside the tunnel. It was too powerful, too bright to be the headlights of a car or the flash of a photographer's camera. It was that intense flash of light, momentarily blinding Henri Paul, that made him lose control of the speeding Mercedes. The vehicle smashed into the third concrete column with a tremendous crash that sounded almost like an explosion. It bounced off, careened farther along the tunnel and then smashed almost head-on into the 13th column some 20 yards farther on, before spinning 180 degrees until it came to rest against the wall on the right side of the tunnel. The vehicle was a tangled, bludgeoned mass of metal and the roof caved in almost to the hood. The front end, which had taken the brunt of the impact, had been pushed back some three feet, but the back seats and the rear of the car were relatively intact.

Dodi Fayed and Henri Paul, who were both on the left side of the vehicle, died — principally from massive trauma to their chests and heads. Diana, thrown about all over the inside of the car as it spun 180 degrees, was lying severely injured on the floor of the car facing backward between the front and rear seats. She was semi-conscious and, at first appearance, it didn't seem as though she was seriously injured. This was the message the late-night duty officer at the British Embassy in Paris was told some 30 minutes after the crash. He immediately passed this information to Buckingham Palace staff on weekend duty who telephoned Balmoral so that Prince Charles, who was staying there with Wills and Harry, could be informed.

The flash of brilliant light had come from the white Fiat Uno that was traveling slowly on the correct side of the two-lane tunnel. As the Mercedes raced into the tunnel, an agent in the rear seat of the Fiat Uno, alerted via a wireless link that the Mercedes was approaching, flashed the blinding light directly into the eyes of Henri Paul. Those high-intensity lights, used by United

States and NATO forces, are designed to blind and disorient people for a few seconds so that they lose control. Driving at such a high speed, probably around 100 mph or more, Henri Paul didn't stand a chance.

The entire trip from the Ritz to the crash scene had taken under three minutes — it would have taken about 10 minutes if Henri Paul had kept to the legal maximum speed. That short time span gives a fairly accurate idea of how fast Henri Paul must have been driving.

Within minutes there was chaos and confusion at the crash scene as 20 or so photographers and their drivers came to a halt near the tangled Mercedes. The nonstop wail of the Mercedes horn, magnified in the confines of the tunnel, added to the chaos and people tried to make themselves heard by yelling above the noise. The photographers flashed away while Romauld Rat, who held a first-aid certificate, checked inside the vehicle to see if anyone was alive. He realized immediately that both Henri Paul and Dodi were dead but, on closer examination, he discovered that both Diana and Rees-Jones were alive.

It was by chance that only three minutes after the crash, Dr. Frederic Mailliez, 36, and an American friend Mark Butt, 42, were returning from a birthday party and chanced upon the crash scene. Dr. Mailliez, an experienced emergency physician, was employed by a private on-call medical service. Having quickly checked the scene, Dr. Mailliez also reached the conclusion that only Diana and Rees-Jones were alive. He called for two ambulances and resuscitation equipment and ran back to the Mercedes with the only piece of medical equipment Dr. Mailliez had in his car, a self-inflating oxygen mask. He clambered into the back of the vehicle and held up Diana's head so she could breathe into the mask.

Five minutes after the crash, two police officers on patrol, flagged down by motorists, arrived on the scene. They called for more police support and then tried to usher away the photographers, who were still at work, and the group of interested bystanders who had arrived on the scene. Dr. Mailliez would say later that at that time he believed Diana's injuries were not life-threatening because there was very little blood coming from her nose and mouth. There were no other visible injuries. She even mumbled a word or two.

Six minutes later, the first ambulance arrived and Dr. Mailliez moved away from Diana so that the ambulance crew could take over. Minutes later, he drove away from the scene reasonably confident that Diana would survive. Dr. Mailliez had no idea the young blond woman was the Princess of Wales.

The ambulance crew quickly ascertained that Henri Paul showed no sign of life, so they concentrated on trying to save Dodi. But after 15 minutes trying to resuscitate him, Dodi was pronounced dead.

It is now acknowledged by most doctors that if Diana had been rushed to the nearest hospital within minutes of the crash it is likely that her life would have been saved. Recovery from such a severe injury is rare and is possible only through immediate hospital treatment. Ironically, if the crash had occurred in the United States or Britain, it is possible that Diana's life might have been saved though, as a consequence of the injury, she may have probably suffered permanent brain damage.

In France, car crash victims are stabilized at the scene before being taken to the hospital. That is why French ambulances are equipped more like mini operating theaters on wheels and are staffed by a fully qualified physician and nurse. In the United States and Britain, the practice is to get the victim to the hospital as quickly as possible and that is why their ambulances are staffed with paramedics.

Diana was carried to the waiting ambulance parked in the tunnel a few feet from the Mercedes and immediately placed on a respirator but her pulse and blood pressure continued to deteriorate. The decision was made to stabilize her before leaving the crash site, but after 40 minutes it was decided there was no option but to take her to the nearby Pitie-Salpetriere Hospital after Diana suffered a major heart attack. She was revived only by external heart massage. The ambulance moved at a snail's pace so that the medics could continue their work. And they didn't want to further risk worsening the condition of the weakening Diana.

She was still unconscious when she arrived at the hospital and once inside the operating room she suffered another heart attack. An emergency thoracotomy (surgical opening of the pulmonary vein) revealed a major laceration to the left pulmonary vein. Damage to such a major blood vessel will usually cause a patient to bleed to death very quickly. Twelve doctors surrounded the operating table. Some surgeons worked on repairing the laceration, others took turns to pump her heart manually, while others pumped blood and other liquids into her bloodstream. After two hours of both internal and external massaging of her heart, Princess Diana was pronounced dead at 4 a.m. Paris time on Sunday, August 31.

Chapter 13

Diana's Secret Mission

$\mathcal{D}$iana's newfound status as an international icon gave her a wonderful feeling of achievement and success. She felt good about herself, and the plaudits she read in newspapers and magazines gave her a feeling of real elation. Sometimes, Diana would read something in the press about herself or watch herself on television and then leap to her feet and walk around the room clenching her fists, her face wreathed in smiles, a look of excitement and determination in her eyes. "Done it, done it" she would mutter quietly to herself between clenched teeth. Those visits to Angola and Bosnia were for Diana the most momentous events of her life because now she could hold her head high for the first time in her life. She had done something to be proud of and the buzz it gave her was like nothing she ever before experienced. She became convinced that she could take on almost anything.

Until that moment, Diana had been craving the adoration of the media and, even more so, those hundreds and sometimes thousands of ordinary men, women and children who came to support and cheer her whenever she stepped out into the public arena. But this caused new problems for Diana. She began to believe the hype that she was receiving from around the globe — pictures, stories and articles about her and her life in innumerable newspapers and magazines and, of course, television news and magazine programs. Praise and acclaim were heaped upon her and descriptions ranged from "Angel of Mercy" to "Savior of the Innocents."

This gave her a feeling of power and real achievement for the first time in her life. She had never before felt so confident or successful. Now Diana came to believe that there was nothing that she could not achieve and, in proving herself to the world, she had succeeded in two of her main aims that she had dreamed of for some years — to destroy Charles' reputation and dominate the royal scene. She had achieved both within a matter of a couple of years. She had ruined Charles' reputation with the great mass of the British people and she was fast reducing both the queen and

Prince Philip to bit players as they went about their dutiful royal tasks as they had done for the last 40 years.

Diana knew that she had become not only the most popular royal in modern times, but had now become the most sought after person in the Western world. As Mike Whitlam explained, "In reality, there were only three world figures in the 1990s who would be welcomed in the great majority of countries for their ability to capture the imagination for humanitarian causes: Mother Teresa, Nelson Mandela and Princess Diana. That was all."

Throughout the 1990s, when royal tours and visits to foreign and commonwealth countries were discussed among diplomats, the only person the host nations wanted to see was Diana. Most countries readily turned down the suggestion of solo visits by Prince Charles and they even found excuses for not hosting tours or visits by the queen and Prince Philip. Of course some visits, scheduled years before, did take place, but new invitations were becoming few and far between. However, if there was the faintest possibility that Diana would visit a country, for a day or a week, the red carpet was immediately thrown down, celebrations organized and there would be an almost tangible feeling of excitement and expectation in the air for weeks before her arrival. Diana loved every minute of it.

Following her legal separation in 1992, Diana was fully aware that she was succeeding in her ambitions to a far greater extent than she ever thought possible. Diana had been in awe of the queen all her life; she had been timid and shy in her presence whenever they met; she respected the queen's remarkable workload and dedication to duty, but now she had succeeded in pushing even the queen, the head of state, to a subsidiary role. Now Diana was carrying the flag, the one person in Britain whom the rest of the world admired and many loved. She secretly reveled in her newfound fame and wallowed in the adoration. It was the most extraordinary achievement, particularly for a shy, reserved, poorly educated girl who had left school without passing a single exam, who had never held down a proper full-time job in her life and who, through adversity and her own determination, had proved herself to be a remarkable young woman.

And it wasn't simply her glamorous, movie star qualities, her beauty, her radiant smile or her acting ability. Diana succeeded so triumphantly because she cared for people and she showed she cared. She was happy to be seen with victims of AIDS, touching and holding the victims of this terrible disease that was frightening and killing so many people; she loved holding and helping destitute, starving children in Third World countries or caring for leprosy victims because she knew it would open people's hearts and their purses and bring some comfort and maybe hope to those poor afflicted victims who had no education, no food, no future and no chance for a better life.

But even Diana wasn't that pure, straightforward or honest. On occasions when Diana left the hospital or hospices where she had been chatting, touching or holding AIDS patients, she would wave goodbye with a look of sadness and compassion in her face, get into the car and, in a trenchant voice tell her chauffeur, "For God's sake drive back to the palace quickly so I can have a hot bath and feel clean again." It might seem vulgar to reveal such negative characteristics, but that was the real Diana; she wasn't totally without a stain on her character.

Diana's unique position of power would only last a short while. Unknown to Diana, the forces ranged against her were becoming ever more fearful of her power to influence people's opinion and to persuade the hoi polloi — electors everywhere — to listen to her arguments and follow her lead. Now, Diana had truly become an unguided missile because there was no telling where she might strike next. There was no plan, no catalog, no list of interests except that she wanted to continue the work she now felt she was destined to undertake from the day she split from Charles. Since her 1995 divorce, Diana was even more confident that she had the popularity and authority to become an ambassador of good causes, roving the world, searching for causes to espouse, humanitarian issues to publicize and innumerable problems to solve.

Throughout the last seven years of her life, Diana had come to the conclusion that she would never find true happiness with a man, though she might fall in love from time to time. And she knew that for the next few years she would continue to flirt and find men she fancied to tease, to titillate, to bed and to amuse her. Diana came to enjoy openly flirting and playing the harlot and not for one moment did she believe that it was wrong in any way to enjoy a sex life with as many men as she wished. She would say, "It's my life and I can do what the hell I like with it."

In some circumstances it seems that Diana didn't care a damn who she hurt in her headlong pursuit of the men she wanted to lay. One such example was Diana's famous public tangle with the English rugby captain Will Carling and his wife Julia. It was played out, blow for blow, in a glare of publicity gleefully fueled by tabloid press during which Diana was labeled a "homewrecker." In private, Diana referred to Julia as "that little tart." For Diana, that affair was both perfunctory and brief though Diana did gain applause and recognition from William and Harry for bringing the English rugby captain home on a number of occasions. For Carling and Julia the affair ended their marriage. Understandably, Julia was not a happy lady though, to her discredit, Diana seemed to take pride in winning the battle for Carling's affections. Then she ditched him.

In her heart Diana could count on the fingers of one hand the number of men she had truly loved. And although Hewitt showed serious interest for a number of years, he hadn't the courage or the willpower to go through with the marriage. Diana understood Hewitt's nervousness because he had come from a quite humble background, a stranger to the life of luxury, power and prestige enjoyed by most of his brother officers in the Brigade of Guards who came from more wealthy families, many following in their father's footsteps and joining regiments in which they had served. Diana understood that Hewitt realized that he was treading on dangerous ground becoming involved with her. Hewitt told her that he had been strongly advised and later chastised by senior officers for refusing to end the affair. She also realized that by continuing their relationship, Hewitt was taking a great risk with his military career. And so it proved. In 1993, Hewitt quit the army but, in fact, he was given little alternative but to resign. Following the initial warning, Hewitt had been advised on numerous occasions to end his affair with the Princess of Wales, whose husband also happened to be Colonel-in-Chief of his regiment, the Brigade of Guards. But Hewitt had not heeded the advice.

And by then Diana had been indulging herself in a number of other love affairs, more illicit relationships with a number of men. And the more she met, socialized, dined, partied and bedded these other men she came to see the flaws in Hewitt's one-dimensional character. She came to understand that Hewitt was not as bright or intelligent as she had first thought; that although he might be courageous on the battlefield, he hadn't the strength of character to take the decision she had wanted and needed in their early years together. And she understood that Hewitt lacked the courage to openly declare his love and show the world he wanted to marry her because he would then once again have to face the wrath of the British people, his brother officers and the British media by admitting that he was the father of Prince Harry. But for some years she continued to enjoy his occasional company and his lovemaking, though she had since discovered there were other men whose company she enjoyed even more and who were equally as wild, romantic, passionate and satisfying in bed.

There were only two other serious lovers in Diana's life — Oliver Hoare and the heart surgeon Hasnat Khan. But Hoare did not want to become more closely involved with a woman who appeared to be suffering serious psychological problems and he was also fortunate in having a loving and beautiful wife waiting patiently at home for him to finish his royal fling. And the handsome Hasnat Khan was far more interested in being married to his job and his career as a surgeon than the limelight, the glamour and the problems that marriage to Diana would have brought.

When Diana's heart was really torn by love and the subsequent desperate feeling of rejection, she would invariably turn to one or two close, personal friends in whom she had great faith. They were her ever-faithful friend and confidant Carolyn Bartholomew, her former roommate and lady-in-waiting, and her dear friend Rosa Monckton. From time to time there were others, such as Sarah Ferguson and Kate Menzies as well as half a dozen other women, including some of her therapists, whom Diana dallied with for a while and then cast aside.

In the last six years of her life, Diana became particularly close to Rosa Monckton, the wife of Dominic Lawson, editor of *The Sunday Telegraph* newspaper, after Rosa had given birth at six months to a still-born baby girl she named Natalia. In a moment of deep sorrow between the two women, Diana suddenly asked Rosa if she would like to bury baby Natalia in her private garden at Kensington Palace, a place which Diana always referred to as "my little oasis."

For a woman whose life was filled with drama and heartache, the internment of a baby in an unmarked grave in her own garden at Kensington Palace must rank as one of the most extraordinary occurrences in Diana's life. It was a thoughtful, deeply affectionate though, perhaps, somewhat bizarre offer of friendship. But Rosa loved the idea and, as a result, baby Natalia's body lies buried today against the garden's west wall.

At the graveside, Rosa read out a verse by Rabindranath Tagore, India's greatest poet and Nobel prize winner, a poem that Diana came to remember by heart and to love.

> *"They who are near me do not*
> *know that you are nearer to me*
> *than they are.*
> *They who speak to me do not know*
> *that my heart is full with your*

> unspoken words.
> *They who crowd in my path do not*
> *know that I am walking alone*
> *with you.*
> *They who love do not know that their love*
> *brings you to my heart."*

As those lines were read out at the short funeral service, Diana once again revealed her huge capacity for unhappiness — one of the reasons she responded so openly to the suffering of humanity — and the tears flowed unchecked.

That sign of such a profound friendship between the two women, who were roughly the same age, cemented their relationship and, as a result, whenever Diana was at a particularly low ebb she would usually turn to Rosa for comfort, solace and understanding. Rosa turned out to be one of Diana's true friends, recalling after her death, "She used to bound down the stairs of Kensington Palace with a huge smile and arms outstretched. But she also had a dark side — that of a wounded, trapped animal who frequently asked for advice but rarely took it."

Throughout her adult life, however, Diana's friends had not always proved so rewarding, though the greater part of the blame for that rested with Diana and her paranoia, which she was never able to shake off or dispel. It was Diana's abnormal tendency to suspect and mistrust others that led to her lifelong tendency to make and break friendships with many people, nearly all of whom were women, all usually for no good reason. The number of women to whom Diana showed great affection, trust, kindness and friendship exceeded a score or more in the last 15 years of her life but these so-called friends would be dropped by Diana without rhyme or reason. And the breakdown in the friendship would usually be sudden and immediate, leaving the friends bemused, disconcerted and somewhat unnerved by the lightning change in Diana's attitude to them.

Diana's infamous mood swings were legendary among her friends and those with whom she worked at Kensington Palace. Nearly everyone who came into regular contact with Diana either witnessed one or many of these mood swings or was at the receiving end of this quite bizarre treatment in which Diana's mood of the moment would gyrate from gaiety, laughter and happiness to a look that could kill or a comment which seemed designed to wound or ridicule the recipient. She could be cruel indeed, a trait which she would have hated if practiced on her by a friend or acquaintance. And these mood swings were still a part of Diana's personality through the last years of her life. No one to whom I have spoken could give sound reasons for these violent swings in her moods, most commenting with a shrug, "That was Diana."

The life of Diana can never be properly appreciated and understood without examining and evaluating her constant need for reassurance and the lengths to which she would go in her bid to control the so-called "demons" in her head that caused her so much stress and anguish.

Diana never enjoyed a peace of mind at any time of her life — from her teenage years onward and she would forever raise the matter with whomsoever would listen until many of her friends became rather bored with the repetitive conversation about the stress in her life, the problems she faced and her desperate search for cures for whatever ailment she was suffering at the time.

To that end, Diana approached a battalion of practitioners, including members of the medical profession, who were all invited to give their expert opinion, their suggested remedies or to exercise their particular skills on a variety of Diana's alleged ailments and her never-ending search for peace of mind in what she saw as her stress-filled life. But for the most part, most members of the medical profession who treated Diana came to the same conclusion — that Diana was simply indulging herself. She would read of the latest fad, some interesting therapy, a new remedy, attributes of an avant-garde treatment and would instantly set about finding out all the details and then try out the fad herself.

Aromatherapy was a constant interest and fascination to Diana and one that she indulged in at least once or twice a week over a period of some 10 years or more. These sessions, undertaken in four different treatment centers in London, made Diana feel relaxed and happy with the world. Diana would experiment with a variety of oils allegedly providing whatever relief she requested at the time, though stress and mental fatigue were the main reasons she gave for seeking any of these treatments.

Acupuncture was another favorite and she became convinced that it was responsible for overcoming her bulimia, her *anorexia nervosa* and her nervousness in company. Diana graciously credited one of her practitioners, Oonagh Toffolo, who would frequently visit Kensington Palace, with saving her life. Diana commented publicly, "I do think Oonagh saved my life. She certainly saved my sanity."

Diana also indulged in colonic irrigation on a regular basis at Chrissie Fitzgerald's London therapy center, despite the fact that she had medical advice telling her there was no need for her to undergo such treatment. She believed the irrigation therapy cleared out the angst and the aggravation that built up inside her, making her more relaxed and at peace with the world. She also enjoyed reflexology, which Diana believed drained the tension from her body.

And there were other treatments that, at one time or another, excited or interested Diana in her life-long quest for peace of mind. She put her faith in osteopathy, which aimed to correct supposed deformations of the skeleton, leading to disease. Her London osteopath, Michael Skipworth, would receive urgent phone calls from a panic-stricken Diana asking for an immediate appointment because she was suffering from a severe headache. Diana came to believe that she suffered from migraines but was reassured that her headaches were not migraines. She would drive to Skipworth's office and found that after 30 minutes of his soothing hands, her headache had disappeared. So for a while Diana put her faith in him.

There were other treatments as well. At one time Diana came to rely on psychotherapy, introduced to her by her trusted friend and therapist Susie Orbach, with whom Diana enjoyed a rewarding relationship during the last four years of her life. Susie Orbach had co-founded London's Women's Therapy Center when she returned after training as a therapist in the United States. Diana met Susie after reading one of her book's *Fat Is a Feminist Issue* published in 1978. In that book Orbach identifies the obsession with weight, shape and food that haunts so many Western women and lays the blame squarely on men for controlling women within unequal partnerships. Diana related to this theory and even more so when she met and talked over her problems with the sensible, down-to-earth Susie.

To educated women, Orbach's theory may have been commonplace but to the innocent, poorly educated Diana who hardly ever read a book, Susie was someone who understood Diana's problem and could offer sound advice through her own experience. Orbach had once suffered from binge eating and its problems but had learned how to control and conquer those urges. Orbach, too, had an unhappy marriage at a young age. Diana believed she had finally met the one person who could *really* understand her, perhaps even shape her life and, as a result, Susie became her guru. Almost dutifully Diana became one of her keenest disciples and she came to rely on Orbach's advice, discussing every problem, every aspect of her life and revealing many but not all of her secrets.

During psychotherapy, the patient transfers emotions connected with people from their lives to the analyst in a bid to deal with the past and eventually forget those emotions that have caused the patient stress. Hypnotherapy can be used for many different aspects of a patient's health and Diana would seek the treatment in a bid to contain her stress level, which she convinced herself she could never overcome. The third treatment — anger therapy — Diana sought after she came to realize that she lost her temper far too often and for silly reasons. She knew that she flew off the handle for no good reason and, in her frustration, would shout, yell, swear and rage around the apartment. It was a well-known fact in Kensington Palace that when the staff heard Diana raging about the place most would try to keep out of her way, fearing a high-velocity verbal attack surrounded by the most lewd, colorful language.

Diana lost faith in anger therapy because she found it wasn't working and she continued to be prone to swearing and yelling fits of temper often for little or no reason. In the 1990s, Diana came to find that her own treatment helped to assuage her violent temper and wild mood swings. She would run to her bed, throw herself on the duvet, thump the pillows with her fists and bury her head in the pillows screaming at the top of her voice, the goosedown drowning her shrieking cries of frustration so that no one could hear her rages.

Like many members of the royal family before her, Diana would also put her faith in astrologers, soothsayers, clairvoyants, mystics, palmists and card readers. Diana would question friends about such people, asking the names and phone numbers of those they trusted and whether they thought the person would be suitable for her to visit. And yet, though Diana did indeed visit many such people, both men and women, she always felt that because they knew to whom they were giving their advice, their opinions, their views of her future, they tempered their true thoughts because they feared she would not want to face the truth. As a result, Diana would feel frustrated, never believing anything promising she was told but preferring to believe the news of her future was always negative, never positive.

Diana would also use her visits to such fortune tellers to seek facts about Prince Charles and his future. She would ask them whether her husband's life was in danger; whether he would die in an accident; whether he would marry again, and whether he would ever be king. In his book, *Shadows of a Princess*, her secretary Patrick Jephson wrote, "Yet she continued to heed her astrologers' predictions, the more dire the better, particularly where the Prince (Charles) was concerned. Sure enough, she was rewarded with regular forecasts of helicopter crashes, skiing accidents and other calamities that obstinately refused to befall him ..."

During the 1990s, when Diana first came to fear that there were people "out there" who wanted her dead she would demand the fortune tellers tell her about her future but, as far as is known, none of them forecast an early death. As a result, she came not to believe their predictions but despite her serious doubts of their competence, Diana continued to seek their prophecies on a weekly basis up to the time of her death.

But there were more down-to-earth friends and advisers who tried for years to wean Diana away from seeking advice from so many different sources, some of whom were dubious though others were well-meaning. As a result of seeking so much advice from so many different people, Diana was constantly confused, leaping from one piece of advice to another. To some who knew Diana well, her search for an answer to her supposed ills and problems was in reality a need for sympathy and attention from strangers who became her "friends." It was also her need for people to slavishly lavish attention on her —

perhaps the only real benefit Diana gained from seeking the advice of so many diverse experts.

After Diana's divorce, Patrick Jephson realized that the princess, to whom he owed total allegiance, needed a strategy of her own now that she was no longer a fully fledged member of the royal family. He recognized that Diana had no experience in planning a public career for herself in the nation's life and, it seemed in late 1993 that she was seriously contemplating and openly discussing with friends and advisers her wish to retire altogether from the public arena, living a totally private life away from the cameras, the media and public attention.

In essence, Diana had had enough. She was fed up with the paparazzi following her every step, every move, seemingly only happy when she broke down in tears. The demands from various charities were increasing as they all realized that Diana's involvement in their particular cause brought in more funds and more interest from the general public. Under so much pressure, Diana felt as though she was running on a treadmill that was accelerating at a faster pace each week and month. She was physically exhausted and wanted some peace for herself, so she made her famous speech at the end of 1993 in which she announced her partial withdrawal from public life.

That speech came as a major shock to almost everyone, including her friends and advisers. *"I hope you can find it in your hearts to understand and to give me the time and space that has been lacking in recent years ... When I started my public life 12 years ago I understood that the media might be interested in what I did. I realized then that their attention would inevitably focus on ... our private lives ... But I was not aware of how overwhelming that attention would become; not the extent to which it would affect both my public duties and my personal life in a manner that's been hard to bear..."*

Diana's decision to cut the number of charities she openly supported struck those charities like a thunderbolt. They were aghast that the wonderful Princess of Wales, who had won the heart of the nation, could contemplate for one minute cutting herself off from the charities that relied on her for their very survival. These charity workers recognized that Diana brought real hope and a ray of light to so many disaffected, unhappy, sick, lonely and dying people everywhere and now she was throwing in the towel. They believed there had to be another reason for Diana's decision because it seemed totally at odds with Diana's love and compassion for people less fortunate. To some of the charity organizers responsible for raising the desperately needed funds, Diana's decision to quit meant that much of their work would have to be curtailed; other charities feared financial disaster.

Yet it soon became apparent to those who worked with Diana that she wasn't really intent on finding time and space for herself at all. Within a matter of weeks, Diana had thrown herself into other interests that she found more attractive than the annual round of what to her had become an endless round of boring, fund-raising charity functions. The world scene had beckoned and Diana was keen to make her mark. Now that she had cleared her decks of mundane work in Britain she was ready to take on the world.

As a result of her decision to pull in her horns, Diana's diary for 1994 was a virtual blank. All the planned visits, meetings, conferences and charity work she had agreed to carry out only weeks and months before had to be canceled. Apologies were written, people were disappointed, events were re-organized or simply canceled. For her part, Diana relaxed and enjoyed herself keeping fit, swimming and visiting her ever-growing list of therapists for her many and varied treatments. She also indulged herself with one or two lovers but Diana, more as an escape than anything else, soon grew tired of these men because in reality she was still in love with her darling heart surgeon Hasnat Khan.

In her heart, Diana *really* wanted Hasnat more than any other man she had ever wanted in her entire life. And she didn't even really know why she so loved him. She didn't even know what attracted her to him above every other man she had ever known or loved. She wondered if the attraction was simply that he spurned her many advances, refused her never-ending invitations to lunch, dinner, a drink or a night together in her bed at Kensington Palace.

Diana tried everything to persuade Khan that her love was real and that he was the only man she ever really wanted. But Khan spurned each and every endeavor Diana could come up with and always for the same reason. He wanted to spend his life working as a heart surgeon, where he felt he could do some good in the world, help people to a better life and, in some cases, to actually save peoples lives by the skills he was learning and practicing each day at the hospital. He told Diana that nothing could compete with that, not even a woman as beautiful as she.

During these years, Diana was having frequent informal chats with the energetic Mike Whitlam of the British Red Cross, who had arranged and organized her visit to Zimbabwe to help highlight the plight of African refugee children. He had also helped to organize her visit to Bosnia, where she would be filmed and photographed calling once again for a worldwide ban on anti-personnel mines. The Bosnia visit would prove another major success for Diana. She was filmed talking to young victims of AP mines about their courageous attempts to live normal lives with an arm or a leg missing, caused by exploding land mines. Once again, her presence in Bosnia speaking with courageous young victims brought down the wrath of ordinary men and women everywhere demanding a worldwide ban on land mines when they saw Diana on their television screens silently and emotionally making the case for the banning of all AP mines.

But now Diana wanted more. Mike Whitlam explained, "Diana would come to see me and we would chat about the problems of the world. She always showed a great interest and concern for refugees, particularly the children, many of whom had no parents and relatives and whose life seemed forlorn and hopeless in the face of simply surviving in such a daunting environment without love, affection or anyone to care for them. Diana felt a natural affection for all refugees regardless of race, religion or color because she felt for them, cut off from family and friends with no home, no country and no place to call their own. She felt in some way that she had a special affinity to refugees and we discussed many visits she might consider making to help the refugee problem wherever it occurred. We had organized a visit to Cambodia but diplomatic problems arose and we were advised by the British Foreign Office that it would be inadvisable if the Princess of Wales visited that country in her quest to highlight the problem of refugee children."

It was during these talks in 1997 that Diana came to the conclusion that one of the world's most intransigent refugee problems was in the Middle East, where millions of Palestinians, many of them children, had been living for some 25 years in makeshift refugee camps in the Gaza strip and the West Bank of the River Jordan.

She decided that she wanted to highlight what she understood was a heartbreaking situation, with children having to face a lifetime of living in wretched camps as refugees with no future and no hope of a better future. In the same way as she visited Angola and Bosnia in a bid to bring an end to the use of antipersonnel mines across the world, Diana now wanted to be seen and accepted as the worldwide ambassador for child refugees. She felt that she had finally discovered a mission in life, something really important which would entail visits to many countries in the world, keeping herself in the limelight of world opinion while carrying out a task which the world could only admire.

She knew that her visit to Zimbabwe had created an interest in African child refugees and now she wanted to create a groundswell of sympathy for Palestine child refugees. She saw herself visiting a refugee camp on the West Bank and posing for pictures with the children, perhaps surrounded by hundreds of children, in an effort to raise awareness of their heartrending plight to the world at large.

Diana was excited by her new project because she believed that in helping child refugees she may have found the cause which would promote her from being a stylish, glamorous, empty-headed princess to someone who earned the respect of people, regardless of their nationality, race or religion. Diana would never have compared herself openly with Mother Teresa, but she hoped that in this newfound work for refugees she might one day be seen as maybe a junior version of the sainted nun.

Mike Whitlam talked to Diana about the life and work of Mother Teresa and about her universal appeal. "Diana never for one moment compared herself to Mother Teresa but she admired her greatly. Diana was searching for a role, a big role for herself and she wanted that role to have a worldwide appeal. There was no doubt that she intended to become someone involved with charity work on the world stage. And she was prepared to do whatever was necessary to reach that position. When Diana spoke like this there was a real determination about her ambition, which had to be admired. I do believe that had Diana lived she would have become a major player in worldwide charity work and, quite possibly, the refugee issue would have become her principal concern. She certainly felt great compassion for the children forced to live in terrible conditions in refugee camps everywhere."

At the time of her death, at age 36, Diana had begun to look at herself more critically in the mirror in the privacy of her bathroom. She was a mother of two children who was nearing 40 and she knew that her looks would not last forever. At the time of her death, she would laugh and joke about that fact and yet it gnawed at her mind. She understood it was time to change her image from that of the glamorous princess with cover girl looks to a more serious, concerned woman of the world who would tackle tough subjects.

AIDS provided Diana with her first major worldwide cause to support and she knew that her efforts in that direction had brought her acclaim, not only from people suffering from

AIDS, but from people in all walks of life who admired the fact that someone like Princess Diana would involve herself in a disease which many people shunned.

She leaped at the chance of highlighting the dangers of AP mines and she was happy to stand behind the cause to ban them. And the more children she had seen maimed by AP mines, the more she knew in her heart that here was another cause where she could make a real difference and win praise for doing so.

Now she hoped that she could prove herself once again as a roving ambassador for humanity — coming to the rescue of thousands of Palestinian children living a life of poverty trapped forever in squalid refugee camps. She believed in her innocence that she could bring them hope for a better future and even succeed in providing not only the necessities for their lives but also better education, better living conditions, better food and all in a more peaceful land.

She had little or no idea whether the Israeli or Palestinian authorities would permit her to enter such refugee camps to push for a better, more secure future for Palestinian children. Nor did she have any idea whether the British authorities or the queen and her advisers would permit her to become involved in refugee causes. She didn't care.

Mike Whitlam explained, "Diana never worried what Buckingham Palace would say after she had been stopped from visiting Cambodia. She told me not to take any notice of palace officials when they raised problems about her intended visit to Bosnia. They feared she may have been become embroiled in politics in pushing for a ban on mines, something which, understandably, Buckingham Palace always fought shy of. Diana would hear none of their objections, asking me to organize everything. In no uncertain terms she made it plain that she was determined to go to Bosnia and pose for pictures with children wounded by mines."

Diana would probably have used the same no-nonsense tactics if problems had arisen of her intended visit to the West Bank. There would have been a necessity for her to obtain permission for such a visit from both the Palestinian Red Crescent and the equivalent Israeli charity. But before Diana had made plans for such a visit, she met her tragic death.

It is probable that the Israeli authorities would not have wanted Princess Diana to make such a visit to a Palestinian refugee camp, though it is highly likely that the Palestinians would have welcomed her with open arms. In her innocence and her ignorance Diana, of course, would not have spared a thought or cared a damn for the politics behind such a visit because she was only thinking of the humanitarian gesture she would be making to help the plight of so many child refugees caught in the crossfire of international politics. Diana did not care a bit about the political and military concerns at the prospect of a worldwide ban on AP mines, and she received rave notices from around the entire world for daring to take on the might of world leaders, the politicians, the world's major military machines as well as the all-powerful arms manufacturers. She was treading on dangerous ground.

Joyful at her new great idea to help refugees Diana, however, had entered the hard world of international politics, blissfully unaware that there might be people out there who would not want her unique power of persuasion to highlight such politically sensitive matters.

Chapter 14

Diana's Revenge

*T*he almost audible sigh of relief from senior members of the royal family and their courtiers at the news of Diana's death changed to exasperation and tightlipped anger a few days later when they were forced to sit and listen in silence to the oration by Diana's brother, Earl Charles Spencer at her funeral service in Westminster Abbey. Charles Spencer pulled no punches.

His tribute — the most courageous and outspoken ever delivered at a royal funeral service — shook the royal family, but earned Lord Spencer huge praise from the tens of millions who listened to the oration. He caught the mood of the nation brilliantly.

He began: *"I stand before you today, the representative of a family in grief, in a country in mourning before a world in shock. We are all* united not only in our desire to pay our respects to Diana but rather in our need to do so. For such was her extraordinary appeal that the tens of millions of people taking part in this service all over the world via television and radio who never actually met her, feel that they, too, lost someone close to them.

"Diana was the very essence of compassion, of duty, of style, of beauty. All over the world she was a symbol of selfless humanity. All over the world, a standard bearer for the rights of the truly downtrodden, a very British girl who transcended nationality. Someone with a natural nobility who was classless and who proved in the last year that she needed no royal title to continue to generate her particular brand of magic.

"We have all despaired at our loss and only the strength of the message you gave us through your years of giving has afforded us the strength to move forward. There is a temptation to rush to canonize your memory; there is no need to do so. You stand tall enough as a human being of unique qualities not to be seen as a saint. Indeed, to sanctify your memory would be to miss out on the very core of your being, your wonderfully mischievous sense of humor with a laugh that bent you double.

"Your joy for life transmitted wherever you

took your smile and the sparkle in those unforgettable eyes. Your boundless energy which you could barely contain.

"But your greatest gift was your intuition and it was a gift you used wisely. This is what underpinned all your wonderful attributes, and if we look to analyze what it was about you that had such a wide appeal, we find it in your distinctive feel for what was really important in all our lives.

"Without your Godgiven sensitivity we would be immersed in greater ignorance of AIDS and HIV sufferers, the plight of the homeless, the isolation of lepers, the random destruction of land mines. Diana explained to me once that it was her innermost feelings of suffering that made it possible for her to connect with her constituency of the rejected.

"And here we come to another truth about her. For all the status, the glamour, the applause, Diana remained throughout a very insecure person at heart, almost childlike in her desire to do good for others so she could release herself from deep feelings of unworthiness of which her eating disorders were merely a symptom. The world sensed this part of her character and cherished her for her vulnerability whilst admiring her for her honesty."

Earl Spencer went on to pledge that the Spencer family would do their utmost to protect

William and Harry from being hounded by the press and he pledged that they would do everything possible to ensure her two sons were not totally immersed in duty and tradition. Those words were intended as a warning to the royal family not to stifle the characters and personalities of the two boys.

The speech, broadcast via loudspeakers to the hundreds of thousands lining the streets of London, produced a huge emotional reaction. Applause greeted parts of his speech, but when Lord Spencer vowed to protect William and Harry, it seemed the entire capital erupted in cheering and yelling. So great and so spontaneous was the feeling that Earl Spencer had hit exactly the right nerve, that unbelievably, and without precedent, those members of Diana's charities inside Westminster Abbey began to clap and then to cheer his words.

No one in Britain ever applauds at funerals of this magnitude, but Diana's funeral was a unique occasion. The crescendo of applause in the streets could be heard inside the Abbey and more joined in. But the applause went on and on until everyone inside the Abbey felt the desire and the necessity of joining the masses outside — prelates and peers, presidents and prime ministers and even members of the royal family applauded.

To some, though, Earl Spencer had gone too far. They argued that if he had a genuine concern for the princess, he would never have issued such damning words. It was a brutal speech but nonetheless brilliant, speaking his mind to the world when one of the targets of his attack — the royal family — was sitting in front of him, unable to escape his withering criticism.

In fact, the queen, Prince Philip and their senior courtiers took great exception to Earl Spencer's oration. In private they were furious, believing his attack bordered on treachery. And, by design, from that day forth William and Harry have hardly seen Earl Spencer or any members of the Spencer family. Far from protecting the boys, who are now of course young men, from a life of duty and tradition, Earl Spencer has hardly spoken to them since. It has been made plain to him that William and Harry need no protection by members of the Spencer family. They are Windsors and would remain Windsors.

Slowly but surely since that fateful day nearly six years ago, the iron will of the royal family has been exercised. No longer do William and Harry live the rather free lifestyle they enjoyed with Diana, instead they have been persuaded to enjoy the traditional royal pursuits of the Windsors — playing polo and hunting, shooting, stalking deer and fishing, everything that their father enjoyed throughout his life. And, save for polo, all these sports were those that held no interest for Diana. In fact, she tried to dissuade her sons from taking them up.

From the moment of Diana's death, it seemed to many that the royal family were exhibiting behavior patterns akin to a feeling of guilt. At the moment of Diana's death, Prince Charles, William and Harry were at Balmoral in Scotland with the queen, Prince Philip and the Queen Mother enjoying the Windsor's customary late summer holiday. The queen, Philip and their advisers decided the family should stay put and continue with their holiday rather than strike camp and head back to London to lead the nation in mourning the "Peoples' Princess." Their only statement was that they were in mourning and "deeply shocked and distressed" by the news.

The nation thought otherwise. Hundreds of thousands flocked to London in that first week, bringing flowers and messages of love and sorrow, leaving them outside the gates of Buckingham Palace. After a few days, the mourners, many with tear-stained faces, became angry and critical, their mood turned ugly and defiant, their unease directed squarely at the queen. Newspapers took up the sentiment of the people. **YOUR PEOPLE ARE SUFFERING, SPEAK TO US, MA'AM** screamed the *Daily Mirror*; **SHOW US YOU CARE**, the *Daily Express* urged and the *Sun* demanded to know, **WHERE IS OUR QUEEN?**

The queen even refused to fly the Royal Standard over Buckingham Palace at half-mast, despite the fact that thousands of flags on buildings across London were doing so. The public took that as an insult to Princess Diana and their mood became even more restive. Some commentators warned of the possibility of mass civil disobedience leading to riots unless the royal family bowed to the demands of the nation.

Little did the nation know of the furious arguments taking place at Balmoral Castle. On the one side was Prince Charles, William and Harry; on the other the queen, Prince Philip and royal advisers. The Queen Mother tried to act as referee, sometimes supporting one side and then the other as the arguments raged. Their various advisers looked on in astonishment but would, from time to time, be invited to give their views on precedence and protocol.

Charles, William and Harry wanted to fly to London and mingle with the vast crowds that were thronging the Mall and Kensington Palace. William and Harry wanted to show their appreciation to those who had traveled to London to say "farewell" to their beloved mother but the queen, urged on by Philip, refused to let them travel.

In one of the most ferocious arguments, Prince Philip decreed that since Diana had taken the decision to leave the royal family some years before, an aircraft of the queen's flight should not be sent to Paris to bring back her body. He demanded that Diana's body should be returned like any other British citizen killed overseas, in a body bag on board an airline flight. Charles was apoplectic at the suggestion, outraged that his father could even consider such a proposal. Voices were raised, swear words exchanged, but Charles refused to back down. Charles threatened to tell William and Harry unless Prince Philip withdrew his proposal. Finally, Charles won the argument and he personally flew to Paris in an aircraft of the queen's flight and brought back her body, the coffin covered in a flag of the Prince of Wales.

The queen and Philip decreed that Diana should only be awarded a simple, straightforward funeral with no pomp and ceremony. Charles and the Queen Mother disagreed totally. More arguments took place, but in the end Charles and his sons once more won the day, and Diana was given a funeral fit for a royal princess. Philip was furious at the decision, but still insisted on walking behind the gun carriage carrying Diana's body to Westminster Abbey with Charles, William and Harry, although the two boys believed he should have been banned from doing so.

The arguments continued to rage at Balmoral and, rather pathetically, the queen issued a statement saying that they had decided to stay at Balmoral to comfort William and Harry in the loss of their mother. Few believed that statement or the sentiment. The great mass of the British public had not been taken in. They were certain that the royal family was feeling guilty.

Only after one week of total silence did the queen finally relent and even then Philip considered her decision "madness." The queen addressed the nation on television; finally, the Union flag was flown at half-mast above Buckingham Palace; the queen traveled to London and Elton John, a longtime friend of Diana's, was given permission to sing at her funeral. Diana's funeral was breathtaking, magnificent, traumatic and harrowing — not only for the million people who traveled to London — but for countless millions who watched the proceedings on television around the world, and silently wept.

Even in death, Diana succeeded in embarrassing the royal family. Neither the family nor their advisers had any idea how they should respond

to Diana's death or the nation's shock, disbelief
and sorrow that the young woman they had come
to respect and, indeed, love had been killed in a
stupid car crash in Paris.

Within days of the last tear being shed and
Diana having been laid to rest at the Spencer
family's ancestral home, the real work began for
the royal minions. It was their duty to ensure that
the memory of Princess Diana did not live on.
And today, some six years after her death, their
task is not yet complete. They are still striving to
obliterate her name and her fame from the
nation's psyche.

Following her death, the British people desperately wanted to honor Princess Diana, many of
whom believed she had been almost a martyr to
the cause of kindness, generosity, love and affection in a world of hatred and prejudice. To that
end they demanded that a magnificent memorial
be erected on a prominent site in London so that
future generations would not forget the princess
who had captured the hearts of their parents and
grandparents. Prime Minister Tony Blair pledged
that his government would honor the princess's
memory. Memorial funds were set up and dona-
tions poured in from people from all walks of life.
Everyone was invited to send in their suggestions
for the ideal memorial for Diana. The govern-

ment's Diana Memorial Committee was formed under the chairmanship of the Chancellor Gordon Brown, its members selected from the great, the good and the privileged of British society. It was their duty to evaluate the various ideas and select the best to ensure that Diana's memory would be forever remembered.

This committee was given a list of odd criteria to test whether the chosen design would be acceptable. The criteria handed down were artistic merit, value for money and practicability; none of them aimed to help keep alive the memory of Diana. Nothing has happened for six long years.

Newspapers have badgered the principal memorial committee to reach a decision and let the nation know what was happening so that the committee's memorial ideas could be subjected to debate and scrutiny. Reasons were given for the lack of progress, some pathetic, others downright insulting. But this is the uniquely British way — the people's will is slowly but surely put to one side and eventually ignored because they are told the correct decision will be made by those qualified to make the right decision. The argument, of course, was utter balderdash, a gigantic confidence trick perpetrated on the British people.

Many of the ideas submitted, some given prominence in newspaper columns, were mostly

intelligent and relevant. They included a magnificent bronze statue of Diana to stand in Trafalgar
Square; renaming Heathrow Airport Princess
Diana Airport in the same way as New York's
airport was renamed for John F. Kennedy after
his assassination, or renaming a major London
thoroughfare, a theater, a sports stadium. All were
quietly quashed. And today, the royal minions are
still at work ensuring that the name of Princess
Diana will eventually be forgotten and compre-
hensively trashed in the dustbin of history.

Finally, in 2002, after years of wrangling and
argument the committee reached their decision
and it was decreed their decision was final. The
people's views and opinions of the committee's
choice were not invited and, to give the decision
credence, it was announced that the queen had
given it her approval. All neatly cut and dried, the
will of the royal family triumphed, the wishes of
the people totally ignored.

The memorial will be a $5 million-dollar foun-
tain, tucked away in London's Hyde Park, on the
site of a disused pumphouse. The ring-shaped
stone fountain, the size of a football field, has
allegedly been designed to reflect the contrasting
joy and turmoil of the princess's life. On one side
of the fountain, water will bubble down a gentle
slope, while on the other it will cascade down,

before the two streams converge into a tranquil pool. There will be a small accompanying plaque bearing Princess Diana's name and the dates of her birth and death.

Future generations will have no statue of Diana to admire and see for themselves what the beautiful, enchanting Diana looked like; no idea of the impact that she made during those 17 brief years that she captured the hearts of the nation; no concept of the impact Diana's fleeting life made on the ordinary men, women and children who had so admired her and gained strength from her courage and fortitude, and no understanding of the charity work she carried out bringing joy and happiness to people forgotten, sidelined or neglected by society.

To many Britons, the decision was indeed unacceptable. Those same people now believe the decision to select a fountain as the nation's principal memorial to Diana was based more on vengeance and retribution toward her than a realistic attempt to keep alive her memory. Others believe the fountain was selected as an important part of the royal family's ongoing efforts to rid Britain of the memory of Diana as rapidly as possible.

However, there is one corner of an English field that will forever hold the essence of Diana.

At Earl Spencer's ancestral home, Althorp, some 80 miles north of London, Diana's brother buried his beloved sister in an unmarked grave on a tiny wooded island in the middle of the Oval Lake. Oak trees surround the grave, shading the monument to her. It is wonderfully peaceful and quiet and, for three months every summer the gates of Althorp House are thrown open permitting visitors to view not only her grave but also an exhibition of videos, gowns and frocks and, most nostalgically, her beautiful wedding dress all housed in a stable block. There is also a room dedicated to her death.

Diana's memory continues to burn brightly in the lives of those unfortunate ones who need help and charitable support. Diana's favorite charities have been receiving substantial sums of money from the $80 million raised by donations from the general public, including much from the United States. Four principal categories of recipients were chosen to benefit: "displaced people," "people at the margins of society," "survivors of conflict" and the "dying and bereaved." In the words of its independent assessor: "It has stuck to its principle of supporting less recognized causes against a number of odds and considerable pressure."

Diana would have approved.

The money is flowing out at the rate of about

$160,000 a week and is likely to do so for at least another 12 years although, inevitably, the charity's income is starting to decline as the demand for Diana memorabilia has lessened in the last year or so.

The ghost of Diana still has the power to burst forth in spectacular fashion, causing uproars and agonies for the royal family. In autumn 2002, Diana once again grabbed the front pages of every British newspaper, dominated the news bulletins and made the headlines, putting the royal family back on the hot seat.

In October 2002, Diana's butler Paul Burrell, 44, faced trial by jury accused of stealing hundreds of items from the estate of Diana, Princess of Wales. The main plank of the prosecution case was that Burrell had possession of 310 items belonging to the princess, the Prince of Wales and Prince William without permission and without informing anyone.

At a meeting at Highgrove in August 2001, the police informed Prince Charles, Prince William and their legal advisers that they had an open-and-shut case. They claimed they were able to produce evidence that some of the princess's items had been sold, that Burrell's bank balance had increased healthily since her death and that an "independent source" told police of photographs of several staff members at a party dressing up in clothing belonging to her.

The sensational trial collapsed dramatically after two weeks when the queen informed the court officials that during a conversation with Burrell shortly after Diana's death he informed her that he had taken some of her papers for safekeeping. Burrell stepped from the dock a free man and sobbed on the shoulder of his lawyer.

Amid emotional scenes outside the court, Burrell declared, "The queen came through for me. I'm thrilled."

Paul Burrell was undeniably one of Diana's most loyal and devoted servants, working happily and conscientiously as her butler for some 10 years. She referred to him time and again as "my rock." When she died, Burrell was distraught and came to see himself as the unique trustee of her life and her secrets.

As Diana's great friend Rosa Monckton explained, "Diana chose to live her life in compartments. It made her feel more secure. I was a very close friend, yet I did not know many of her other friends. I certainly did not know any members of her family. Only Paul had the key to all the doors. Not only was he her butler, but he was also the custodian of her life's secrets."

Allegedly, the queen mentioned to Prince

Charles, as they were driving across London together during the second week of the trial, that she recalled a meeting she held with Paul Burrell shortly after Diana's death in which he had told her that he had taken some of Diana's belongings and letters to his home for safekeeping. It was explained that Charles immediately urged his mother to make contact with the court and reveal what Burrell had told her. However, there were not too many people convinced that the queen's remarkable and sudden revelation was accurate and many believed that Burrell had never told the queen any such thing in any conversation. It is a well-known fact that Queen Elizabeth, despite being more than 70 years of age, has a most remarkable memory.

Burrell claimed later that his conversation with the queen, which took place in 1998, lasted for three hours and the queen stood while the two chatted. Senior Buckingham Palace staff have told this author that the conversation actually lasted less than 10 minutes!

The real reason the queen decided to make her sensational intervention and speak out was simply a dramatic attempt to bring the trial to a halt and permit Paul Burrell to walk free. Evidence heard during the first two days of the trial showed that if Burrell elected to give evidence in his own defense and went into the witness box he would be forced to reveal royal secrets under oath that could be seriously damaging to the royal family.

The queen, Prince Charles, Prince Philip and all their advisers knew there would be a very good chance that the evidence Burrell would have given would have, more likely than not, been pro-Diana and, consequently, anti-royal family. They couldn't take such a risk. They were well aware that Paul Burrell was Diana's confidant and he certainly knew most of her secrets as well as the names of most, if not all, of her lovers. After all, he had met most of them at one time or another. It is quite possible that Burrell knew of Prince Harry's parentage. The last thing the queen would have wanted was for that fact to be revealed under oath in an English criminal court. A way had to be found to shut Burrell up and stop him speaking out. The queen knew it was important to silence Paul Burrell – so much so that she was prepared to risk her own reputation and come to the rescue even if her intervention made her look less than wise, or even injudicious.

Within days of the trial collapsing, Paul Burrell sold his story for $500,000 to the *Daily Mirror*, a tabloid newspaper, but he was careful not to reveal too many of Diana's secrets. Some of his revelations, however, did raise eyebrows and

Buckingham Palace staff read every word, looking for secrets they would prefer to be kept under wraps.

In a bizarre revelation of his conversation with the queen, Burrell claimed that the queen warned him to be vigilant explaining how his unique closeness to Princess Diana left him exposed to people who wished him harm. She told him, "Be careful, Paul, nobody has ever been closer to a member of my family than you were to Diana. There are powers at work in this country about which we have no knowledge."

This revelation has been discussed and examined ever since. Some royal insiders believed that the queen was simply trying to put the fear of God into Burrell to stop him revealing royal family secrets by gossiping or writing his memoirs. Others believed that the queen was simply using rather quaint phrasing to describe Britain's secret intelligence services without actually suggesting that such organizations exist.

The queen's apparent allusion to dark forces raised concerns that parts of British life were being run by an unelected secret organization. Such fears, which have been raised from time to time throughout the queen's reign, have always been dismissed as fantasies of conspiracy theorists. The queen's remarkable claim seemed to suggest that Britain's secret intelligence agencies work goes beyond anything sanctioned by the monarch, the highest authority in the land.

The British establishment and all successive British governments have always dismissed such theories surrounding Britain's own security services though it must be said that, even today, Britain's security services operate quite independently with little or no real political restraints, though the politicians might deny this.

Paul Burrell was well aware that Diana was of the firm belief that her phones and her apartments at Kensington Palace were bugged and that was the reason she hired the services of a private security firm to sweep every room in her home for bugs. The Squidgygate saga had confirmed her suspicions and right up to the time of her death Diana was certain that her phones were tapped.

During her conversation with Burrell, the queen took the opportunity to impress on Burrell her concerns for Diana and the considerable efforts she made to encourage a warm, friendly relationship. But she was, in fact, trying to alter the record of her relationship with Diana, trying to persuade Burrell that she had always tried to establish a good relationship with Diana and was unhappy that her well-intentioned efforts had not been reciprocated by her daughter-in-law. Burrell said that the queen told him, "Before Diana died, I tried to reach out to her so many times."

He revealed that the queen and Diana used to write short letters to each other right up until the time of her death but there was no suggestion of their contents. He did say, however that Diana would always begin her letters, "Dearest Mama."

Burrell added, "People have always said there was a chronic rift between the queen and the princess but that is so wrong. The queen would write a letter at a turbulent time for the princess and she, in turn, would write a letter reconfirming her respect and allegiance to the monarch. Her Majesty is not capable of hurting people. Diana knew that when she died, the queen was not one of her enemies. There was never any hatred between the two of them, never any animosity. Both parties knew in their own particular ways how to communicate — and they did. The world knows of the relationship breakdown but Diana and the queen shared one wish — to have a happy family."

Many people who know Burrell and his close relationship with Diana believe that he, who, though married with children, is allegedly bisexual, was in love with Diana or, perhaps infatuated by her. Some at Kensington Palace described Burrell as being "overawed" by her, others that he was "besotted" by her.

Burrell also spoke of the rift between Diana and her mother, Frances Shand Kydd, as well as with other members of the Spencer family. He recalled a phone call Diana received from her mother in early 1997, when she hurled obscenities and swear words at her daughter in a slurred voice because she could not accept her in the company of Muslim men. Allegedly, the phone call left Diana crumpled on the sitting room carpet in front of the marble fireplace at Kensington Palace, sobbing into her white bathrobe and vowing never to speak to her mother again. That conversation took place exactly six months before Diana was killed and she never once spoke to her mother again. Mrs. Shand Kydd wrote more than a dozen letters to Diana in that time, but Diana had ordered that they should all be returned, unopened. The contents of those letters are not known.

Paul Burrell also took the opportunity to accuse the Spencer family of the gross hypocrisy of not wanting to know Diana during her life but being happy to claim her in death. He stated, "The Spencers found Diana unacceptable in life. But after her death they found her very acceptable at $15 a ticket," referring to the entrance fee for visitors to the Spencers' ancestral estate, Althorp House.

He wrote of Mrs. Shand Kydd's envy, her per-
verse desire for control and her bitterness toward
her daughter and what he described as the
hypocrisy of her brother Charles in his funeral
oration to Diana. Paul had never forgotten that,
following her separation from Prince Charles,
Diana had asked her brother if she could rent one
of the family cottages in the grounds of Althorp
House for her, William and Harry to use during
school holidays. Her brother Charles refused,
saying that it would bring press intrusion to
Althorp and might be upsetting for his children.

Paul Burrell also told the world of the feuds that
had torn apart the Spencer family and the disastrous affect her parents' divorce had on Diana's
entire life, giving that as the reason for her emotional and physical problems. Burrell claimed, "I
don't think the princess ever recovered from the
thought of being abandoned. She desperately wanted to be loved. She believed that's why she had so
many problems — the anorexia, the bulimia. She
recognized it was the root of all her problems."

Diana had not spoken to her sister, Lady Jane
Fellowes, for two years before her death, despite
the fact that she lived next door to her in
Kensington Palace. Diana felt resentful that Jane
appeared not to support her when her marriage
broke up. It may simply have been that Jane was

married to Sir Robert Fellowes, the queen's private secretary and chief adviser. Diana frequently clashed with Sir Robert over a hundred and one minor issues and she may have feared her sister Jane supported her husband rather than her sister.

Burrell believed the relationship between Diana and her other sister Sarah was always awkward because Sarah had been Prince Charles' lover 12 months prior to Diana first dating Charles. She always wondered whether that had created a feeling of jealousy. On the morning of Diana's wedding, Sarah famously said to her, "I once thought all this would be mine."

Ever since Diana's death, however, Paul Burrell has made a good living giving talks about Diana and her life, lecturing to passengers onboard luxury ocean liners and working on committees promoting her memory. He also equipped his modest home as a shrine to Diana's memory with presents she had given to him during the 10 years he worked as her butler; numerous photographs of himself with Diana as well as his favorite photographs of her. He strived to become the world's greatest authority on Diana and every aspect of her life.

But the secret Burrell has never revealed is the fact that for some six months before her death he was actively searching for a new job. He told friends that he was fed up with his life as Diana's dog's body and wanted out. He was hoping to secure a job as a butler to a wealthy American family, preferably in California. He was convinced that finding a job in the United States would be quite easy because of the fame attached to him after working for the princess for 10 years. However, what Burrell did not reveal was the fact that he was only looking for a new job because Diana was fed up with him and she wanted to be rid of him. Diana found him too cloying, too obsessive, too involved with every aspect of her life and she did not like that. She wanted her freedom back.

In his memoirs, Burrell wrote, "People don't understand what we had. I dream of her. I adored her. I can't escape her. She haunts me. I know I have a problem here. I know that it is sad — a grown man not able to get over a woman who died five years ago."

Burrell accepts that he is "nutty" and "obsessive" about Diana. He knows he has been unable to adjust to the fact that she is gone forever. He admits that his obsession for Diana makes life very difficult for his devoted wife Maria, by whom he has two children, Alexander and Nicholas. "My wife doesn't like this," Burrell said, "but there will never be another woman I will be as close to as Diana. But she knows it. When Diana used that quote about there being three people in her marriage, Maria pointed out that that was her saying! The princess had stolen it."

Burrell continued, "To me the princess always came first. I might have put her above my wife and children but there are reasons for that. She needed me; they didn't. Maria and the boys might have been at home while I was with Diana, but they have always been strong. Maria is from a very close family. She always had her family around. She always had people she could depend on. Diana had nobody."

The trial of Paul Burrell threw up further embarrassment for the royal family on the subject of gifts. As with every other head of state, visits to other countries usually end with the host head of state giving a present to the visitor. In most cases, gifts are exchanged and pleasantries spoken. Understandably, the queen, who has been Britain's head of state for more than 50 years has received an inordinate number of gifts, many of which she may have liked and wished to keep. But there have been hundreds, if not thousands, of such gifts which she had no wish to keep. The problem at Buckingham Palace has always been what should be done with the unwanted gifts. Of course it would be out of the question to decline a gift.

The queen has had to be most careful in recycling such gifts in case the person who gave the present should hear of its disposal.

That is where the Crown Jeweler can be most useful to members of Britain's royal family. It is an honorary position awarded to a distinguished jeweler who is acknowledged in his profession as an expert. For decades it has been accepted in royal circles and within London's jewelry trade that such gifts are recycled through the hands of the Crown Jeweler. People wanting to purchase a gift and seeking something expensive, different, perhaps unique and tasteful would be directed to the Crown Jeweler's shop in London's fashionable Bond Street and would often leave very happy with their purchase. Discretion is perhaps the most important part of the Crown Jeweler's role in this trade of unwanted royal gifts — he would never let on to purchasers of these gifts where they came from or who had passed them on to him for sale. It was a question that was rarely asked and, if requested, never revealed.

Burrell's trial brought to the surface this little-known trade in royal gifts, and the tabloid press and the majority of the nation considered such practice scandalous. The general public had not the faintest idea that such a practice existed. The public did not take kindly to the fact that gifts

handed to members of the royal family by distinguished foreigners were later either handed over
to their servants or, even worse, handed to the
Crown Jeweler to sell for cash, the money from
the sale of those items duly handed over to the
family member. Some of these goods, often
unique and priceless, were sometimes sold for
tens of thousands of dollars.

Evidence from the Burrell trial suggested that
the selling of gifts for cash was practiced only by
Prince Charles and, as a result, his reputation
was bruised as the tabloid and the quality press
reacted with shock and horror to the scandal. But
that is not the case — all members of the royal family, including the queen and Prince Philip and nearly every other member of the family carry on the
gifts-for-cash practice. Usually, the trusted aide or
palace servant who is asked to take a gift to the
Crown Jeweler and hand them over for sale is
usually recompensed with a tip or a small present.
Whether this recompense is made because the
trusted servant has carried out a task outside his
or her usual job description or to ensure the trans-
actions remain secret is not known.

It seems beyond belief that the queen, one of the
wealthiest women in the world who, by an accident of birth, lives a life of unimaginable wealth
and privilege, could be reduced to pawning gifts

for cash. Throughout her reign, the queen has done a magnificent job of convincing the British people that she is a middle-class housewife who frets about the cost of central heating in Buckingham Palace. But this revelation that their head of state sells gifts for cash and keeps the money may not be well-received by her subjects.

Hanging over the heads of the queen and her family like a Damocles sword ever since Diana's death is the figure of James Hewitt. They had no idea when this wretched man would once again enter the public domain, but they feared that it could only bring further embarrassment to the family.

In 1999, Hewitt decided to publish his memoirs, *Love and War*. Hewitt chose to concentrate mainly on himself, his views, his opinions, his understanding, his life, his military career, his attitude to his affair with Diana and not so much on revealing Diana's secrets, and certainly very few secrets of their love life. In his memoirs Hewitt, understandably, wanted to show the world that throughout his love affair with Diana he acted as an officer and a gentleman. He set out to show that he was not the cad the world had dubbed him and to a great extent his memoirs achieved that.

But Hewitt remained a potential danger to the royal family because they knew that he held an ace up his sleeve — 64 letters and notes Diana had

written to him at various times during their on-off
affair. Buckingham Palace officials had learned
the letters contained Diana's most closely guarded
secrets, the intimate details of her love life with
Hewitt and the way that sex played a vital role in
their relationship. Those letters contain the most
personal and explicit sexual references, including
deeply intimate revelations by a vulnerable young
woman to the man she loved and worshipped. The
palace knew they were dynamite for if they were
published in a newspaper or magazine the whole
Diana-Hewitt affair would hit the headlines, once
again causing huge embarrassment to Prince
Charles, Prince William and Prince Harry and
also the queen.

The existence of the letters first emerged in
1998, when Hewitt's former lover, Anna Ferretti,
allegedly stole them from his Devon home and
tried to sell them to a newspaper. That deal was
foiled and the letters handed over to Kensington
Palace. Hewitt insisted he wanted the letters
back and threatened to sue Diana's estate for
their return. Lawyers acting for the estate
advised that the 64 letters could not lawfully be
kept from Hewitt so her family reluctantly handed them back. In a 1998 statement issued through
his then-solicitor Mark Stephens, Hewitt said, "I
would never sell letters from Diana."

In December 2002, however, Hewitt changed his mind. He had come to realize that he might be able to sell the letters for as much as $10 million — to Hewitt that was a fortune. He would be able to buy a smart London home, a house in the country and live comfortably on the income for the rest of his life. To a man who had found it difficult settling down to a routine civilian life after his army career, it seems the lure of easy money leading to a life of leisure proved irresistible. He decided to sell the letters to the highest bidder on the condition that the contents of the letters were never revealed to the general public. Of course, even Hewitt would have realized that once the letters had been sold and had become the property of the purchaser he had lost all control over them. The purchaser could, if he so wished, publish and be damned for doing so. "I've decided to sell the letters to the highest bidder," Hewitt confirmed in January 2003.

Many thought it despicable that Hewitt could stoop so low as to sell the letters revealing intimate details of Diana's sex life, the woman he professed to love. Others could not contain their anger that Hewitt should consider such a sale for the effect they might have on William and Harry.

Almost six years has passed since the fatal crash and there are still judicial procedures to be settled. Immediately following the accident, Judge Herve Stephan was appointed to probe the causes, normal procedure following a fatal car crash in France. He ordered that the Mercedes S280 should be sent for a thorough investigation to an Institute of Criminal Research authorized by the French National Police. As a result, the Mercedes was taken to the only private unit in France that deals with technical examination of vehicles involved in fatal crashes. The team of experts confirmed that the cause of the accident was "excessive speed" and their secret report on the car was forwarded to Judge Stephan. This author has attempted to obtain a copy of this secret report but was refused.

It can be confirmed, however, that the Mercedes was totally taken apart, piece by piece, and not put back together again. The bits and pieces were examined by specially trained technicians, then placed in a sealed container and taken away by police. The owners of the institute have no idea of the whereabouts of the container; nor do they know whether the remains of the Mercedes have been crushed and disposed of. Publication of Judge Stephan's report, believed to be some 6,000 pages long, is still awaited, though it was completed in 1999. He has said, however, that the facts reveal that alcohol, drugs and high speed were to blame for the crash. For some extraordinary and unknown reason, no date has even been set for the full report to be published. What mystifies people is why the French judge did not publish his report at least three years ago after receiving the secret report from the technicians. All police inquiries were completed by the year 2000 — there appears no reason for further delay.

There is also the matter of inquests into the deaths of both Diana and Dodi. In British law, an inquest should be carried out in every case where a body is returned to the country following a death abroad. The inquest would establish the cause of death and when and where the person died. It is understood that the inquest has been held up by the two-year French investigation and, perhaps more pertinently, by legal objections by Mohamed al Fayed.

In 1997, the inquest into Diana's death was formally opened and immediately adjourned to a later date. At the full inquest, the results of the post-mortem examination carried out by a Home Office pathologist will be published. Also at the inquest, interested parties can ask to give evidence and put questions to any witnesses called. It may well be that Dodi's father would ask some very interesting and probing questions as to the causes of death. It may be that Fayed has evidence he would want to put before the coroner for further consideration. Ever since the crash, Fayed has alleged that the deaths of Diana and Dodi were not an accident but the result of action taken by Britain's security services. Fayed may have some questions to ask that could prove embarrassing to the royal family.

The verdicts in the princess' case could only be chosen from the following: accidental death, an open verdict or unlawful killing. And the longer the delay in holding the inquest, the more critical and probing questions may yet surface.

And no matter what efforts are made by those in positions of power to erase the memory of Diana, there is no chance that they will succeed for generations to come. For waiting in the wings is the handsome young William, heir to the throne. Without doubt, one of the most damaging legacies that Diana could have bequeathed to the House of Windsor sends shivers down the spines of those dedicated to the preservation of the monarchy and, in particular, the Windsors.

Prince William is second in line to the throne and, all things being equal, he will be crowned on the death of Prince Charles, who is nearly 60 years old. At what age he will succeed to the throne is of course not known unless the queen, now age 75, decides to abdicate. Nor of course does anyone know how long Charles will reign or want to reign. The fear among some senior members of the royal family is William's present-day negative attitude at the prospect that one day he might be king. In 2000, William summoned up the courage to tell his father that he did not wish to remain heir to the throne and wanted to renounce formally all claim to the throne.

"It's his mother's influence, of course," was the sneering comment of one senior royal aide. It probably is Diana's influence that still tends to dominate William's thinking. In numerous con-versations with his father, William insisted that his rejection of his title and his claim to the crown was no teenage rebellion, something that would pass with time, but a decision he had been mulling over for a couple of years.

In straight-talking discussions, William told his father, "I don't want to be king. I don't want the job."

Despite such open defiance, Charles remains quietly confident that his son's opposition and discontent with the role he has been destined to fulfill in life is only a youthful flickering of disloyal rebellion that will pass with time. Nonetheless, Charles decided to inform the queen of his conversations with William and seek her advice. The news of William's negative attitude to the monarchy and his unwillingness to take seriously his responsibility to the family horrified her.

The queen's first reaction was to instruct Charles to "get a grip" on his wayward son and instill in him the meaning of the word "duty." She told Charles to pass on her message to William, telling him in no uncertain terms that there could be no rejection of his role of heir to the throne and that he should banish all such thoughts from his mind. Charles was asked to pass on to William the message that his role in life had been predetermined by an accident of birth. He had been born into the royal family — a hereditary monarchy — and, as the eldest child of Prince Charles he is the heir to the throne and nothing can change that.

The queen then turned on Prince Charles, blaming him for not bringing up William to understand that he has never had a choice as to whether he does or doesn't want to be king. He was born to be king and, as far as the queen is concerned, nothing that William has said has changed that fact. Nor will it, come what may.

Secretly, however, the queen was aware that the blame lay more with Diana than with Prince Charles. She knew that Diana had exercised considerable influence on young William and now she began to worry that Diana's influence may be too ingrained in William for her to do anything about it.

The queen understood that Diana had instilled in both Wills and Harry a sense of freedom, an understanding that they did have a say in their future. Diana also suggested to them that it wasn't necessary in this day and age to sacrifice one's entire life to one's nation. Diana accepted that duty was an essential part of being a privileged member of the royal family, but she believed one also could make a choice as to the extent one had to sacrifice one's life for duty.

From the queen's perspective, Diana had walked away from her responsibilities to the monarchy and turned her back not only on her marriage, but also on her duty to the crown. The queen believed that Diana did know before her wedding what was expected of a future Princess of Wales. But Diana had decided to go her own way when she came to the conclusion that she didn't want to accept the responsibilities that came with the privileges of being a royal.

Throughout his young life, William saw the disdain that his mother showed to the queen in private, though she toed the line in public and always in the presence of the queen. William had seen his mother making jokes about the queen and Philip, mimicking their voices and their mannerisms, making them appear foolish, overblown characters living in a time warp, divorced from the real world outside the close confines of royal palaces. Indeed, mimicking the queen became one of Diana's more famous party pieces, leaving everyone present not knowing whether to laugh with her or leave the room in embarrassment. William knew that his mother believed the whole royal business was little more than a gigantic charade that she believed had passed its sell-by date. William knew that Diana thought the monarchy should be dragged into the 21st century if it was to survive, rather than remain stuck in the 19th century.

Following his mother's death, William thought more deeply of everything she had talked about; relived those many occasions when she would be critical of the royal family and most of its members; when his mother found it almost impossible to talk to the queen because she never received any feedback and when she made any suggestions she never received a reply. Indeed, William remembers his mother telling him that she thought the Queen Mother, whom she greatly admired, was making most of the decisions and that part of the reason for the queen's constant equivocation was simply that she didn't want to make a decision until after she had consulted the Queen Mother.

Diana also told William that the Queen Mother did not approve of her and that she rarely talked to her because she felt she was always disapproving. One reason, of course, was that Charles was the Queen Mother's favorite grandchild and there had always been a close bond between them. Diana never mentioned, however, that she always felt guilty when talking to the Queen Mother because she thoroughly disapproved of Diana taking a lover within a couple of years of her wedding.

And Diana did not mention to William that another reason for the Queen Mother's disapproval was Diana's brazen attempts to persuade the nation that Charles was unfit to succeed his mother and that the crown should instead pass directly to William. But Diana was killed before she had thought out her plans. One can only speculate, but it is likely that Diana would have persuaded William to push through a root and branch reform of the British monarchy, modernizing and transforming the crown into a more European, less-formal style.

Diana's death removed her growing influence over young William much to the relief of the queen, Prince Philip and senior courtiers. They now felt they could concentrate on William, applying discreet but increasing pressure on him to come to heel and toe the line. Privately, however, senior courtiers confirm that the queen, and particularly Prince Philip, have been deeply concerned by William's desire to abdicate his responsibilities and they are not certain that William has yet come to the belief that he will one day be king, come what may.

Prince Charles decided that he should permit William to leave Britain and travel the world for a year as he so wanted to do. Charles considered Wills would benefit from seeing the world from the same perspective as other young people did during their gap year between school and university. Charles was keen for William to see different societies, different peoples, different attitudes, differing lifestyles so that he would then be able to judge how Britain compared to other countries.

It was vital that Charles should select the right person to accompany young William on his travels, someone who was not a member of the royal family nor someone who lived a similar privileged lifestyle. Charles chose Mark Dyer, a burly, rugby-playing, red-haired former Welsh Guards officer. During that 12-month stint, William and Mark got along famously. Mark dated Tiggy Legge-Bourke, who was then working as a sort of social secretary, adviser and friend to Wills and Harry. More importantly, William respected this tough, no-nonsense, down-to-earth man who once described himself as William's companion and mentor. It was a good choice.

Charles called Mark for a chat some time after he had accompanied William to Belize on a two-week jungle survival course with the Welsh Guards. Charles asked him if he would accompany William both to the island of Mauritius in the Indian Ocean, on a scientific and ecological research program run by the Royal Geographical Society and later on safari trip to southern Africa. But before those trips, William chose to spend 10 weeks in Patagonia in South America where he taught English and carried out tough volunteer work helping the local people.

These trips went famously and William particularly enjoyed roughing it in Patagonia. He insisted on living exactly like all of the other 40 young teenagers whose main task was to build a series of sturdy wooden walkways above the marshland linking the villagers' homes and to construct an extension to the one-vehicle village fire station. Wills, a well-built, strong young man 6-foot-3-inches tall and weighing some 200 pounds, volunteered for the toughest jobs, like carrying the heaviest logs and slogging away at digging the trenches and holes even after his hands blistered. He also lived in exactly the same conditions, doing his share of the mundane domestic duties, eating the same food including taking his turn cleaning out the lavatories and scrubbing the floors. He shared the communal cold-water washing facilities and slept with 10 others on the floor of one of the rooms. That was not something that either Charles or the queen would ever have approved. It worried them.

William would say later, "What I really enjoyed was being treated like everyone else. In Patagonia the local people didn't know me from Adam and treated me the same as everyone else. I didn't want to be treated differently. I didn't want any privileges and I never got any. Great!" That sentiment also worried them.

Before Wills went on safari, however, Charles called in Mark Dyer and asked him to talk to William about his future responsibilities, to sound him out about his thoughts of his future, and of his duty and responsibility to the royal family. Charles confided in Mark that Wills stated that he never wanted to be king and didn't want the job at any price. Dyer agreed to help. During their eight weeks on safari where they tracked, hunted and shot game in the scrub and deserts of Botswana, Dyer and William spent hours chatting beneath the stars when they camped for the night.

Since beginning his studies at St. Andrews University in Scotland, some 800 miles from London in September 2001, it does seem that

William has settled down and is working reasonably hard at his studies — though he does like to escape most weekends whether to go shooting or stalking deer around Balmoral or fishing in the River Dee. William, now 21, has two more years at St. Andrews. After that Wills may well join the British Army, probably the Welsh Guards. If he does so William would spend at least three years, if not six or more in the army. He has no wish to follow in his father's footsteps and opt for a career in the Royal Navy, which during the past century has been selected by former British kings. Once again, it seems William is opting for a more egalitarian career in the services.

William believes that a career in the army will shield him from being exposed to media attention or the curiosity of ordinary people, something he treats with trepidation if not horror. He still has no wish to seek the limelight or expose himself to public scrutiny, in fact, he seeks to shun such attention at all times. He hopes that the army will give him that protection and a feeling of anonymity. "When you're wearing a helmet and dressed in battle fatigues no one can recognize you," he has pointed out to friends.

The question of succession is now hardly ever mentioned. The family believes the question is best left dormant in the hope that a more mature

William will in time come to understand that he has no real option but to one day become head of state, king of England. William has agreed to study the rather boring subject of the British Constitution, which Charles also had to study in his days at Cambridge University, learning how the nation works and the laws that govern the country. Apparently, Wills is not at all keen on those studies, much to the embarrassment of Charles and the annoyance of the queen.

Since Diana's death, young William has indeed become more of a royal. His favorite sports are now shooting, fishing and stalking, playing polo and hunting, so very different from his earlier interest in more egalitarian sports such as football, swimming, rowing and tennis, which his mother had urged him to take up.

Prince Charles is fearful that William has not yet accepted the fact that one day he will be crowned king. Charles understands that Wills can be obstinate and rebellious, much like his mother, and Charles is equally aware that if Diana did not want to do something she simply refused. If, indeed, William does one day refuse the crown, Diana would have achieved the sweetest possible revenge.

Bibliography

All published in London unless otherwise stated.

P.D. Jephson, *Shadows of a Princess*, 2000.

Inspector Ken Wharfe, *Diana: Closely Guarded Secret*, 2002.

Lynn Picknett, Clive Prince and Stephen Prior, *War of the Windsors*, 2002.

Philip Zeigler, *Mountbatten*, 1985.

Andrew Morton, *Diana: Her True Story*, 1992.

James Hewitt, *Love and War*, 1999.

Anna Pasternak, *Princess in Love*, 1994.

Nigel Blundell, *Windsor v. Windsor*, 1995.

Vernon Bogdanor, *The Monarchy and the Constitution*, 1995.

Basil Boothroyd, *Philip: An Informal Biography*, 1971.

Lady Colin Campbell, *The Royal Marriage: Private Lives of the Queen and Her Children*, 1993.

Jonathan Dimbleby, *The Prince of Wales: A Biography*, 1994.

Tim Heald, *The Duke: A Portrait of Prince Philip*, 1991.

Robert Lacey, *Majesty: Elizabeth II and the House of Windsor*, 1977.

Elizabeth Longford, *Elizabeth R: A Biography*, 1983.

Trevor Rees-Jones with Moira Johnston, *The Bodyguard's Story: Diana, the Crash and the Sole Survivor*, 2000.

Ida MacAlpine & Richard Hunter, *George III and the Mad-Business*, 1969.

Other royal books by Nicholas Davies:

Diana, A Princess and Her Troubled Marriage, 1992, USA.

The Princess Who Changed the World, 1997.

Diana: The Lonely Princess, 1996, USA.

Queen Elizabeth II: A Woman Who Is Not Amused, 1994, USA.

Elizabeth: Behind Palace Doors, 2000.

William: King for the 21st Century, 2000.

William: The Rebel Prince, 2001.

Index